Elizabeth Harrower

SYDNEY STUDIES IN AUSTRALIAN LITERATURE

Robert Dixon, Series Editor

The **Sydney Studies in Australian Literature** series publishes original, peer-reviewed research in the field of Australian literary studies. It offers engagingly written evaluations of the nature and importance of Australian literature, and aims to reinvigorate its study both locally and internationally. It will be of interest to those researching, studying and teaching in the diverse fields of Australian literary studies.

Alex Miller: The Ruin of Time
Robert Dixon

Colonial Australian Fiction: Character Types, Social Formations and the Colonial Economy
Ken Gelder and Rachael Weaver

Contemporary Australian Literature: A World Not Yet Dead
Nicholas Birns

Elizabeth Harrower: Critical Essays
Ed. Elizabeth McMahon and Brigitta Olubas

The Fiction of Tim Winton: Earthed and Sacred
Lyn McCredden

Shirley Hazzard: New Critical Essays
Ed. Brigitta Olubas

Elizabeth Harrower

Critical Essays

Edited by Elizabeth McMahon and Brigitta Olubas

SYDNEY UNIVERSITY PRESS

First published by Sydney University Press
© Individual contributors 2017
© Sydney University Press 2017

Reproduction and Communication for other purposes

Except as permitted under the Act, no part of this edition may be reproduced, stored in a retrieval system, or communicated in any form or by any means without prior written permission. All requests for reproduction or communication should be made to Sydney University Press at the address below:

Sydney University Press
Fisher Library F03
University of Sydney NSW 2006
AUSTRALIA
sup.info@sydney.edu.au
sydney.edu.au/sup

National Library of Australia Cataloguing-in-Publication Data

Title:	Elizabeth Harrower: critical essays / edited by Elizabeth McMahon and Brigitta Olubas.
ISBN:	9781743325599 (pbk)
Series:	Sydney studies in Australian literature.
Notes:	Includes bibliographical references and index.
Subjects:	Harrower, Elizabeth--Criticism and interpretation.
	Women novelists, Australian--Criticism and interpretation.
	Authors, Australian--20th century.
	Women and literature.

Cover image: Elizabeth Harrower photographed returning to Australia in 1959 on board the *Southern Cross*. Courtesy of Elizabeth Harrower.

Cover design by Miguel Yamin.

Contents

Acknowledgements		vii
Rediscovering Again: Reading Elizabeth Harrower Across Time		1
1	Harrower's Things: Objects in *The Watch Tower* Michelle de Kretser	9
2	Elizabeth Harrower in Sydney Fiona McFarlane	13
3	A Really Long Prospect: Elizabeth Harrower's Fallen World Ivor Indyk	17
4	Sydney in the Fiction of Elizabeth Harrower Elizabeth Webby	23
5	A Wrong Way of Being Right: The Tormented Force of the Harrower Man Nicholas Birns	33
6	"The wind from Siberia": Metageography and Ironic Nationality in the Novels of Elizabeth Harrower Robert Dixon	49
7	Weather and Temperature, the Will to Power, and the Female Subject in Harrower's Fiction Kate Livett	65
8	"White, fierce, shocked, tearless": *The Watch Tower* and the Electric Interior Brigid Rooney	81
9	Addiction, Fire and the Face in *The Catherine Wheel* Brigitta Olubas	97
10	Projecting the Sixties: Mediation and Characterology in *The Catherine Wheel* Julian Murphet	107

11 Traversing "the same extreme country" in *The Watch Tower* and *Daniel Deronda* 119
    Megan Nash

12 Moments of Being in the Fiction of Elizabeth Harrower 133
    Elizabeth McMahon

Contributors 145

Index 149

Acknowledgements

This collection of essays began as a symposium titled Rediscovering Christina Stead and Elizabeth Harrower held in the School of the Arts and Media (SAM) at the University of New South Wales in December 2015. The Harrower event was held on the second day of the symposium and comprised sessions of scholarly papers and a writers' panel chaired by Ivor Indyk and including Michelle de Kretser and Fiona McFarlane. This symposium constituted the first sustained scholarly engagement with Elizabeth Harrower's fiction. All of the contributors included in this volume participated in this event, and we thank SAM and its Creative Practice Lab at UNSW for supporting such a memorable and historic occasion.

We thank our authorial subject Elizabeth Harrower for her wonderful writing and for her generous assistance in preparing this volume by granting permission to quote from her letters to Shirley Hazzard, and by answering emails checking facts. We are keen to know her responses to the engagements with her work published here.

We thank the anonymous referees who provided sharp insights and valuable suggestions for the improvement of the essays, reminding us again of the benefits of this process in the production of scholarly research. We also thank Kate Livett, who created and implemented a style guide and subedited the manuscript for submission.

We thank Text Publishing, who undertook the republication of Harrower's backlist, the collection of her short fiction, and the initial publication of *In Certain Circles* (2014). Text's project successfully returned Harrower and her fiction to wide public attention and this collection is one such response. We also thank our publishers, Sydney University Press, in particular Robert Dixon, who commissioned the volume, publisher Susan Murray, and our editor Denise O'Dea.

Introduction
Rediscovering Again: Reading Elizabeth Harrower Across Time

2014 saw the long-awaited first publication of Elizabeth Harrower's final novel, *In Certain Circles*, written nearly four decades earlier and withdrawn by the author shortly before its scheduled publication by Macmillan in 1971.[1] This belated publication itself enacted a form of literary revival, not least in bearing the impress of international endorsement in the form of a "Rediscovering Harrower" essay by James Wood in the *New Yorker*.[2] Just ahead of this publication, Harrower said in an interview with Susan Wyndham that part of the reason she withdrew the novel from publication might have had to do with the death of her mother, which had left her "frozen" with grief; she also claimed to have forgotten the novel, and to be no longer interested in it, or in her writing life, or indeed in writing at all.[3] Two years earlier, she had spoken about the recollected novel with some finality and an intimation that it was somehow futural, yet to be (or not be) authored: "There are a lot of dead novels out in the world that don't need to be written",[4] a point which plays suggestively alongside her claims not to remember the novel: "I looked up the blurb and it said it is 'an intense psychological drama', and I said, 'That sounds like me'". She was more explicit, if also casually ironic, in the account she gave of changing her mind in the face of repeated requests from Michael Heyward, the publisher at Text, to see the manuscript, returning again to the figure of mortality as the natural frame for a writing life: "And I'd say, 'No Michael', just automatically, and finally I thought, well, I'll be dead soon and he'll be able to look at it then, so if it would please him, yes, have a look, Michael". Harrower's chatty, canny shifts in tense here work to create a temporal space – an anticipated, inevitable future and a conditional readership – for that (long-lost), last novel, while at the same time her thoughtful locution invites readers to reconsider the question of a writing career as a larger arc of moving in and out of the public eye.

The publication of her short story "Alice" in the *New Yorker* in early 2015 came with an attached audio file of Harrower reading the story, a performance of writerly presentness

---

1   Elizabeth Harrower, *In Certain Circles* (Melbourne: Text Publishing, 2014).
2   James Wood, "No Time for Lies: Rediscovering Elizabeth Harrower", *New Yorker*, 20 October 2014. http://bit.ly/1Cqu4W0.
3   Quoted in Susan Wyndham, "Elizabeth Harrower Doesn't Want Spoilers to Her Own Novel", *Sydney Morning Herald*, 3 May 2014. http://bit.ly/2mJmnJn.
4   Quoted in Helen Trinca, "Novelist Elizabeth Harrower Has Lived Dangerously but Kept Her Words to Herself", *Australian*, 27 October 2012. http://bit.ly/2nXG9lE.

and liveness – even aliveness – that resonated with those intimations of loss and mortality from the previous year. The recording of Harrower's voice brought the fineness of her prose sharply into the present. It also inflected and complicated the apparent diffidence of her interview commentary and the tenacity of her withdrawal from the writing life through the signing of her work with death and forgetting; it announced her as a writer of the present and at the same time a voice from the past. Later in 2015, Text published *A Few Days in the Country*, a collection that includes Harrower's first but hitherto unpublished story "The Fun of the Fair" alongside stories previously published in various Australian magazines and anthologies, and "Alice", published in the *New Yorker*, as noted above. In the years just before this, Text had republished Harrower's four earlier novels: *Down in the City* (1957; 2013), *The Catherine Wheel* (1960; 2014), *The Long Prospect* (1958; 2012), and *The Watch Tower* (1966; 2012). These late and fortunate reappearances of Harrower's work inflect the longevity of her writing career; they invite her readers to read *with* her work *across* time, to consider questions of duration in relation to the practices and purposes of writing, and to attend to the shifting contexts of her work in real time.

The years in between the two main periods of Harrower's publishing career – from the mid-1960s to her 2014 return to literary prominence – provide a further set of coordinates for her readers, along with the conundrum of what we are to make of her four decades of apparent literary silence. The often-quoted inscription from her great friend Patrick White – "To Elizabeth, luncher and diner extraordinaire. Sad you don't also WRITE"[5] – might intimate, provocatively, a criticism of her deployment of time through these years; however, this should not be taken at face value. It might rather be seen in the context of the extraordinary range of literary friendships that she maintained across her adult life: with White, famously, but also with Christina Stead, Kylie Tennant, Judah Waten, David Malouf, Shirley Hazzard, Vivian Smith, Antigone Kefala and many others, along with a large number of artists, arts writers, journalists and significant figures from the left of Australian politics. While Harrower's circles are more properly the focus of a biography, their extent and depth should be noted here, as they help deepen and inform any understanding of her profile and significance for contemporary readers. The letters she wrote to Shirley Hazzard across those four decades provide an extraordinary record of these networks of friendship,[6] and of the literary and political life of the period. The correspondence between the two writers merits mention here for the ways it shows their negotiation of national and international letters, art and politics. Indeed, Harrower's letters provide a wealth of sharp and informed insight into the upheavals of the artistic and political worlds in the wake of the 1972 election of the Whitlam Labor government, and the enormous changes wrought by this across the nation. Her exhilaration speaks to the keenness of her understanding of the shared public spaces where politics are lived, which sit in apparent contradistinction to the intense and tortured interior spaces of her novels, but which are nonetheless, as she intimates here, always of a piece with them:

---

5   Quoted in Wood, "No Time for Lies". White's comment was of course intended to be provocative, and to be viewed within the context of a close and supportive friendship.
6   Harrower's letters to Hazzard are in Shirley Hazzard's papers, currently held by Hazzard's executors, to which Brigitta Olubas has been given full access; Hazzard's letters to Harrower are held with Harrower's papers at the National Library of Australia, currently under embargo.

> I must tell you that I . . . and half the population are THRILLED about the change of government. At last. And they are speaking so rationally, simply, unaggressively, unoratorically – it's heaven. It can't last perhaps, but it has started very, very well. From not being able to read an Australian newspaper, I am reading four a day. You become so used to living in a condition of public shame, vicarious shame, that you forget what – no, have never known what – it might be like to agree with those who speak for us. I found myself in a little local bus – all strangers, all Labor voters . . . all so varied, we were bosom friends by the end of the journey . . . It had to happen, but it seemed too miraculous. And that's how it continues.[7]

Later letters from Harrower, often with clippings from the Australian press, record the devastation of the left after the dismissal of the Whitlam government on 11 November 1975, but also provide wider commentary – always informed and engaged – on international politics, and on local and international arts. Harrower's thoughts and observations are everywhere evident in the essays that Hazzard went on to publish about Australia, often as a direct, though unacknowledged, source.[8] As well as informing our sense of the depth and density of Harrower's place in the Australian scene through this period, and the sharpness of her insights, this correspondence speaks to her complex position as a writer working both within and outside Australia, and in international literary contexts. Harrower takes up this point in one of her earliest letters to Hazzard, where she muses on the view, expressed by an acquaintance about Hazzard but clearly applying just as aptly to Harrower herself, in a comment which illustrates her acuity as a reader. It provides a further reminder to her readers of how her fiction speaks of and to the larger world through the domestic and the intimate:

> Someone was arguing the other night to the effect that Australian writers had to live abroad if they were to write anything of any consequence. Your name was then brought in to support this idea . . . If people write about public events, I suppose this is true, but if they write about people, the only handicap here or anywhere else is a lack that no change of continent would be likely to alter. Since your work seems to me at all times extremely private, I was taken aback to hear this, and could only feel that you had been misunderstood by my acquaintance.[9]

Elizabeth Harrower: Critical Essays takes up the invitation to read and re-read Harrower's fiction offered by her new books and the republication of her earlier work. The collection opens with eloquent tributes by two acclaimed contemporary novelists, Michelle de Kretser and Fiona McFarlane. Their reflections, as writers of fiction working and publishing, like Harrower, in Australia and internationally, bring the complex and inflected labour of reading firmly into view and remind us of how important it is for the work of a great and still-living author to be available to readers. De Kretser traces the delicate imbalances of *The Watch Tower*'s presentation of the inner and outer worlds of her characters, their psychology and the material objects with which they surround themselves through the "flickering glamour" and "dangerous magic" of the commodity form. She

---

7 Elizabeth Harrower to Shirley Hazzard, 5 December 1972.
8 See in particular Hazzard's "Letter from Australia", *New Yorker*, 3 January 1977.
9 Harrower to Hazzard, 16 November 1966.

uses this to observe that Harrower is writing of her contemporary world, the 1960s, even though her plot is set two decades earlier, and she opens up the questions of timeliness and anachrony that resonate across Harrower's publishing career. McFarlane's point of departure is the astonishing quality of Harrower's evocation of place, particularly Sydney, which she reads through the lens of her own departures from and returns to the city. She notes the "very tangled and very tender" knowledge of place invoked in the reader and wonders, resonantly, "if this knowledge gives Harrower a special access to *me* as a reader". Her comment, and the insightful connections de Kretser draws between Harrower and her location in an earlier period, provide an appropriately thoughtful starting point for the rest of this collection.

The shifting sense of writerly time and place plays out across all the essays, with several critics taking up quite directly the extended time frame demanded by the project of reading Harrower; the differing ways her work has come back into focus across the last several decades. Ivor Indyk notes the different effects that the dire expressivity of her prose has had on him over time; its intensity leading him in recent re-readings to "step back from the closeness with which she observes the emotional restlessness of her characters", and to examine larger questions such as morality, godlessness and the processes of human thought. Elizabeth Webby draws on the longevity of her experience of reading and teaching Harrower to reflect on the remarkable record these novels provide of specific social and historical periods, of the topographical and experiential spaces of postwar Sydney and their changing vistas. Webby is particularly interested in the ways that female characters are placed in these spaces, with the interest in the changing experiences of women a particularly salient feature of the mid-century in and of which Harrower was writing.

Nicholas Birns on the other hand traces the centrality of masculine power in Harrower's novels through the historical lens provided by feminist politics. Here is another instance of the ways Harrower's work provides diverse and historically rich perspectives, ways which are also always complicated by the insights and priorities of later, or different, points of departure; her fiction takes us into recognisable historical moments while at the same time recalling to us the contingency of those moments and sites. Robert Dixon offers a broad perspective on Harrower's work and the range of contexts within which it has been produced and consumed, but turns attention to the ways that these novels scope the international worlds across which they move in terms of "metageography", that is, using representations of physical space to unsettle and complicate understandings of national and communal forms and entities. Dixon approaches Harrower's novels via the rubrics of Neal Alexander and James Moran's argument that modernist novels "shuttle restlessly between multiple and overlapping spatial frames: local, regional, national, and international", through the operations of irony, and in the process outlines the formal mechanisms by means of which this work opens itself and its readers out to the world.

There are therefore larger arguments to be made about the working of time and space in Harrower's fiction, and these are most resonant when approached through a consideration of the whole of her work. The republication of Harrower's older novels alongside a new novel and stories provides us with an oeuvre which constructs a dynamic, multidimensional map of the world and of experience; a vision of being in the world that is itself embedded within the structures of her fiction. The opening lines of the first story Harrower ever wrote, "The Fun of the Fair", wire a single experience of an unloved child into the vastness of the earth's weather systems and then into cosmic blackness.

This centrifugal expansion operates to highlight both the insignificance and the grave importance of one young girl within the magnitude of space and time. Across the oeuvre, narrative dimensions and processes constantly collide, misalign, obscure and illuminate each other. The narratives dilate, contract and traverse domains from the individual and everyday domestic experience to societal formations, world history and the cosmos. Importantly, the dimensions and energies of this global and cosmic, this *natural* world, are not ahistorical constructions in Harrower's fiction. Rather, the elements of fictional construction – character, plot, figuration – are animated by the particular energies of the postwar, Cold War mid-century. The dark night experienced by the young girl in "The Fun of the Fair", for instance, is produced by both an electrical storm and an electrical blackout; that is, electricity appears as both meteorological event and modern technology.

The myriad forms of connection across space, time and experience in Harrower's narratives challenge understandings that they can be treated separately in fiction and, indeed, in human history. Megan Nash's reading of *The Watch Tower* takes up the explicit association made between that novel's tyrant, Felix Shaw and the historical figure of Adolf Hitler, arguing that this association does not deny the magnitude of difference in terms of effect between the two, but rather that it refutes a mutual exclusivity of domestic and political tyranny. Elizabeth McMahon notes the charged coming together of forces in the epiphanic moments that recur throughout Harrower's fiction, in which characters connect across conventional boundaries designed to separate them. In these moments, McMahon argues, there is often a shift to a more poetic register, which draws the reader into these intense moments of contact. For instance, in the final scene of the short story "Alice", a young bride visits the elderly Alice in an acknowledgement of friendship: "Even after the girl left, in clouds and drifts of white, nothing seemed substantial. A buoyancy, an airiness, something quite amazing surrounded Alice. She had no idea what it was called".[10] The final sentence here returns both Alice and the reader to the everyday world of grounded reason from the poetic interlude of an "airy" lightness of being.

The novels trace the effects of these moments as they play out over time – and in forms quite different from that of the fleeting epiphany. In *Down in the City*, the fairytale awakening of Esther by the gaze and touch of Stan at their first meeting proves to be the prelude to a narrative of her prolonged debasement. In *The Long Prospect*, the immediate, profound recognition between twelve-year-old Emily and the adult Max, which occurs in the half-shadows of Emily's cinematic fantasies, is ultimately shut down and Emily is transplanted into the tedium of suburban realism. These epiphanies are part of a larger experiential discrepancy traced in Harrower's work between interior and exterior realities, between domains of fantasy – including sanctioned entertainments such as the cinema and fairytale – and quotidian routine. The points of these intersections are often perilous, as we see played out repeatedly in the "romance" thread of her narratives, and the confusion regarding their translation into daily life and in its fictional forms. Julian Murphet's reading of *The Catherine Wheel* in terms of "generic interference" historicises this point to argue that the novel stages a "qualitative leap out of the lumbering ethical narratological circuits of 1950s fiction" into the future of new media and new ways of being.

The figurative constructions of Harrower's fiction also perform complex and dynamic interconnections that serve to mark, *inter alia*, her position at the crossroads between

---

10   Elizabeth Harrower, *A Few Days in the Country and Other Stories* (Melbourne: Text Publishing, 2016), 30–1. All subsequent references are to this edition and appear in parentheses in the text.

modern and postmodern relationships to the world and experience.[11] In these texts, modern people and modern energies are both produced by and part of the postwar industrial world.

New technologies actively enter into the minds and bodies of characters, and the spaces they inhabit and traverse. Harrower can be read in the naturalist tradition of a steely-eyed, forensic, realist dissector of human experience. But her characters are nonetheless almost cyborgian in their interconnection with the atmosphere around them, as Kate Livett argues; with contemporary technology, with telecommunications, and with cinema and postwar media. The telephone is a prosthetic "extension" of Clem's body in *The Catherine Wheel*; and, again in *In Certain Circles*, when Zoe receives the phone call telling her that Anna is in fact alive, she is described as being "only astonishment and relief listening to sounds through a black machine"; and in Christian's repeated invocation of "Stella, Stella" in *The Catherine Wheel*, character and text are merged with the cinema and *A Streetcar Named Desire*, as Murphet argues.

Three essays address the significance of the interconnectivity of electricity and media, linking the specificity of Harrower's mid-century locations to wider, elemental dimensions. Brigid Rooney investigates the centrality of electricity in *The Watch Tower* and *The Long Prospect* to show "how modern circuitries of electrical power reconfigure the relationship between urban and suburban spaces". Moreover, Rooney claims, electricity is an "analogy for the emotional truth" in Harrower's fiction. However, as she argues, connectivity and emotional truth do not necessarily create expansion, potential or enlightenment. On the contrary, the grids of connection create matrices that hold the female protagonists captive. "Shocks" of human connection and insight do not necessarily produce the momentum needed to reach a space outside the grid. Brigitta Olubas argues that alcoholic addiction is tied to electricity as a mode of self-articulation, "a form of connectivity, a flow, like the telephone; declarative but distracting, misleading, unreliable", and ultimately necessary for the illuminations of art and thought to be generated. Through the mechanics of fire, which is linked to both alcohol and electricity, the novel strains towards the articulation of mythic dimensions of quotidian existence. Murphet reads Christian Roland as a character primarily from cinema, even a radio signal. He is part of "a speculative cultural future woven of electronics, mass mediation, and an utterly transformed public sphere". Accordingly, Murphet argues, he is "less a literary character than a loosely assembled media construction projected into Clem's two rooms by the power of electrical circuitry", a point which gestures again to the contrasts of scale and reach that characterise Harrower's larger view. Harrower's profoundly modern understanding of the world does not, then, negate or underestimate primitive and elemental forces. Her characters are propelled by the imperatives of myth and, as Indyk notes, by primitive emotions. In her discussion of the will to power in Harrower's fiction,

---

11   See Ihab Hassan's classic list of the distinctions between modernism and postmodernism in *The Postmodern Turn: Essays in Postmodern Theory and Culture* (Columbus: Ohio State University Press, 1987) in which metaphor is the defining mode of relation in modernist thought whereas metonymy is the defining relationality of the postmodern (48, 91). In Harrower's fiction, for instance, the metaphoric connection between human experience and electricity undergirds *The Long Prospect* and *The Watch Tower*. However, this connection is also metonymic in that human experience and electricity are not only terms of comparison but each is also a part of the other. Further, these metaphorical and metonymic relations are constantly shifting in terms of scale, as seen in the tropological chain of electrics, alcohol and thought in *The Catherine Wheel*.

Kate Livett charts how human drives are connected to "the meteorological fluctuations within and without the human person" in a relationship of profound mutual elementality. Here, too, we find the complicating shifts between metaphor and metonymy with the weather as a symbol of the contest of human wills as well as being co-material with the human in a relationship of mutual interactivity.

In this interplay of forms, genres and figures, both readers and characters are required to shift from the literary contract set up by the conventions of one system of meaning to those of another – and then another. In this maze of systems and their attendant conventions, the heroines of Harrower's fictions find that the truths of one system, one narrative, one domain of experience, are not transferable to others. In this intensely dynamic literary imaginary, characters become stuck in the interstices of form. Some seize opportunities to escape or, at the very least, to participate in a script of their own choosing. Most often, this proves to be destructive but it does allow the exercise of will. Occasionally, also, her protagonists experience moments of clarity, but not coherence. The publication of *In Certain Circles* in 2014 provides a great revelation as to how Harrower envisages these moments of insight might be translated into the world. It is a revelation full of time, including the time of our waiting.

References

Harrower, Elizabeth. *A Few Days in the Country and Other Stories*. Melbourne: Text Publishing, 2016.
———. *In Certain Circles*. Melbourne: Text Publishing, 2014.
Hassan, Ihab. *The Postmodern Turn: Essays in Postmodern Theory and Culture*. Columbus: Ohio State University Press, 1987.
Hazzard, Shirley. "Letter from Australia". *New Yorker*, 3 January 1977.
Trinca, Helen. "Novelist Elizabeth Harrower Has Lived Dangerously but Kept Her Words to Herself". *Australian*, 27 October 2012. http://bit.ly/2nXG9lE.
Wood, James. "No Time for Lies: Rediscovering Elizabeth Harrower". *New Yorker*, 20 October 2014. http://bit.ly/1Cqu4W0.
Wyndham, Susan. "Elizabeth Harrower Doesn't Want Spoilers to Her Own Novel". *Sydney Morning Herald*, 3 May 2014. http://bit.ly/2mJmnJn.

1
Harrower's Things: Objects in *The Watch Tower*

Michelle de Kretser

The Watch Tower (1966) is typically read as a psychological novel, an exemplary study in abuse and entrapment that returns to and intensifies the central subject of Elizabeth Harrower's fiction. Like everyone else who reads it, I am riveted by the forensic brilliance with which Harrower details Felix Shaw's systematic destruction of the lives of the women in his household. Yet this focus on individuals and psychology risks blinding us to other things that are going on in the novel, one of which is a preoccupation with, well, things. So I'd like to look a little closer at objects in *The Watch Tower*.

I'll begin by considering two brief passages from the novel. The first describes the house Felix has recently bought in Neutral Bay:

> It was a lovely single-storeyed colonial house painted white, with a roof of grey slate and long shady verandahs decorated with old wrought iron. There were lawns. There were daphne and camellia and gardenia bushes with dark shiny leaves. In the garden behind the house there were fruit trees, two of which were hung with enormous lemons, sweetly scented.
>
> Inside the rooms were large and cool, and stood awaiting furniture and embellishment at the hands of their new owner. A pattern of leaves, criss-crossed and winking light, blew and shivered on the empty white wall of the sitting-room as the poplars at the side of the house shook and sent shadows indoors.[1]

The second passage reflects on the visit of one of Clare's young friends to the house:

> Clare recalled Ruth wandering, inquisitive, about her bedroom, pausing to admire the impersonal array of covers, brush, comb, Royal Doulton pin trays and small crystal vase that Laura and Felix had bought for the dressing-table. Ruth examined and saw every expensive artifact with an acuteness of interest that fascinated Clare. Clearly, Ruth would remember for months, years, perhaps forever, the thin blue-grey china trays that she had turned about in her plump white hands. She found them worthy of coveting.

---

1   Elizabeth Harrower, *The Watch Tower* (1966; Sydney: Angus & Robertson, 1991), 31. All subsequent references are to this edition and appear in parentheses in the text.

[. . .] A small explosion had revealed to Clare that she was a person to whom one thing was much the same as another, interchangeable because unspeakably unimportant. Another explosion had revealed the alarming fact that this was the way her companions treated *people*. (59)

After Felix has proposed to Laura, she receives a flow of presents from him: "chocolates, nylon stockings, silver trays and wine glasses" (45). The house in Neutral Bay is the costliest and most dazzling of the objects Felix dangles before her, and it serves to quieten Laura's doubts about him. "[A]gainst all her silly, invisible fancies, she had to set the very real white house" (45). Giving more weight to the "real white house" than to her "fancies" proves an error that will ruin her life. In the moral economy of the novel, Laura pays dearly for her susceptibility to desirable objects.

Her marriage to Felix locks her and her sister into a circuitry that reverses the value of people and things. Within hours of the ceremony, Laura feels "like an object" (43). Clare deplores the materialism she observes around her, but in order to survive will herself choose to become an object: the stony, observant watch tower of the title. As for Felix, he is the incarnation of a ghastly little figurine of Bluebeard, his very own "china image" whose "malicious smile never tires" (46).

Even the natural world isn't safe from the drive to reify and possess. Sydney Harbour, "dead from being over-admired by its suburban landlords" (99), is gloated over by Felix as if it belongs to him. The Shaws' beautiful garden, described in the first passage above, becomes a sweatshop in which all in the household labour, eradicating weeds and ensuring the perfection of those glossy flowering shrubs, which come to seem not so different from the artificial flowers produced in one of Felix's factories.

I would like to say three things about all this.

In the first place, I'm struck by the sheer quantity of objects mentioned in *The Watch Tower*. Harrower evokes cars, neon signs, clothing, jewellery, household objects, patent drinks, shop window displays. One reason Felix attracts narrative disapproval is because he is a manufacturer: i.e., someone who puts more things into the world. The gifts given in the Shaw household at Christmas and on birthdays are itemised, since objects stand in for loving kindness in Felix's world. "To the extent that he gave, he atoned and acquired new virtues, to the extent that he received, he was admired, loved and respected" (80). In Felix's perverse reckoning, a gift is an expression not of generosity but of aggrandisement and control. Among the gifts he gives Laura for marrying him, and on subsequent occasions, is a quantity of silverware; Judas' thirty pieces of silver come irresistibly to mind.

My second point is that while disapproval of this world bereft of ideals and stuffed with things is strongly marked in *The Watch Tower*, the rhetoric of the novel is entranced with objects. One has only to consider the lovely, seductive language in which Felix's house is described in the first passage above. I ask you: who wouldn't want to live in that house? Laura is punished for desiring it, but look how Harrower's sentences caress it, down to the shifting leaf-shadows on that wall.

In the second passage above, Ruth "covet[s]" the objects on Clare's dressing-table. The verb is telling: "covet" is an old word, an Old Testament word, one that we hear preceded by "thou shalt not". Unlike Ruth, Clare, the moral centre of the novel, dismisses objects as "interchangeable" and "unimportant" (a judgement that dismisses Ruth along with the objects she covets). Yet those pin trays are evoked with ekphrastic precision. They are "Royal Doulton", fashioned from "thin blue-grey china": four adjectives, one a brand name, lavished on those "interchangeable" and "unimportant" objects. Throughout the novel, Harrower treats objects to precise descriptions – a precision that suggests enthralment. It doesn't exactly undo her moral argument, but I think it serves to complicate it.

My final point is that this complication seems to come very much out of the rapidly burgeoning consumerism of the early 1960s. Although *The Watch Tower* is set in the 1940s, I think it couldn't have been written then. In its appalled fascination with objects, the novel partakes in the commodity consciousness that accompanied the postwar flood of consumer goods and found its most famous artistic expression in Andy Warhol's soup cans. In the realm of fiction, *The Watch Tower* has affinities with Georges Perec's *Things / Les Choses* (1965).[2] As Perec's title suggests, consumerism is central to his novel, which is one of social analysis, and he sets out to satirise commodity fetishism through hyperbolically detailed descriptions of the costly objects his protagonists yearn for but can't afford. Harrower's evocation of objects appears incidental in a novel predominantly concerned with the psychological, yet as in *Things*, *The Watch Tower* suggests that the rise of consumerism leaves its imprint on consciousness, normalising the fetishisation of objects and its corollary, a deadening of affect in human relations. Nevertheless, both Perec and Harrower describe objects in alluring prose: the flickering glamour of the commodity, its dangerous magic, is rhetorically embedded in both books.

References

Harrower, Elizabeth. *The Watch Tower*. (1966) Sydney: Angus & Robertson, 1991.
Perec, Georges. *Things: A Story of the Sixties*. Translated by Helen Lane. New York: Grove Press, 1967.

---

2   Georges Perec, *Things: A Story of the Sixties*, trans. Helen Lane (New York: Grove Press, 1967).

2
Elizabeth Harrower in Sydney

Fiona McFarlane

It seemed especially fitting to re-read the work of Elizabeth Harrower in Sydney in November, the season of the jacaranda, when Sydney is perhaps most perfectly and most ludicrously itself. Because Harrower is one of the great novelists of Sydney, and it's impossible – I find it impossible – to think of her work without also thinking of the suburbs of the lower North Shore, of Kings Cross, and again and again of Sydney Harbour.

Even the Ballowra of *The Long Prospect* (1958) (modelled on Newcastle) and the London of *The Catherine Wheel* (1960) are so deliberately and self-consciously not-Sydney, and their not-Sydneyness plays such a role in how the events of those books unfold, that they're haunted by Sydney, read through Sydney, and in this way participate in a complicated kind of homesickness that very palpably conjures Sydney.

If I'd read *The Watch Tower* (1966) or *In Certain Circles* (2014) or *Down in the City* (1957) while I lived overseas, it would have been in an agony of homesickness; and this despite all the ways in which those books make of Sydney a very beautiful prison, the scene of enormous crimes of personality, to the point that, in *The Watch Tower*, the splendours of the view from the house in Neutral Bay are tainted for Clare simply by Felix's having gloated over them – Felix who knows he should see *something* as he looks over the Pacific at Bulli, but can only see "water and bush",[1] just as Lilian in *The Long Prospect* is unimpressed by the view from Thea's seaside flat (and this is one of my favourite Lilian moments):

> There, below, and straight ahead, was that much-praised view of the sea. A lot of water, yes, but nothing to make a fuss about. She had once said, "For all I care the Pacific can jump in the lake." It had been a success. On the strength of that success she now relaxed her mouth at the Pacific and admitted that it was blue.[2]

Sydney Harbour, in *The Watch Tower*, "glitters" with "brilliance", but it's "blinding", "eye-straining" – the harbour's surface is "fiery white", and the "dazzling light" forces people to take shelter (274). Sydney's beauty is brutal, excessive, and often wasted. It's rarely

---

[1] Elizabeth Harrower, *The Watch Tower* (1966; Melbourne: Text Publishing, 2012), 274. All subsequent references are to this edition and appear in parentheses in the text.
[2] Elizabeth Harrower, *The Long Prospect* (1958; Melbourne: Text Publishing, 2012), 4.

visionary; the light of Sydney doesn't illuminate, it overwhelms, it blunts the senses: there is the inference that men like Felix Shaw and Stan Peterson are allowed to flourish – or at least endure – in part because of the casual carelessness with which the majority of Australians, drunk on sunlight, are prepared to ignore what is, for Harrower, the great question: "how should human beings treat each other?"

My response to the Sydneyness of Harrower is of course an emotional one – I was born in Sydney, I grew up here, and I first read Elizabeth Harrower just after I returned home from many years overseas and was being reminded every day of Sydney's beauties and its limitations. I've recently been reading the American poet and scholar Susan Howe on the snarls and pleasures of reading about a place with which you're very familiar. This is from Howe's book *Spontaneous Particulars: The Telepathy of Archives*: "I experience, through an occult invocation of verbal links and forces, the qualities peculiar to our seasonal changing light and color. It's a second kind of knowledge – tender, tangled, violent, august, and infinitely various".[3]

That was a moment of recognition, reading those sentences and thinking about Elizabeth Harrower's Sydney while surrounded by purple trees – yes, there is another kind of knowledge involved, very tangled and very tender. (I don't think this knowledge gives me – or other people familiar with Sydney – any kind of special access to Harrower's work. But I do wonder if this knowledge gives Harrower a special access to *me* as a reader.)

Along with the emotional, my response to Harrower's Sydney is a creative one, because it's impossible to underestimate the enormous gift it is, as a writer and a reader, to have your own city illuminated in prose as lucid, wise, and relentless as Harrower's. And I see the impact of that gift when I read the prologue of *Down in the City*, and its breathless description of Sydney – which reminds me in some ways of the opening section of Christina Stead's first novel, *Seven Poor Men of Sydney* (1934); both of these passages being designed to introduce Sydney to the reader not familiar with it. It's strange to think that, chronologically speaking, the world's first encounter with Harrower's writing, which is so extraordinarily interior, was in this uncharacteristically distant passage. There's something a little nervous, a little sheepish about that *Down in the City* prologue – the writing is wonderful, of course, but so insistent, so deliberately bold and colourful, stuffed with names and objects, so determined to be bright and noisy, that it makes me think of a tour guide who loves a monument but worries her clients will need some convincing. I can't help but feel that Harrower really wants *Down in the City* to start with the second chapter, which opens just as all her other novels do, *in medias res*: "What was never known for certain was *why* David Prescott acted as he did".[4]

I wonder if this is a reflection of the fact that Harrower wrote *Down in the City* in England – did the act of writing Sydney from London in the 1950s require this kind of conjuring? Was there an anxiety, walking down the much-written streets of London, that a place like Sydney might have to work harder to be the location of a literary novel; that Sydney, unlike London, required some scene-setting before a reader even got to the name, let alone the point of view of a main character? You can see in the later books the way Harrower relaxes about this: the opening of *In Certain Circles*, for example, does give us a description of Sydney (though not until page 4), but it's from Zoe's privileged perspective,

---

3   Susan Howe, *Spontaneous Particulars: The Telepathy of Archives* (New York: Christine Burgin/New Directions, 2014), 59.
4   Elizabeth Harrower, *Down in the City* (1957; Melbourne: Text Publishing, 2013), 10.

as if Sydney has been arranged for her pleasure (and in many ways it has). The exterior map of Sydney we receive at the beginning of *Down in the City* becomes interior and multiple and much more complicated once it's no longer a beautiful, knowing travel guide and reaches us, instead, as character opinion, experience, prejudice and privilege. I can imagine Harrower finishing the prologue and thinking, well, that work has been done, now I can hang up my tour guide's hat and get on with being a novelist, and Sydney can become a remarkable place to play with, to distort and reimagine, to praise and to love and to make fun of and to criticise.

When I think about what Harrower means for me as a writer, I keep returning to Sydney and the question of what to *do* with it: how to approach the gift it is to be tenderly and variously familiar with this particular city. Harrower's Sydney is never simply picturesque; it's always complicated, contradictory, born out of violence – those convict shackles Zoe Howard and her classmates "disbelieve entirely".[5] It's never fixed – just as the characters who live with Harrower's narcissists can rarely be pinned down, are always responding with "I wouldn't say that *exactly*", Sydney shifts and changes depending on class and sex and personality, and all these prismatic surfaces are like lenses Harrower is constantly adjusting throughout her work.

And she's very definitely a writer of adjustments – the way she revisits particular wounds, dwells on the violence of a certain kind of personality, is constantly puzzling out the faulty mathematics of all forms of narcissism – so she adjusts the lens and sees one thing, and then adjusts again and sees another. It's as if personality, human nature, exists on a scale too big for actual use and, knowing this, Harrower has become the genius of a particular segment of it. And Sydney – glorious, banal, oblivious, transcendent, overbearing, contradictory, full of weed-choked parks named after city councillors and the Pacific stretching out to "hazy infinity" (*The Watch Tower*, 274) – Sydney is a gorgeous mirror for Harrower's characters. It reflects the limitations of some, the magnificence of others; it astonishes, it bores, and it's taken for granted, and this is so true of how people live in a city.

Having spoken so much about Sydney, I'll finish with the act of leaving it – Clare as she takes the train from Central out into the bush at the very end of *The Watch Tower*. The Sydney of this section is very different to that of the *Down in the City* prologue, or the bright, terrifying harbourside and inner-city suburbs of most of the novels, including most of *The Watch Tower* itself. These are the outer suburbs of Sydney, the greater part of Sydney, and these suburbs are marked, mostly, by the time it takes to pass through them, and by their formal, funereal dreariness – they're likened to cemeteries, cities of the dead, and described as if they're already the ruins of a lost civilisation. There are no humans in them, only relics. There's no attempt, in this catalogue, to act as tour guide or cartographer; this version of Sydney must be endured in order to reach the release of the bush. When, abruptly, the city ends, the light is no longer dazzling or overwhelming; it is, very simply, "wonderful".

---

5   Elizabeth Harrower, *In Certain Circles* (Melbourne: Text Publishing, 2014), 6.

References

Harrower, Elizabeth. *In Certain Circles*. Melbourne: Text Publishing, 2014.
——. *The Watch Tower*. (1966) Melbourne: Text Publishing, 2012.
——. *The Catherine Wheel*. (1960) Melbourne: Text Publishing, 2014.
——. *The Long Prospect*. (1958) Melbourne: Text Publishing, 2012.
——. *Down in the City*. (1957) Melbourne: Text Publishing, 2013.
Howe, Susan. *Spontaneous Particulars: The Telepathy of Archives*. New York: Christine Burgin/New Directions, 2014.

3

A Really Long Prospect: Elizabeth Harrower's Fallen World

Ivor Indyk

When I first read *The Long Prospect* (1958) some thirty years ago, what impressed me was the expressivity of Harrower's writing, its power in capturing the drama and surge of emotion. It strikes you immediately, in the first pages of the novel, which have the formidable and oppressive grandmother Lilian intruding into the flat of her one-time boarder, the young scientist Thea, with "her eyes on swivels" – and not just her eyes working overtime, but her eyebrows too, "one ironic eyebrow cocked and ready to greet Thea", and "one drooping disdainfully".[1] As so often in Harrower, the drama of emotion is played out in the face – the characters constantly scan each other's faces, they twist incredulously or curve maliciously, they beam with admiration or are bleached with dismay. Their mouths are similarly expressive – close-lipped with resolution, quivering with anger, clamped shut with rage. They exhibit several different kinds of laughter, smiles, grins and giggles – most of them fairly chilling. And then of course the eyes – cold, downcast, brightly sullen, wild with accusation or fixed with tension, "frank and yet guarded" (125). Within moments of her intrusion into the younger woman's flat, Lilian's face and indeed the nervous, endlessly mobile dispositions of her body in the confined space, have registered a whole parade of emotions: disdain, resentment, disapproval, wonder, disappointment, incredulity, anger, excitement, annoyance, jealousy, awe and derision.

If you think of understatement or irony as key features of Australian writing, especially when it comes to emotion, then it is easy to assess Harrower's expressivity as valuable in itself. Only Patrick White shows this kind of discrimination in portraying the emotional lives of his characters, and this kind of dramatic intensity and motility. But when I read *The Long Prospect* again recently, in light of the large and renewed claims that are now being made for Harrower's writing, I found it difficult not to step back from the closeness with which she observes the emotional restlessness of her characters, and to see them from a more distant perspective. I don't go looking for God in Australian fiction, but I don't think I've had a stronger sense anywhere than in Harrower's novels of characters set adrift in a godless universe, free to expend their energy in the domination of others, for want of any higher aim, or to subject themselves to domination by others, to go limp with

---

[1] Elizabeth Harrower, *The Long Prospect* (1958; Melbourne: Text Publishing, 2012), 3. All subsequent references are to this edition and appear in parentheses in the text.

the expectation of a retribution that never comes, or to administer it themselves, to exist without morality, or to assert principle without vitality. At the heart of their fretfulness is a terrible fear of emptiness, and at moments of awareness, when their emotions run high, and they exhaust themselves with anxiety, it is not the emptiness within that triggers their fears, for that is readily filled with emotion, but the emptiness all about them. In short, there is in their restlessness a strong sense that they are doomed.

Or damned, rather than doomed – for although theirs is a godless world, you feel the absence of God, or even just a sustaining moral code, most acutely. In part this is due to the oppressive spell cast by tyrants like Lilian, and Felix Shaw in *The Watch Tower* (1966), whose domination and manipulation of their dependants is so grandiose and cruel, it is as if they have expanded to fill the void left by the absent God, in their arbitrary exercise of power. They can get away with anything now, so why not?

On the other side, there is the acquiescence – not without struggle and anger, not without theatrical displays of helplessness – exhibited by Harrower's victims. I think James Wood is right when he refers to the "Protestant masochism"[2] of Harrower's female characters. In *The Long Prospect*, the emotional territory is marked out as Protestant, not by direct assertion, as it often is in Patrick White's novels, and in his autobiography *Flaws in the Glass* (1981), but by implication. In fact Harrower gets her most powerful effects by implication, invoking the influence of something huge, which is however never visible or present. This is how she describes the relationship between Lilian's daughter Paula and the man she will have to marry. "Their world was Greenhills, their literature and philosophy Hollywood. Young, unthinking, they were nevertheless conscious of having transgressed; until they married, their fear was genuine. By guilt they were estranged before they properly knew each other" (16). As so often in Harrower you have to pinch yourself to be sure she has said what you think she might have said, so slippery is her prose, so quick to accuse or disparage, precisely as it expands the scale of the judgement it prepares to hand down. "How far back must one go to find the root of human imperfection?" Thea wonders, as she attempts to trace the guilt back to its source, and forward to its consequences. "And in which direction first?" (18).

The cause in this case, ubiquitous in *The Long Prospect*, is sex. It is the smell of sex that drives Lilian into Thea's flat, "her eyes on swivels" (3). You have to work it out – "[b]y guilt they were estranged before they properly knew each other" (16) presumably refers to the fact that Paula had thrown herself into the arms of a local boy and got pregnant, but the absence of explanation allows the implication to be much larger. Guilt seems to be the precondition of existence, at the heart of every relationship. In this respect the taint of paedophilia which hangs over the relationship between Thea's one-time lover Max and young Emily is symptomatic of the hold the horror of sex has over the characters. And yet they seem chained to the act, as if sex and self-abandonment were something they were damned to repeat endlessly. The sexual licence in *The Long Prospect* is breathtaking, and all the more shocking for being implied rather than stated.

> In a private room they mixed drinks, ate oysters and quarrelled, changed partners and returned from an absence on the beach, the women to smear soft lipstick on mouths

---

2   James Wood, "No Time for Lies: Rediscovering Elizabeth Harrower", *New Yorker*, 20 October 2014. http://bit.ly/1Cqu4W0.

suddenly pale, the men to blow noses on fishy handkerchiefs, have another drink, and pat their friends on the back with the generosity of self-congratulation. (48)

It is a merciless or indifferent light from the distant heavens that often in Harrower signals the state of damnation, just as, at other times, it is the glittering light off the sea, or sunlight entering a room, which offers a transient moment of grace. So when Lilian, her woman friend, and their lovers, head out for another night of prawns and partying, they step "into a blaze of moonlight that gave to houses, fences, and telegraph poles the sharp transparency of a negative held close to the light" (198). Harrower presents the parade of souls as if it were a *Totentanz*, the women going over on their heels and clutching each other's arms, while "their lovers plodded after them, stolid, dead, and – when the procession to the garage was abruptly halted – bewildered, as if wakened from a deep sleep" (198).

On the other hand, when grace falls on the characters, it does so in heavenly colours, transfiguring the scene with the promise of a momentary redemption – though the question always remains, is this an ironic promise? Thus, in the midst of the grief caused by the forced separation of Max and Emily on the suspicion of their irregular sexual attraction, there is grace – of a kind:

> At that moment the big square window filled with sunshine: the room was lightened, warmed. Sunlight fell on the young girl curled up on the floor against the bed, kindled the brilliant dark-blue of her gown and hung over her uncombed hair: her right cheek, her right hand, were touched by it. And, he too, was covered in light, made suddenly round and whole, brought back to recognizable life, made again her kindest friend, breathing, brown-skinned, looking down at her, leaving her, sent away from her . . . (220)

The moment recedes before it properly gets underway, and changes nothing for either of them. There is a similar promise offered, and immediately negated with irony, in *The Watch Tower*:

> It was one of those magnificent days that people are inclined to think unique, perhaps the most exquisite they are ever destined to see, a day to wring superstitious vows from any who wander into it with untroubled eyes. They will remember this earthly radiance for ever! (They forget the regularity of days fit for trumpet and angels.) (166)

Max, it needs to be said, is a Catholic, and in *The Long Prospect* it is his intrusive presence that first marks the territory out as explicitly Protestant. Max is already married, but that is not the issue – that doesn't register at all in the scheme of things; there isn't a couple in the novel that isn't adulterous – the real problem is that he is a Catholic. A Catholic! "What you need's a man – not a Catholic" (21), Lilian tells Thea, as if Catholics weren't really human. And there is also a barely stated, but to me unmistakeable, Jewish "implication" in the novel, in the presence of Rosen, Lilian's latest boarder-lover. Rosen is an English Jewish name, an abbreviation presumably of Rosenberg, or Rosenbloom, or Rosenbaum (again, White is rather more explicit than Harrower, with his character Rosetree in *Riders in the Chariot* (1961)). Rosen is alternately obsequious and preening, and Lilian treats him like a dog she can kick around at will. Her granddaughter Emily, despite her young age and her principles, gets in on the act too, "eager to go on with the fun of Rosen-baiting"

(26). Max the Catholic has no surname, Rosen has no Christian name – he is simply Rosen throughout. Felix Shaw in *The Watch Tower* is another of those vaguely foreign figures that haunt the borders of the Protestant imagination: his eyes are so dark they have almost no whites, he is swarthy, and in appearance, "like a Turk or a Persian" (21).

There is also something of the Protestant tradition of self-examination in the incessant elaboration of feeling, and the dwelling on motive and thought, which characterises Harrower's style. Susan Sheridan has drawn the comparison between Elizabeth Bowen and Harrower,[3] and *The Watch Tower* features an extract from Bowen's *The Heat of the Day* (1948), which is uncannily like Harrower's own writing in its cadences and discriminations – but I think the echoes go further back, to those nineteenth-century English novels in which the heroine, beset by an unyielding sense of dependency, engages in endless rounds of analysis and reflection – or further back still, to Samuel Richardson's *Clarissa*, for that particular combination of self-scrutiny and attenuated oppression which is also a characteristic of Harrower's writing. Obviously Harrower's novels aren't quite as attenuated as Richardson's – but they can seem so at times, given the relentless nature of the negation to which her characters are subject. It's as if the examination of feeling and thought gets its mandate from oppression, and also its urgency. It is not in its interest to escape the subjection which gives it its rationale. In *The Watch Tower*, just when you think Clare and Laura's subjection to Felix has reached its limit, and the possibility of at least Clare's release from his domination seems imminent, Harrower introduces the pathetic figure of Bernard the presser into the mix – orphaned, impoverished, ill – to ensure that Clare renounces the possibility of removing herself from bondage, by committing herself to his care.[4] The continuation of her subjection, against all the odds, requires some engineering, but that is the point in a way – it gives reason an opportunity to take up the scrutiny of motive afresh, and to judge the self as wanting.

> Clare had needed help always, craved understanding and, above all, had longed to appreciate. When it was manifest that she was not to receive these blessings, her resolution to survive was adamant. She would not be disposed of. However, she had to remain a person whose entire strength was required to maintain her own equilibrium. She stood upright without support; in the circumstances, it was the best she could do. She did apprehend other people and feel them with clarity and depth, receiving information about them involuntarily from her intuition. She had never known what this gratuitous news was for. She wished her fellows well, but it had never entered her head that she – pusillanimous, vicious, sustained only by a peculiar sort of pride and insurmountable determination – could be useful to anyone. If it had been suggested, it would have seemed the cruellest joke. Interest and sympathy she had given easily but acts had always, obviously, been impossible. She had no authority.
>   Now everything was reversed . . . (262)

That sense of analysis, of reason itself, not only as an expression of self-reliance in a world which renders all other rewards uncertain, but as a bulwark against despair, is articulated

---

3   See Susan Sheridan, "Pity's Cost", review of *In Certain Circles* by Elizabeth Harrower, *Sydney Review of Books*, 12 August 2014. http://bit.ly/2pVSKKW.
4   Elizabeth Harrower, *The Watch Tower* (1966; Melbourne: Text Publishing, 2012). All subsequent references are to this edition and appear in parentheses in the text.

again in *The Long Prospect*, when Max argues at length to save Emily's innocence in the face of her grandmother's machinations, only to admit to doubt:

> He knew that he was pedantically occupying, and would continue to occupy, himself with every implication of the evening's scene – moral, metaphysical, sociological, psychological – that he would consider the effect on Emily, on Lilian's relations with her, on his own with Lilian; that, in short, he would do anything to postpone that inevitable flooding of his consciousness by the futile, insistent desire that the catastrophic emptiness of the past years should not be allowed to continue into the future. (153)

The wonder is that Max, or indeed any of Harrower's characters, is able to postpone that chilling combination of "futile, insistent desire" and "catastrophic emptiness" as long as they do.

It should be noted also that Emily, purportedly the developing moral centre of *The Long Prospect*, is by no means an innocent. No one can be innocent in Harrower's world, certainly not those that are victims, given their intimate experience of the exercise of power. The child is no exception, subject to the self-interest and ignorance of parents and grandparents. Emily's awareness of this from a very young age is startling in its knowingness.

> They spoke to her from unreason and were frightening. Having no way of expressing her intuition in lucid thought, she simply knew that they were amateurs. This sensation brought with it a sensation of complication being passed from ignorance to ignorance; of complication handled by indifference; of complication on the verge of being dropped to the ground where it would inevitably shatter. (32)

There is little that Emily doesn't know. She knows how to stage her feelings, and each of her transitions in the novel, from childhood to adolescence, is to a new awareness of power and how it might be used. When her mother abandons her yet again to the care of her grandmother she wails – "I want a mother and father like everyone else" – with an exasperation that is said to be "only half-feigned" (37):

> This was a familiar line. Years ago she had said it and meant it; now she only put herself off, made herself sick, made herself wail again, miserably conscious that though she might be acting, there was a coldness somewhere about things that was reason enough for misery. (37)

There is that big implication again, the long cold prospect. As when Max departs, and Emily dwells repeatedly and theatrically on the black and yellow taxi that bore him away:

> With widened eyes she looked at her dusty fingers, along the quiet street, at the corner round which he had gone away – and the scene was ordinary, familiar. Yet somewhere in the midst of it her intangible opponent had suddenly unveiled himself to her, disported in her tears and weakness. And he was very big. (237)

And invisible too, and probably not even there.

There is another dimension to Harrower's fallen world that deserves commenting on, and that is its primitivism. It's not just the power exerted by the evil tyrants in her novels that has this character, as when it is said of Felix Shaw, "His eyes were rather peep-holes through which a force could be glimpsed, primitive, chilling, subterranean beyond definition" (277). There is also the primitive comfort afforded by objects when the character exhausts himself or herself in tracing the complications of thought or emotion. The garden gate offers continual solace to Emily when she is growing up, parentless – she sucks its frame, she swings on it, she rocks herself backwards and forwards. It is similar to the function performed by the fence post that Thea encounters when, late in the novel, she returns to the scene of her earlier life:

> She was so stirred by what she saw, by what she had been told, by her isolation on this particular hill on this hot Saturday afternoon – most of all by memories – that she could have embraced the post, would have been relieved to weep against it, sleep beside it, waken healed and unmoved. (239)

But most of all there is the sense that the emotions – for all the work that is done on them, to trace their contours, to explain their convoluted logic, to give them a rational air – are themselves essentially primitive. A fallen world is, virtually by definition, a world surrendered to primitive impulses. The human is little better than animal, perhaps worse in some respects. Sexual desire is chief among these impulses – but there is also greed, the lust for power, the opposing drive for self-preservation – which leads to subjection – and cruelty and fear. In this light, what is most striking about Harrower's description of Lilian's reactions, as she rampages through Thea's flat at the beginning of *The Long Prospect*, is not its expression of emotion, but the way she presents Lilian as possessed by emotion, as a monster, an ogre.

References

Harrower, Elizabeth. *The Watch Tower*. (1966) Melbourne: Text Publishing, 2012.
——. *The Long Prospect*. (1958) Melbourne: Text Publishing, 2012.
Sheridan, Susan. "Pity's Cost". Review of *In Certain Circles* by Elizabeth Harrower. *Sydney Review of Books*, 12 August 2014. http://bit.ly/2pVSKKW.
Wood, James. "No Time for Lies: Rediscovering Elizabeth Harrower". *New Yorker*, 20 October 2014. http://bit.ly/1Cqu4W0.

4
Sydney in the Fiction of Elizabeth Harrower

Elizabeth Webby

The recent publication by Text of two new works by Elizabeth Harrower, along with their reissuing of all her earlier novels, some out of print for over fifty years, provides an ideal opportunity to study the development of various themes and preoccupations in her fiction. I have chosen here to focus on her fictional representations of Australia and Australians, and in particular how the city of Sydney, where she has spent most of her life, figures in her work. The previous difficulty of accessing Harrower's novels has, no doubt, been one of the reasons why they have received little detailed critical study. Most essays published to date have discussed *The Watch Tower* (1966), using a variety of perspectives but rarely mentioning its Sydney setting. In 1990, when editor of *Southerly*, I published an essay on *Down in the City* (1957) by Rosie Yeo, based on her Honours thesis which I had supervised, to draw attention to this then largely forgotten novel. While the differences in class and attitude of those who live in various parts of Sydney are especially important in this novel, the city appears in all of Harrower's works, even those not primarily set there.

Re-reading Harrower's books in the order of their first publication, I was struck by the more direct and critical comments on Australia and Australians in her two earliest novels, especially when compared with her two latest ones, both written in Australia. *Down in the City* and *The Long Prospect* (1958) were written in London, where Harrower had gone in 1951, initially to study psychology, later to try to become a writer. There, like Clemency James in Harrower's third novel *The Catherine Wheel* (1960), she seems mainly to have spent her time at her desk, living as cheaply as possible. In one of her rare interviews, conducted by the then editor of *Meanjin* Jim Davidson in 1980, Harrower said: "I was drawn to write about Sydney because I'd been absent from it for some years. I used to love it".[1] Perhaps as a result of being written in London rather than Sydney, coupled with Harrower's inexperience as a writer, there is a much more overt and deliberate setting of the scene in *Down in the City* when compared to her later novels.

Unlike these later novels, *Down in the City* does not plunge the reader immediately into the world and minds of its central characters. Instead, it opens with a descriptive prologue designed to establish and contrast the very different areas of Sydney inhabited by Esther Prescott and Stan Peterson. Although geographically quite close, since both are

---

[1] Jim Davidson, *Sideways from the Page: The Meanjin Interviews* (Melbourne: Fontana, 1983), 252.

situated to the east of Sydney's CBD, the places in which they live could not be further apart in terms of class, wealth and respectability:

> It is three miles and as many worlds from the peaceful high-walled streets, the tennis-courts and golf-course of Rose Bay to the hill of glamour and fostered disreputability that is King's Cross. One holds the white-brick, blue roofed mansions and landscaped gardens of the managing directors and senior partners; the other, the craggy hotels and flats, the furnished rooms and cement courtyards of the ambitious and the seekers of anonymity.[2]

The prologue goes on to provide a more detailed picture of Kings Cross in the immediate postwar era, with its German delicatessens and Italian fruit shops overflowing with imported delicacies and "cornucopias of paw-paw, passion-fruit and pineapple", its foreigners and racketeers, its "long-haired boys, mascared women and powdered men" (5). But it does not stop there, moving into the city centre to sketch little vignettes of various classes of Sydneysiders going about their daily business: the affluent couple, who already own a boat and a beach house, discuss taking a trip to Europe while waiting in their car for the traffic lights to change, two bank clerks ponder which horse to back on Saturday, three golden debutantes scan the social pages for news of their latest parties, six girls from a clothing factory plan an evening out dancing. Finally, we meet another girl busily dispensing milkshakes to thirsty crowds:

> Stella has had three jobs already this summer and she won't be in this one much longer. The trouble is they all expect a girl to give up her private life to her work. But not Stella. If Jacko has a day off and says, "Come on!" she goes. There are other jobs, and she's young this year. (8-9)

Down in the City was first published in London in 1957 by Cassell and Co. with a front cover featuring a photograph of trams and cars going to and from the city, down what must be Oxford Street as it was in the 1950s. There are tram wires criss-crossing above the street and advertisements for Penfolds wine and Capstan cigarettes on top of two of the buildings that line it. The back cover features blurbs for two other recently published antipodean novels by now forgotten authors, Florence Preston's *Harvest of Daring* and Frank O'Grady's *Hanging Rock*. Preston published four novels with Cassell during the 1950s; all but one were historical romances set not in a city but on "a New Zealand sheep-farm". O'Grady, brother of the better-known John, author of *They're a Weird Mob*, also published in 1957, had three historical adventure tales published by Cassell during the 1950s; all had Australian bush settings. He later published three more with Angus & Robertson in the 1960s.

As a contemporary novel set in the city rather than the bush, Harrower's *Down in the City* was therefore very different to most books about Australia and New Zealand published in Britain in the 1950s. But no doubt the view of Sydney Harrower offers in the prologue, as a place with plenty of sunshine, exotic food, abundant jobs, wealth and leisure, would have provided an attractive alternative for British readers still coping with austerity in the aftermath of World War Two. In *The Catherine Wheel*, published by Cassell in 1960,

---

2   Elizabeth Harrower, *Down in the City* (London: Cassell & Co., 1957), 5. All subsequent references are to this edition and appear in parentheses in the text.

England is generally portrayed as cold and wet, with most of the characters struggling to survive financially. At one point, Clemency, the first person narrator, thinks nostalgically of "Sydney smelling of sun and sea and roast coffee beans".[3] At another she comments on the depressing effects of the English climate, contrasting it with Australia where "life is lived in the open" (189).

While the prologue to *Down in the City* seems to reflect something of Harrower's own nostalgia for Sydney, it is also possible that her publishers requested she add this introductory description of the city, because it was an aspect of life in Australia still largely unknown in England. Kings Cross, for example, is equated by Harrower in the prologue to an area of Paris more familiar to British readers: "It is Montmartre: it is bright and wicked" (5). Some readers, indeed, may have been disappointed to find little of this aspect of the Cross, especially nothing more about the "mascared women and powdered men", in the rest of the novel! But in its ethnographic overview, the prologue also demonstrates a highly critical attitude to Harrower's fellow Australians, similar to that displayed in Patrick White's well-known essay "The Prodigal Son", first published a year after *Down in the City*:

> In all directions stretched the Great Australian Emptiness, in which the mind is the least of possessions, in which the rich man is the important man, in which the schoolmaster and the journalist rule what intellectual roost there is, in which beautiful youths and girls stare at life through blind blue eyes.[4]

White wrote this essay to explain why, despite the all-pervading mindless materialism and hedonism, he had returned to Australia in 1948 and continued to live there. After her own return in 1959, Harrower clearly shared White's concern about the attitudes to life of most Australians but was also overwhelmed by the natural beauty of Sydney: "I thought, my god, this is not a serious country. On the other hand at Balmoral, where I went, it was so beautiful, it was gorgeous. I thought if everyone in Europe knew how gorgeous it was, they would all want to come".[5] And interspersed between the vignettes of unthinking Australians in the prologue to *Down in the City* one finds this passage describing the natural beauty of the country:

> On the beaches and cliffs of the coast the breakers crash. The Pacific, white-flecked, stretches out to hazy infinity. The dark, dusty bush waves in the sea-breeze. South, the irrigated orchards, long miles of fruit trees, flourish, and in the north, the tropical plantations, the sugar-cane. Beyond the mountains to the west great plains of yellow wheat bend and rise acre on acre under a gentle wind, under the deep blue sky, unmarred by hill or cloud, wide as the continent. (7)

The prologue ends with an image of the night sky: "Away from the city and the glimmer of neon lights the vast black heavens overawe the earth with incandescent stars" (9). Often in Harrower's fiction the natural world, especially the night sky, provides what is the

---

3   Elizabeth Harrower, *The Catherine Wheel* (1960; Melbourne: Text Publishing, 2014), 114. All subsequent references are to this edition and appear in parentheses in the text.
4   Patrick White, "The Prodigal Son", in *Patrick White Speaks* (Sydney: Primavera Press, 1989), 15.
5   Ramona Koval, interview with Elizabeth Harrower, *The Monthly Video*, October 2014. Transcript at http://bit.ly/2pGhjKU.

only source of escape for characters constrained by pressures placed upon them by their circumstances and by others. At times, too, her characters' failure to perceive beauty in a scene is used by Harrower to reflect either their tension and despair or their lack of interest in anything that is not central to their own narrow world view.

An example of the latter can be found in Harrower's second novel, *The Long Prospect*, which also contains passages that clearly reflect Harrower's critical opinion of most of those she had left behind in Australia. This novel does not have a descriptive prologue but takes us directly into the thoughts of one of its characters. Lilian finds that the door to the flat where her former boarder Thea is now living is ajar and enters, "her eyes on swivels".[6] This marvellous phrase immediately establishes Lilian not only as a determined busybody but an unsympathetic character, something confirmed when she has no time for natural beauty, as shown in her "contemptuous dismissal" of the flat's ocean view: "A lot of water, yes, but nothing to make a fuss about. She had once said, 'For all I care the Pacific can jump in the lake'"(5-6). After this dramatic opening, the narrative needs to backtrack to fill in the details of Lilian's daughter's hasty marriage and its failure, in order to explain why her granddaughter Emily is living with her. And, as in *Down in the City*, Harrower also needs to set up the main contrast on which the novel depends. Whereas Harrower's first novel presents a clash between old and new influences and aspirations, as reflected in the class differences between Rose Bay and Kings Cross, the contrast in *The Long Prospect* depends more on attitude and education. This is how Thea is described in a lengthy passage marking out her difference from most of those around her:

> Adult, intelligent, feeling, the opposite of frivolous and yet not earnest, she was the opposite of the popular ideal of her place and time. Then and there, in the cities, great wealth marked a naïvety one would hesitate to call childlike. A contradictory striving after perpetual adolescence, sophistication, and an accumulation of wealth were the motives of action. The chief conviction was one of superiority; this was brought about by the Pacific isolation of the continent, and, contrariwise, by trips to a Europe where all the famous treasures were old and frequently dirty, where there were peasants, and the city-dwellers were peculiarly poor. What the fuss was about Europe few Australians could imagine. Not all of them believed in its existence.
>
> To be one of the self-critical minority was to be not so much politically unsound – for there was very little, it seemed, to be political *about* – as thoroughly, disagreeably, un-Australian. (101-2)

Like the prologue to *Down in the City*, this is a much more direct reflection of Harrower's own view of Australia and Australians than anything in her later fiction. Not surprisingly, there are clear echoes here of the prologue, where the main purpose of a trip to Europe was to buy the latest Paris fashions and so become "the best-dressed woman in Sydney"(6). For Harrower and others of her generation who belonged to "the self-critical minority" with intellectual and artistic interests, however, Europe was the place to be. Harrower dates a change in her own attitude to 1972 and the coming of Gough Whitlam, when "[m]any people who were very isolated in that uncongenial sort of Australia found themselves at home in their country for the first time".[7]

---

6   Elizabeth Harrower, *The Long Prospect* (1958; Melbourne: Sun Books, 1966), 5. All subsequent references are to this edition and appear in parentheses in the text.

Certainly, most of the characters in *The Long Prospect* seem determined to prove they are very much Australian in their love of drinking and parties, and their contempt for people like Thea and her former lover Max, who prefer reading to carousing. Through Max, Emily is introduced to the wider world of books and knowledge, becoming by the end of the novel, a member of the "self-critical minority", with a look that is "a provoking compound of scepticism and understanding, impatience and calm" (186) as she is forced to play along with her parents' games. Likewise, in *The Watch Tower*, Clare is forced to take part in her sister Laura's placating of Felix, her cruel and demanding husband, even though "Laura confused what was with what ought to be in a way that deeply antagonized her uncompromising sister".[8] Like Emily, Clare is a reader who longs to find people with whom she can communicate:

> Now with Chekhov's, Dostoevsky's, Tolstoy's Russians, who were all more recognizable as people than people were, you could sit on a fine day, or a day of storms, and discuss even the weather with exquisite joy in the company of fully-grown human beings who had eyes set straight in their heads. (69-70)

Of course, these are Clare's thoughts, rather than the narrator's, as in Harrower's first two novels, and readers will remember that many of the characters in Russian literature also fail to have "eyes set straight in their heads". Hence there is more than a little irony in the later reference to Clare as "the only Russian in Sydney", but her sentiments do echo those in *The Long Prospect*, even though now presented more dramatically.

In the passage just quoted, Clare is travelling by ferry to her workplace in the city centre. As she wonders where she will ever find someone else from her tribe, "Clare sighed and stared at the everlasting harbour" (70). In the remainder of this chapter I look at how the physicality of Sydney, its characteristic sights, sounds and smells, are used by Harrower to provide insights into her characters' thoughts and feelings. Returning to *Down in the City*, near the beginning we are told that Esther, who has been brought up in splendid isolation by her father after her mother's early death, has two pleasures: initially, "to be hot, to be alone in the sun, to notice the gradual deepening of her tan". When she gets older she comes to love visiting the city centre, to "smell the coffee, the flowers, the rich expensive leather, the cosmetics. She looked through ruby glass in antique shops, and handled heavy satins from abroad" (14). From this, we are alerted to the deep sensuality that lies beneath Esther's innocent gentility, something that, combined with her loneliness, leads to her marriage at thirty-three to Stan Peterson, "after having known him for two weeks" (15). When Esther and Stan go out for the first time, on what she feels is "a night of unusual magnificence" (24), they drive across the bridge to the North Shore and eventually into a reserve on the harbour: "at night, when the bush – an aromatic mixture of scrub and gum, old as the continent – rustled on its perimeter, and the black water lapped against the retaining wall, it had mystery and beauty" (26). And it is here, after some hours with Stan, that Esther agrees to marry him.

Esther's life is radically changed; after her isolated years in secluded Rose Bay her move to Stan's flat at Kings Cross brings her new friends in Laura Maitland and Rachel

---

7 Davidson, *Sideways from the Page*, 252.
8 Elizabeth Harrower, *The Watch Tower* (London: Macmillan, 1966), 43. All subsequent references are to this edition and appear in parentheses in the text.

Demster, who live in the same building. Though outwardly charming, Laura is eventually revealed as a busybody whose narrow-minded prejudices anticipate those of Lilian and her friends in *The Long Prospect*. Rachel, a seventeen-year-old orphan who lives with her aunt and uncle, anticipates Emily and Clare in her love of reading and need for affection and is initially won over by Laura. Like Emily at the end of *The Long Prospect* she feels that there is nothing in life to look forward to, something reflected in her jaundiced view of her surroundings. Walking with Esther near the water, she sees some teenage girls and boys laughing together:

> Contempt and envy vied for a place in Rachel's feelings. She looked away from them to the dark blue harbour. She hated the colour of the water: it was not a colour at all. If she were to scoop a handful up, the watery blueness would remain behind. It was as spurious as life itself – second-rate. (47)

For Rachel, salvation arrives in the form of a new job where she meets Luigi Roberto, "a former classics master from Milan", who she finds "treated her as an adult, and liked her to say what she thought" (90). In her reaction to their relationship, the cracks in Laura Maitland's seemingly charming façade begin to appear as she displays her prejudices: "'But a foreigner! – I won't even call him a new Australian – I don't suppose he's even naturalized'" (90). Harrower, however, is happy to use the term in a passage shortly afterwards which represents Australians from the perspective of the newcomers: "Earnest and snubbed, the old-young New Australians went unsmiling through the streets, despising and fearing the lotus-eaters among whom they now lived, despised and feared by them" (117).

Down in the City is the only one of Harrower's novels to depict local reactions to the postwar changes to Australia's population mix. Two of the stories in *A Few Days in the Country* (2015) do, however, deal with this. Although there is no indication when they were written, both focus on young women working in Sydney in the years immediately after World War Two. In "The City at Night", after her first day at work Janie goes for a meal with Leonie, who arrived in Australia from Lithuania as a baby. She is disliked by the other women at work because she is "different" but it is this very difference that appeals to Janie. As the meal progresses, they discover they have much in common in their liking of swimming, reading and going to plays and are, in Harrower's words, like "two lonely Martians meeting unexpectedly on Earth".[9] While this story has a happy ending rare in Harrower's work, this is not the case with the following one, "Summertime". Here, the young Claire Edwards is working as a clerk in a clothing factory owned by a Miss Frazer. Like Laura Maitland in *Down in the City*, though she claims to act in Claire's best interest, Miss Frazer is an interfering busybody who wishes to control the younger woman. Claire has remained friends with a former employee, Annette, another who arrived in Australia as a baby, though is still seen as inexorably foreign by Miss Frazer. Like Laura, she complains about Annette not being naturalised and succeeds in destroying the friendship when she tells her that she does not deserve to be Claire's friend. The prejudices here are shown to operate in both directions, however, since Annette refuses to invite Claire to parties at her house because the other guests will all be foreigners: "Her eyes would shine

---

9   Elizabeth Harrower, *A Few Days in the Country and Other Stories* (Melbourne: Text Publishing, 2015), 39. All subsequent references are to this edition and appear in parentheses in the text.

with remembered fun, and Claire would feel, but not say, that there was nothing that she would like better than a party, 'all foreigners'" (49).

The young women of these stories resemble Clare from *The Watch Tower*, where it is a foreigner, the young Dutch refugee Bernard, who is the catalyst for her eventual escape from the constraints of her dysfunctional family triad with Laura and Felix. Nicholas Birns notes that in Harrower's fiction the city is seen as confining rather than liberating.[10] This is particularly true of *The Watch Tower*, where not even the beauty of the harbour survives the deadening effect of Clare's forced confinement. After she has tried unsuccessfully to escape the beautiful house at Neutral Bay, in which she is sentenced to live with Laura and the cruel and demanding Felix, she looks at the city with very jaundiced eyes:

> In a way, all she had was herself and the sky. If she looked down from it, there were asphalt streets, cement footpaths, tight little bungalows, ripe gardens and scratchy ones, hovels, crowded reverberating streets in the city, advertising, dust, nothing wonderful, no work of genius, only the monotonous harbour, dead from being over-admired by its suburban landlords. (99)

Here the night sky is the only part of the world to offer Clare consolation. Shortly afterwards, when Felix has made another failed attempt to win the company and friendship of a younger man through an over-generous business deal, Laura also recognises that her dreams of a different life, one where she is not constantly working, will never be realised. In despair she travels into the city centre and walks aimlessly up and down the streets:

> The city looked tawdry, dirty, flimsy as a fun-fair, grit falling from half-demolished buildings, deserted scaffolding rising above those still under construction . . . Neon signs hung low overhead from low awnings and stretched into the diminishing distance – a printed roof of glowing signs in queer off-reds, pinks, yellows, blues and greens, mis-spelling lunatic messages with demented jocularity, letters jumping, flashing and changing, messages from things to no one, silently chattering over the blighted streets. (108)

The "lunatic messages" here mirror the "screaming emptiness" in Laura's mind, her sense that she must escape from her marriage to Felix but her inability to think of a way to do this. Later she buys a newspaper and reads through the advertisements, hoping to find a job and somewhere else to live. But she has no qualifications and very little money in her purse, so eventually all she can do is go back to him. When Clare finally does manage to escape at the end of the novel, it is significant that she does not go overseas but leaves the city for the country. As her train travels away from Sydney it passes through the inner suburbs: once again, the description of them is filled with images of hardness, death and decay:

> black rotting terraces, narrow walls and fences leaning askew. Dismal relics of clothing blew damply on clotheslines. The outer suburbs marched up, crowded, formal and hard as nineteenth-century cemeteries. (219)

---

10   Nicholas Birns, *Contemporary Australian Literature: A World Not Yet Dead* (Sydney: Sydney University Press, 2015), 57.

After passing through more outer suburbs with their "hills and valleys of roofs", their "hard shapes" and "graveyard architecture", the train finally arrives in the bush:

And there were trees suddenly, swift-moving past – blossoming eucalyptus, pines. Alone in the compartment, Clare jerked the window up and leaned out into the day. The light was wonderful. Waves of air beat against her face, and it smelled of grass, or clover, or honey. (219)

Towards the end of *In Certain Circles* (2014), Zoe, one of its four central characters, travels into the city centre to have lunch with her brother Russell. This is one of the very few occasions where the novel's action is not confined to the harbourside suburb where they have grown up. Written after *The Watch Tower* but withdrawn from publication by Harrower in 1971, its action covers twenty-three years from the end of World War Two to the late 1960s. The postwar rebuilding of the city described in the passage from *The Watch Tower* quoted earlier, while still underway, is seen here in a more positive light as scaffolding is removed:

Buildings Zoe had known all her life had disappeared since the previous week. The wreckers were out; cranes hung over the city. Scaffolding that had come to seem a permanent hazard to pedestrians had been whisked away to reveal skycrapers, fountains, minatory sculpture. Naming the restaurant where he had booked a table, Russell had added the qualification, "If it's still there."[11]

Here the changes to the city Zoe has "known all her life" anticipate the major changes in both Russell's and her lives that are shortly to follow, thanks to the shock of the apparent suicide of Anna, Zoe's sister-in-law, and the revelation of the longstanding though suppressed love between her and Russell. This in its turn leads to the breakup of Russell's marriage to Lily as well as that between Zoe and Stephen, Anna's brother. Despite, or perhaps because of this, *In Certain Circles* also ends on a positive note, in this case without the need for Zoe to leave Sydney for the country as Clare had done in *The Watch Tower*. For Zoe, "the day was lovely. And now she could move on" (152).

Although there is little description of the built environment of Sydney in *In Certain Circles*, as in Harrower's earlier novels the physical environment is employed throughout to reflect the characters' feelings. The novel opens on a hot day near to Christmas, with the seventeen-year-old Zoe's innocence and self-preoccupation amusingly on display: "If you could believe what you read, Sydney was one of the largest cities in the English-speaking world. In this place – Sydney – then, that the newspapers of the city were always praising, Zoe's mother and father held moderately conspicuous positions" (7). And since her parents, whom strangers regard as special, see Zoe herself as even more special, "Zoe took attention and praise for granted, as though they were part of the public utilities, like running water and electricity" (7-8).

When we meet her later, in part three of the novel, Zoe is forty; fifteen years of marriage to Stephen have worn away her innocence and self-confidence, thanks to his refusal to be happy and his constant criticism of her. Her view of the possibilities of life has now become much more limited and realistic, as reflected in Sydney now being described

---

11 Elizabeth Harrower, *In Certain Circles* (Melbourne: Text Publishing, 2014), 200–1. All subsequent references are to this edition and appear in parentheses in the text.

as "the world's twenty-eighth largest city, with a population more or less equal to Rome" (183). Now, too, Zoe's mind is occupied not with the harbour view in front of her but with images of the "ruins of blackened smoking cities" (183). When, a few days later, Lily, devastated by the loss of her twin daughters who have gone to London on ballet scholarships, comes over to complain, Zoe is less than sympathetic. In response, "[g]iving her a glance of purest hatred, Lily turned ostentatiously to stare at the well-known view, which filled the room like a rather too-literal painting of itself" (191). Like Zoe's earlier, Lily's emotional turmoil is reflected in her failure to see what is in front of her; the harbour view is not appreciated for its beauty but regarded with as much disdain as an inferior work of art.

Seen from outside rather than inside the house, however, the physical world can allow for a momentary truce between Stephen and Zoe as they walk on the beach and swim. And their final discussion about the end of their relationship occurs as they sit in the sun outside, where Stephen has gone to "contemplate the view" (242). Unlike the wives in Harrower's earlier novels who remain trapped in the various disasters that are their marriages, Zoe is able to recover from her poor choice of husband and prepare to "move on", though not necessarily to leave her Sydney home.

Although, as cited earlier, Harrower has pointed to changes in Australia following the election of the Whitlam government in 1972, she has not to my knowledge said anything about the influence of feminism on her work. Yet *In Certain Circles* does allow women more agency than they had in Harrower's earlier fiction. Although Anna, whose status as an orphan most closely resembles that of Laura and Clare, marries David to escape the grind of office work and poverty, she is freed by his early death and later becomes a successful potter. Both Lily and Zoe have supportive families, attend university and pursue professional careers. While not continuing with these after their marriages, with Lily choosing to devote herself to her daughters and Zoe to Stephen, they do establish a translation business, even though there is no need for them to earn money. The constrictions that dominate women's lives in Harrower's earlier novels are less apparent here, as reflected in the greater emphasis on exterior rather than interior scenes, with characters gathering on the verandah, going for drives in the country or walking along a beach. One can only wonder about the ways in which Harrower might have responded, had she continued writing, to the continuing changes in women's roles, in Sydney and in life in Australia after 1972, and regret her long silence.

References

Birns, Nicholas. *Contemporary Australian Literature: A World Not Yet Dead*. Sydney: Sydney University Press, 2015.
Davidson, Jim. *Sideways from the Page: The Meanjin Interviews*. Melbourne: Fontana, 1983.
Harrower, Elizabeth. *A Few Days in the Country and Other Stories*. Melbourne: Text Publishing, 2015.
——. *In Certain Circles*. Melbourne: Text Publishing, 2014.
——. *The Watch Tower*. London: Macmillan, 1966.
——. *The Catherine Wheel*. (1960) Melbourne: Text Publishing, 2014.
——. *The Long Prospect*. (1958) Melbourne: Sun Books, 1966.
——. *Down in the City*. London: Cassell & Co., 1957.
Koval, Ramona. Interview with Elizabeth Harrower. *The Monthly Video*. October 2014. http://bit.ly/2pGhjKU.
White, Patrick. "The Prodigal Son". In *Patrick White Speaks*. Sydney: Primavera Press, 1989.

5

A Wrong Way of Being Right: The Tormented Force of the Harrower Man

Nicholas Birns

Elizabeth Harrower's fictions are often severe and enigmatic, and, although riveting in their surface action and exquisite in their style, do not immediately disclose their meaning. Yet it could well be said that if Harrower has a subject it is gender. All her novels are about gender relations and hierarchies. Indeed, the only way to ignore this is if we persist in seeing gender as a minor and provincial sphere, not heeding to the way that, as Raewyn Connell puts it, gender institutions affect all social institutions. This is even more salient as we realise how, in Connell's words, gender differences can appear in one sense so "stark and rigid" and in another so "fluid, complex, and uncertain".[1]

Harrower's characters, at least until her most recent novel, live in a world where gender tends to be reduced to the stark and rigid. In Ann Snitow's terms, "male and female are both forced by circumstances to caricature themselves".[2] Feminism, indeed, reframed the masculine by making it contingent, even provincial. And it is only from such a contingent standpoint that we can understand the men in Elizabeth Harrower's fiction.

Forced by Circumstances

A Harrower man is a discrete type, one which, perhaps, her fiction has already made archetypal. Felix Shaw in *The Watch Tower* (1966) is the *mal idéal* of this type. Felix marries the hapless Laura Vaizey when her mother Stella has returned to England and she is left on her own. Felix quickly reveals himself as domineering and megalomaniac. In this, he is exemplary of the Harrower man. Harrower men establish heteronomy. In other words, they rule others, particularly women, control them, deprive them of autonomy.

Yet Harrower men also cannot exercise self-control; they are ironically, as Naomi Riddle has outlined, hysterical, and cannot sustain their own centre.[3] Riddle critiques previous analyses of Harrower's work for assuming that the women in Harrower's novels

---

1   Raewyn Connell, *Gender: In World Perspective* (London: Polity, 2009), 3.
2   Ann Snitow, *The Feminism of Uncertainty: A Gender Diary* (Durham, NC: Duke University Press, 2015), 185.
3   Naomi Riddle, "'Turning inward on himself': Male Hysteria in Elizabeth Harrower's *The Watch Tower*", *Southerly* 72, no. 1 (2012): 204-13.

are passive victims of authoritarian, domineering, self-contained men. Arguing against this, Riddle exposes the vulnerability and inconsistency of Harrower's male characters.

I would like to pursue the point that Harrower's men become authoritarian precisely because of their vulnerability. The force they try to exercise over women is a result of their own feeling of having been forced by circumstance. Furthermore, the women gravitate to them precisely out of a tragic hope that these men will exercise force on their behalf rather than against them. What Natalya Lusty calls the "emotional and psychological vulnerability of men" leads Harrower's male characters to try to reinforce the tottering frame of their own self-conceived power by being abusive and domineering towards the women in their lives.[4] Thus the behaviour of men such as Felix, the sadistic-hysterical chocolate-factory owner who marries Laura Vaizey in *The Watch Tower* stems from his own feelings of fear, loss and inadequacy.

Harrower's men are important as an index of gender because they are very much at a transitional point. They at once continue and alter the tradition of difficult men in Anglophone fiction. There are cold, distant, controlling men, like Soames Forsyte in the early volumes of John Galsworthy's *Forsyte Saga*, who wants to possess and objectify women, largely because he lacks the capacity for empathy. There are men like Mr Casaubon in George Eliot's *Middlemarch*, Mr Gradgrind in Charles Dickens' *Hard Times*, and Mr Dombey in Dickens' *Dombey and Son*, who have very different types of pathologies and narcissisms, but all of whom are repressed and suffocated by their own personae.[5]

What I will call the classic Harrower men – Felix Shaw, as well as Christian Roland in *The Catherine Wheel* (1960) and Stan Peterson in *Down in the City* (1957) – are aggressively masculine. But unlike Gradgrind or Soames or Casaubon, their problem is *not* a lack of feeling. They are indeed overflowing with emotion, in the form of resentment and rage. Though authoritarian, seeking to subordinate the women in their lives, they are filled with an anxiety, a fear of their own inadequacy. But they are also insurgent: they are lower middle class or working class, they often feel the world is conspiring against them, so that their oppression of their women inflicts on them their own sense of oppression and subjugation. One might think in this context of Marlon Brando, James Dean, the early Elvis Presley, Stanley Kowalski in Tennessee Williams' *A Streetcar Named Desire*, perhaps the "American crooners" that threaten to drive out the local talent in Harrower's *Down in the City* (1957).[6] But arguably the ultimate source for the Harrower man is D.H. Lawrence, especially the Lawrence extolled by F.R. Leavis, who stands, as described by Susan Reid, for "organicism, humanism, and resistance to industrialization".[7] These ideologies produce a masculinity that is at once brutal and rebellious, subversive and domineering. As Susan

---

[4] Natalya Lusty, "Introduction", in *Modernism and Masculinity*, ed.Natalya Lusty and Julian Murphet (Cambridge: Cambridge University Press, 2014), 5.

[5] See John Galsworthy, *The Forsyte Saga* (1922; Hertfordshire: Wordsworth Classics, 2001); George Eliot, *Middlemarch* (1872; Hertfordshire, UK: Wordsworth Classics, 2000); Charles Dickens, *Hard Times* (1854; New York: Dover Thrift Editions, 2013); Charles Dickens, *Dombey and Son* (1848; New York: Random House, 2003).

[6] Elizabeth Harrower, *Down in the City* (1957; Melbourne: Text Publishing, 2013), 7. All subsequent references are to this edition and appear in parentheses in the text.

[7] Susan Reid, "Idylls of Modernity: D.H. Lawrence's Subversive Pastoral", in *New Versions of Pastoral: Post-Romantic, Modern, and Postmodern Responses to the Tradition*, ed. David James and Philip Tew (Madison, NJ: Fairleigh Dickinson University Press), 85.

Bordo said of Stanley Kowalski, the man becomes "the abusive but sexually vital king of his household".[8]

Harrower men in general have the strengths and weaknesses of Lawrence as filtered through Leavis: the aggressive, forceful rebel who wants to overthrow the system but also to be himself authoritarian and domineering. These men have a clear view of the world, an obdurate certainty as to the nature of the universe. But they are so determined to control others' choices – to rule – that they end up suborning even their own autonomy.

It is easy for us to condescend to these men. Economic conditions have changed; the chocolate factories in Sydney and the working-class solidarity they produced are no more. While Harrower's men had to fight to receive any education, it is assumed now that everyone will be educated. Harrower's men either work with their hands themselves or run a business supervising the manual labour of others. Today, readers are more likely to wonder what Harrower's women saw in these men, and to thank their stars men today are not like that. The consensus is that masculinity has changed now, such that it is not considered a political imperative to denounce or decry these earlier men.

In addition, whereas formerly the macho outsiders – the Norman Mailers, Jack Kerouacs and Charlie Parkers – were valued, today there is more value given to the geek, the nerd, as seen in the *Harry Potter* books or the television comedy program *The Big Bang Theory*, or Junot Diaz's novel *The Brief Wondrous Life of Oscar Wao*, or, consummately, Steve Jobs and Bill Gates. F.R. Leavis spent fifty years in academia yet was determined not to come off as a geek, and used words coded with machismo even as he acclaimed George Eliot to be the greatest English novelist. Today, geek chic is a watchword, and geek chic has, as Sherrie A. Inness has argued, not only freed men from violent, aggressive stereotypes but also allowed the idea of the smart woman to take a culturally plausible hold.[9] Furthermore, the prominence of transgender discourses in today's world, and the way the gender of an individual is not fixed, permanent or definitive, has made the very categories of male and female less fixed and more supple. In this laudably more gender-fluid world, the enraged male outsider of the Harrower model is neither extant nor a figure for emulation.

I will divide my discussion between the three Harrower novels with classic male antagonists – *The Watch Tower*, *Down in the City* and *The Catherine Wheel* (1960) – and the two outliers: *The Long Prospect* (1958), which has a female antagonist, and *In Certain Circles* (2014, originally written late 1960s), which features men in a more qualifiedly positive light. The classic men, though, are rapacious and unstable, aggressive and temperamental. If these men seem so obviously undesirable now, why did Harrower women take up with them back then? One possibility: the women who fall in with the three classic men are all looking for an escape from stasis. As an expatriate Australian in the late 1960s Earl's Court era, Clemency James in *The Catherine Wheel* is an outsider, a "wild colonial girl", and finds it difficult to crack the inner ring.[10] As a result, Clemency feels an affinity with the crude if boisterous Christian, also an outsider, if in a social rather than geographic sense. Lewis, Clemency's more cerebral and technocratic alternative to Christian, is described as "reasoning, contending, convincing, unaware that his

---

8   Susan Bordo, *The Male Body* (New York: Macmillan, 2000), 111.
9   Sherrie A. Inness, *Geek Chic: Smart Women in Popular Culture* (New York: Palgrave, 2008).
10 Elizabeth Harrower, *The Catherine Wheel* (1960; Melbourne: Text Publishing, 2014), 207. All subsequent references are to this edition and appear in parentheses in the text.

expressions were not mirrored in my face, unaware of any impression he might be making, conscious of himself for the moment" (204).

In *Down in the City*, Esther Prescott's "feeling for the city, for the tall light buildings and narrow streets and crowded pavements" (14-15) images her split from her bourgeois family of origin. In addition, in her late twenties, she feels she is ageing out of marriageability. Stan Peterson is both Esther's best chance and an expression of the affection she feels for urban Sydney, which brings with it "sea and sun", "wealth and glamour" but also, significantly, "strength and fickleness" (15). Though Stan's crude power is a reduction, a reification, of the dynamic, pluralistic urban tumult Harrower evokes in Kings Cross, it does have a felt relationship to it. Stan is certainly both strong and fickle. Stan's rebel-without-a-cause quality seems a correlative for Esther's desire for "the newest of the new" (5), with all its hectic anarchy. This hectic anarchy is symbolised by the memorable description of Kings Cross at the very beginning of *Down in the City*. Even though Stan's authoritarianism is designed to trammel just this dissent, his energy temporarily deludes Esther into thinking otherwise. Laura Vaizey in *The Watch Tower* has a mother who has fled back to London and a younger sister still a minor, and Felix seems like the ideal surrogate father. As Betty Friedan notes in *The Feminine Mystique*, woman's worth at that point in time mattered *only* in her ability to be ensconced in a domestic sphere – and Felix can both supply that sphere and, seemingly, make authoritative decisions within it.[11]

But here emerges the dark secret of the Harrower men. Felix is not the businessman he claims to be, but a woman-hating, deeply closeted homosexual who is not only oppressive, but also vulnerable and incoherent. He not only does not wield his authority over others for good, he is not a benevolent despot or paterfamilias, and cannot even wield authority meaningfully, for good or bad. Thus when Clare, his sister-in-law, demands to be free from his domination, it is both because Felix is oppressive and because his incompetence has fomented anarchy.

Gender and Force

However irrational the women's attraction to these men, it is not unaccountable. Katie Roiphe has argued that the insurgent men of the 1950s and 1960s were precursors to feminism in their self-assertion, and (with a more leftist and feminist valence) Barbara Ehrenreich, in *The Hearts of Men*, links mid-century male rebels to the unravelling of gender hierarchies: both involved the breaking down of the static structures of late-modern authority.[12] The women are thus attracted to the men because in a world where they cannot exercise agency the men, even while oppressing them and annealing their literal agency, are in another way vicariously exercising that agency on their behalf. The men are a response to the women's parents or to their milieu of origin, their natal milieu, which had never appreciated them and which has seen them as excess baggage, superfluous, as problems to be solved rather than individuals to be encouraged. One

---

11   Betty Friedan, *The Feminine Mystique* (New York: Norton, 1963).
12   Katie Roiphe, "The Naked and the Conflicted", *New York Times Book Review,* 3 January 2010, 8; Barbara Ehrenreich, *The Hearts of Men: American Dreams and the Flight from Commitment* (Garden City, NY: Doubleday, 1983).

can see this in the late 1950s and early 1960s in Australian contexts as well, from the cane-cutters of Ray Lawler's *Summer of the Seventeenth Doll* (1957) to the character of Brownie in Criena Rohan's *The Delinquents* (1962) – a social rebel but also a normative heterosexual matinee idol.[13]

It is as if for women to achieve self-expression in that era they had to become attached to a charismatic if insurgent man, as occurs in Rohan's novel, and as is the most a woman can hope for from heterosexual love in Lawler's play, which ultimately scuttles any manifest hope of a sustained heterosexual partnership. This situation is better today. Theoretically, women are no longer limited in earning power, vocational possibility, volition, or social expression, as were the heroines of Harrower's novels. Indeed, Harrower's novels stand as an argument for why what we now call Second Wave feminism absolutely had to unfold: that it was not an option if a civilisation in any way humane and rational was to emerge in our time.

But even such a committed feminist as Nancy Fraser has warned that feminism is in danger of co-opting gender equality in a way that reinforces the economic inequalities of capitalism and neoliberalism. In Fraser's view, neoliberal forces "succeeded" in defusing the "radical potential" of feminism.[14] This may be the underside of positive developments such as the way that, in Australian culture, undesirable male archetypes like that of the "ocker" are no longer so actually prevalent. As Anne Summers writes, "[t]hey not only look (and smell) different, they are – overwhelmingly – very different from their fathers and grandfathers. Men today routinely wear wedding rings – and plenty sport earrings. They plaster themselves with cologne and aftershave and hair product, often overdoing it in their quest to avoid 'ponging'. They mostly care what they wear, and will shop for themselves".[15] But, bearing in mind Fraser's point, there is a similar danger of the new, more sensitive man becoming a medium through which the male is assimilated into the dominant social system. In addition, Arlie Hochschild has argued that, even as women have moved into the workplace, they still continue to undertake most domestic chores in the context of heterosexual relationships, in effect doubling their workload.[16] This leaves us with the complicated scenario of reading Harrower's novels with a potentially complacent backward eye, aware that the situation is better now, but yet not perfect or entirely changed. Just as women's roles have changed so that, unlike Lilian Hulm, the grandmother in Harrower's *The Long Prospect*, they do not have to exercise their power only in secret, the consensus is that men have been transformed too, that they now change diapers and sing sensitive emo ballads and can, as Summers describes, manifest a range of gender expression no longer restricted to macho inarticulacy and rage of the old Stanley Kowalski variety. Felix and Stan and Christian might have been better people had they been allowed to sample this broader range of gender possibility. But men are also more transparent, lacking the secrets of the Harrower men, even if those secrets were dark ones.

---

13 Ray Lawler, *Summer of the Seventeenth Doll* (1957; New York: Samuel French, 2011); Criena Rohan, *The Delinquents* (1962; Melbourne: Text Publishing, 2014).
14 Nancy Fraser, *Fortunes of Feminism: From State-Managed Capitalism to Neoliberal Crisis* (New York: Verso, 2013), 1.
15 Anne Summers, "Men Change, the Stereotypes Stay the Same", *Age*, 10 April 2011.
16 Arlie Russell Hochschild with Anne Manning, *The Second Shift: Working Parents and the Revolution at Home*, revised edition (1989; New York: Viking Penguin, 2012).

The very transparency of the geeky and the nerdy men renders them open to neoliberal financialisation, to a rote, data-driven, smart tabulation of excellence.[17] As C.D. Blanton, Colleen Lye and Kent Puckett note, financialisation may seem to be limited to an economic sphere of the reassertion of free-market economics, but also raises "cultural questions".[18] Even the imagination today is financialised in concepts such as Richard Florida's idea of the "creative class", which privileges individuals who think outside the box, exemplified by the "free agent" and "entrepreneur" who is imaginative but who uses that imaginative edge to conquer the market.[19]

Neoliberal men and women can have their talents objectively assessed and valued, but at the cost of the "force" that, to allude to the way that word is used in Simone Weil's essay on *The Iliad*, both shadows the lives of humans yet gives them value. Force is also a principle in Harrower's work, if in a different way. If force, as Weil argues, is "that x which turns anybody subjected to it into a thing", then Harrower's women certainly gravitate to men who exert force to objectify them.[20] Weil sees force, whether it kills instantly or over a long term, as wholly negative. This is generally how "force" is used in Harrower's oeuvre, especially *The Watch Tower*, where the word comes up a dozen times. Felix's eyes "were peep holes through which a force could be glimpsed, primitive, chilling".[21] When Felix begins to visibly manifest his psychological deterioration, Clare feels "an amorphous, cold awareness of the existence of some force, and not a friendly one, powerful, invisible, voiceless armed with shears and choppers, ranging the world for hope to kill" (148). In both these citations, force is hard, amoral, and associated with masculine power, in line with Weil's characterisation of force as the keynote of Homer's inherently male-dominated epic.

But there might also be a countervailing, more positively feminist idea or avatar of force, or at least in the way women can seize some of the momentum of the killing force of male warfare for their own agency. When Felix first realises that his sister-in-law Clare and her boyfriend Bernard together have the power to withstand him, he did not appear "to notice that he had almost been knocked to the ground by the force of their excitement" (305). Here, the bully realises that there are countervailing forces aloft even in his self-limited world, forces in which women can participate on equal terms with men. Clare has the autonomy her sister does not. But the dark truth is that this sort of positive autonomous force was just what Laura was searching for. Though it is far too crude to read the novel as a national allegory, that Laura turns to Felix after her mother, Stella, who was born in India under the Raj, "returns" to England marks Felix as an intermediate state between colonialism and a democratic commonwealth. This emerges in the novel's one scene that is remotely pastoral:

---

17 I take the term "financialisation" from C.D. Blanton, Colleen Lye and Kent Puckett, "Introduction: Financialization and the Culture Industry", *Representations* 126 (2014): 1–8.
18 Blanton, Lye and Puckett, "Introduction: Financialization and the Culture Industry", 1.
19 Richard Florida, *The Rise of the Creative Class: And How It's Transforming Work, Leisure, Community and Everyday Life* (New York: Basic Books, 2002), 165.
20 Simone Weil, "The Iliad, or the Poem of Force", trans. Mary McCarthy, *Chicago Review* 18.2 (1965): 7.
21 Elizabeth Harrower, *The Watch Tower* (1966; Melbourne: Text Publishing, 2012), 277. All subsequent references are to this edition and appear in parentheses in the text.

> At Bulli Lookout, forty-four miles south of Sydney, Felix drew the car up and there was a moment's stocktaking silence. "Whew!" He turned to Bernard, searching his eyes. "It's no easy thing holding a car like this in, I can tell you. Takes a lot of practice." "It's a beauty." Bernard ducked down suddenly to feel the loose sole of one of his brown suède boots. Giving his rusty laugh, Felix climbed out of the car and led the way across to the platform high above the ocean. Bernard waited for Laura who had sat alone in the back, insisting that she preferred it. (274)

There is a sudden avowal of Australian nationalism, all the more striking for the novel as a whole being so explicitly unconcerned with the condition of Australia. Also notable is that this is one of the few moments in the novel when Felix is in any way expansive or affirmative, especially since this is near the end of the book when his fortunes are beginning to tumble. There is some sort of mutual reinforcement between Felix and the Australian nationality projects in that both are insurgent, vitalist, anticolonial, subversive and masculinist. If Felix is hardly expressive of a Lindsayan affirmation of rousing, vernacular sensuality – he is too unhappy and too chthonic for that – he finds the language of Australian nationalist affirmation a cognate to his own. Felix goes on to say: "'[D]oes this beat the Mediterranean hollow or doesn't it? Leaves Capri for dead, I'd say.' Of course he has never been to the Mediterranean" (274). Though Felix may be, from a twenty-first-century vantage point, intermediate and basically untenable in world-historical terms, he is hardly intermediate in Laura's own life situation: he is all she has. As oppressed by Felix as she is, Laura turns to him to try to find, vicariously, by proxy, some sort of force for herself. One thinks of the use of the word "force" in Wordsworth's "Lucy" poems:

> No motion has she now, no force;
>   She neither hears nor sees;
> Rolled round in earth's diurnal course,
>   With rocks, and stones, and trees.[22]

Harrower's women are not like this. They are not dead; they are sensate, articulate and volitional; they make mistakes and end up in dire predicaments, but they do so out of a desire to live and as a manifestation of life. Harrower's women, in seeking out her men, are trying, however ill-advisedly, to equip themselves with this sort of force, and, though this means their decisions are tragic, they are certainly not pathetic.

Harrower's short fiction also reveals a distinction between the two types of force: in the first instance male force and female force but really more generally a force of brutality and a force of resistance or self-assertion. In "A Few Days in the Country", Sophie finds love "is a force in her compared with which any other was slight indeed".[23] But in "Lance Harper: His Story", the title character, trying to improve himself, watches an educational speaker on television, who "really smoulders with conviction" and "uses all his force to prove that a man who knew his classics knew everything worth knowing" (127). This is particularly indicative as presumably a speaker on the classics only needs intellectual

---

22 William Wordsworth, *Selections from the Poetical Works of William Wordsworth*, ed. Hawes Harrison Turner (Charleston, SC: Nabu Press, 2010), 11.
23 Elizabeth Harrower, *A Few Days in the Country and Other Stories* (Melbourne: Text Publishing, 2015), 201. All subsequent references are to this edition and appear in parentheses in the text.

authority, but to make an impression on Lance he needs also a more visceral, charismatic authority. We see here a male and virtual audience feeling the same impact via television that Harrower's women often feel vis-à-vis Harrower's men – that their force can inspire, liberate, strengthen them, even though it is not their own force, but the force of another. Materially, the two kinds of force in Harrower are gendered female and male; conceptually, though, they are divided between the force of autonomy and the force of heteronomy.

Geordie Williamson says of Lilian in *The Long Prospect* that her "toughness" inspires "grudging admiration as well as fear and dislike".[24] This grudging admiration is the same magnetism that draws Harrower's women to her men; and it is useful to note that, as Williamson's reference to Harrower's leading female antagonist Lilian indicates, this dichotomy of force can manifest itself in gendered terms but is not definitely bound by them. Furthermore, the same force in the antagonists that draws their victims to them is also a token of their weakness and vulnerability. Lilian, though, may be a special case in that, as a post-menopausal woman, she is in a sense exempt from the most rigorously patrolled gender scenario, of the nubile and reproductive female, and can in effect age into quasi-manhood. Notably, Paula, the female of reproductive age in the three generations, has the least autonomy, even less than her pre-teen daughter Emily, who has a feasible autonomy if only in the long prospect. Lilian is an interesting exception to a rule of gender that is still generally oppressive for the Harrower woman.

The women in Harrower's novels end up oppressed by what they thought would liberate them. But that they reach for and attach themselves to the men in the first place is out of an attempt to shake up the system, in much the same way that in Henry James' *The Portrait of a Lady*, Isabel Archer's terrible choice was also a search for ethical and aesthetic integrity, even if at the cost of succumbing to what Sigi Jottkandt terms "the exigency of the phallus".[25] Harrower has been compared to James, though the Jamesian formalism of her third-person limited-point-of-view narratives about personal relationships is, as Gelder and Salzman argue, undergirded by a sense of "realism with a political purpose".[26] Gender may be the place where form and politics meet in Harrower. As James Wood has put it, the Harrower woman often strives for choice, but like Isabel Archer, ends up as merely "an obedient shadow" of herself.[27] Meg Brayshaw has described Harrower's men as "vampiric", and the paradigm of the vampire, of a man who drinks his victim's blood and gains force from that, is the sad inversion of what Harrower women think they are getting from the relationship: a vital force that will recharge their agency and lead them to greater self-assertion, if only by proxy.[28] In these hopes, Harrower's women are fundamentally deluded; and this delusion, at least in the three "classic" cases of *Down in the City*, *The Catherine Wheel* and *The Watch Tower*, leads to their betrayal and diminution.

That being said, one feels that the problems in Harrower's books are not the women, but the men, and that this is different from earlier fiction of women's lives. In *Middlemarch*,

---

24   Geordie Williamson, *The Burning Library* (Melbourne: Text Publishing, 2012), 161.
25   Sigi Jottkandt, *Acting Beautifully: Henry James and the Ethical Aesthetic* (Albany: SUNY Press, 2005), 141.
26   Ken Gelder and Paul Salzman, *After the Celebration: Australian Fiction 1989–2007* (Melbourne: Melbourne University Press, 2009), 201.
27   James Wood, "No Time for Lies: Rediscovering Elizabeth Harrower", *New Yorker*, 20 October 2014. http://bit.ly/1Cqu4W0.
28   Meg Brayshaw, "'No light, no land or sea': A Geocritical Reading of Elizabeth Harrower's *Down in the City* (1957)", http://bit.ly/2q11CiB.

Casaubon is a limited and deluded person, but he is not the problem of the novel; it is the gap between Dorothea's aspirations and the possibilities available to her, and indeed Barbara Hardy has argued that Casaubon is sexually impotent, quite the reverse of the problem of the Harrower man.[29] In *My Brilliant Career*, it is Sybylla, and her being caught between the controlling alternatives of marriage and creative life, that is the problem. That, in Jill Roe's words, Sybylla's story "ends where it began" is less because anything is wrong with the perfectly agreeable Harry Beecham but because Sybylla does not wish to inclusively define herself through matrimony, and, as Roe puts it, "declines to marry into the squattocracy".[30] But the crisis in Harrower's books is a crisis of masculinity, a crisis of men from which the women in the books suffer. James Gilbert has argued in *Men in the Middle* that the 1950s presented a crisis of masculinity as, simultaneously, masculinist ideologies sustained and even renewed by two world wars and the global rise of a suburban lifestyle uneasily played off a growing awareness of queer and dissident sexualities as well as a sense of the rising power of women, who had shown their ability to perform competently in the workplace during those same world wars.[31]

In an Australian context, Robin Gerster speaks of how the Australian participation in the military occupation of Japan in the late 1940s and early 1950s created a particular style of masculinity whose exaggeration of its white, male privilege bespoke an anxiety about contamination by Asian and queer discourses.[32] It is against this background that the Harrower male protagonists such as Stan in *Down in the City*, Christian in *The Catherine Wheel*, and Felix in *The Watch Tower*, with their curious combination of vigour and panic, self-confidence and paranoia, swagger and hysteria, can be most productively understood.

Precarious Men

Now, there are other sorts of males in Harrower's works besides the classic Stan-Christian-Felix model. But they are in a precarious position. This is instanced by the plight of Max in *The Long Prospect* (1958). Max is a chemist by training, working in a sleepy industrial town as a visiting scientist. He might be a model geek. But in what John Colmer terms the "shoddy society" of Harrower's version of mid-century Newcastle still in the days of Broken Hill's corporate monopoly over that city and its concomitant state-managed industrial capitalism, Max is an anomalous figure who is not perhaps quite a man and certainly cannot crack the authority wielded by ferocious Lilian.[33] Indeed, *The Long Prospect* – like *In Certain Circles* – does not have a charismatic man, and its Felix, in effect, is Lilian Hulm. It is this redoubtable grandmother who manipulates and controls people, and holds her granddaughter at bay.

---

29 Barbara Hardy, *The Appropriate Form* (London: Bloomsbury Academic, 2013), 109.
30 Jill Roe, *Her Brilliant Career: The Life of Stella Miles Franklin* (Cambridge, MA: Harvard University Press, 2009), 77.
31 James Gilbert, *Men in the Middle: Searching for Masculinity in the 1950s* (Chicago: University of Chicago Press, 2005).
32 Robin Gerster, "Travelling Is Victory: Australian Military Tourism and the Occupation of Japan", in *Occupying the "Other": Australia and Military Occupations from Japan to Iraq*, ed. Christine de Matos and Robin Gerster (Newcastle, UK: Cambridge Scholars Press, 2009), 107–22.
33 John Colmer, review of *The Watch Tower* by Elizabeth Harrower, *Australian Book Review*, 5, no. 11 (1966): 218.

But this has to be looked at a bit more closely. One cannot assume that just because on a readerly level Lilian occupies the same role in *The Long Prospect* as Felix does in *The Watch Tower* she is in fact as powerful as he is. Although she is indeed villain, oppressor of the character with which we most sympathise, and figure for an irrational and arbitrary power structure, Lilian wields her power most significantly over her granddaughter, Emily, whereas the three paradigmatic Harrower men all wield their authority over women who might – especially in the case of Felix and Laura in *The Watch Tower* – be younger than they but are still adults and consenting sexual partners. This is very different from Lilian's domination of her granddaughter. Meanwhile, the adults who Lilian dominates – her daughter Paula and Paula's husband Harry, Max and his on-again, off-again girlfriend Thea – are all more or less manipulable only because of Lilian's control over the child. It is assumed that Lilian also exercises a dominant role in her relationship with her lodger and paramour, Mr Rosen, whom at one point she derides as a "real old woman",[34] and whose Jewish – or, as he claims, Welsh or Irish – ethnicity also leaves him outside conventional, hegemonic masculinities. But their relationship is very much at the periphery of the book. The overall point is that it is fallacious to assume Lilian is as powerful as Max, because the limitations imposed on her gender initiate a degree of cultural constraint even if her temperament is similar to her male counterpart. Jackie Byers, writing of Hollywood films of the 1950s, warns that not just melodrama but also realism has "a tendency to obscure power relations" between men and women by a "focus on individuals" which "represents larger social conflicts in terms of the personal".[35] Harrower's novels, which can be said to oscillate between melodrama and realism, are indeed three-dimensional stories with their own internal dramas, not just proof texts of cultural gender roles and shifts. But the specific can be indicative. While *The Watch Tower* can be said to represent the gender politics of the era in the marriage between Felix and Laura, Lilian's authority over her granddaughter, and her ability to manipulate Max, Thea and Paula insofar as they are psychologically involved with the child, is a one-off, arguably a fluke. Moreover, it is no accident that, whereas the three novels with authoritarian male antagonists are set in metropolitan centres – Sydney or London – it is the book with the female antagonist that is set in the more provincial mid-sized industrial city, as if female authority can only be wielded in a very restricted sphere. Thus Lilian Hulm's boarding house becomes Newcastle writ small.

We also should not assume that masculine power gets off scot-free in *The Long Prospect*. Max may seem not controlling and authoritarian, but the other kind of man, a benevolent man, the benefactor. Max tries to save Emily. But in trying to do so he not only furnishes grounds for the adults to interpret his interest in Emily as untoward, he also actually crosses the line from inner feelings about the child Emily to outward expression of those feelings, which are indeed inappropriate and draw him towards the stance of a prurient pervert. Although Max does care for Emily as a person, recognising her precocity and promise, and treating her as a person while the other adults treat her as chattel or as an object to manipulate, Max still wants from Emily more than he can have: a true meeting of the minds, impossible between an adult and child. Even at the end, as he urges Emily to communicate with him when she is college-age or on her own, he is trying to sow

---

34 Elizabeth Harrower, *The Long Prospect* (1958; Melbourne: Text Publishing, 2012), 25. All subsequent references are to this edition and appear in parentheses in the text.
35 Jackie Byers, *All That Hollywood Allows: Reenacting Gender in 1950s Melodrama* (Chapel Hill: University of North Carolina Press, 2011), 5.

5 A Wrong Way of Being Right: The Tormented Force of the Harrower Man

the seeds for a later equal relationship, which given the initial power imbalance of their encounter, is exceedingly implausible. Finally, Max is not a family member, and however unfair and oppressive Emily's actual family is to her, he cannot intervene. Max puts himself in an impossible position. As a sensitive, non-controlling man, he is a harbinger of a new, less conventional and domineering kind of man than his counterparts in other Harrower fiction. But not only is he there before his time, he also cannot divest himself of the male privilege he has always assumed with regard to Emily.

Max abuses his authority, not out of an excess of insurgent charisma, but out of an excess of benevolence. The would-be new man, this "chemist man", this not-yet-geek who, because he is still locked in an industrial economy, expresses his benevolence crudely (20). Women in that era want a different sort of masculinity. Thus, although the reader gets the impression Max settles for Thea, Thea also, it has to be said, settles for him. Max is ineffectual: a man with "few, and no visible, ties" (96) whose "vital times" (96) are already, even though he is at a still-young age, permanently in the past. Max cannot be a part of Emily's story in the context of the structures of domination that Emily not only comes to expect, but on one level requires as a way to identify with a desirable insurgency. As long as Emily has been socialised to compliance, Max will never rise to the occasion. A woman, Lilian, may be the villain of the book. But its chief male character has nearly as dire a flaw. He does not and cannot achieve the status of hero. Max, like Felix, is both privileged and vulnerable. He is kind and confused, rather than brutal and confused like Felix. But the same paradoxical lack of self-control is there.

This is not to say that Harrower's characters are permanently locked within an inescapable patriarchal world. Harrower's five published novels register slow processes of social change, and no more so than in her latest and most recently published novel. *In Certain Circles* (published 2014; written late 1960s/early 1970s) is a novel of transition and adaptation, from the old patriarchy to a world of greater dignity and equality glimpsed but not yet realised in its pages. In fact it could be said that the long prospects of *In Certain Circles* are dual. One is of a society with increasing pay equity, job equity, and gender role equity. The other is a further future, what Luce Irigaray calls a "future perfect", where the patriarchy, which took millennia to assemble, will be finally disassembled.[36] This is demonstrated in the book's central situation, the marriage of the upper-class Zoe Howard to the working-class Stephen Quayle, and in the way in which Zoe's brother, Russell, and Stephen's sister, Anna, are affected by this relationship. Anna says, "[w]omen are still in their early days".[37] Zoe in turn says: "Isn't it marvellous that men are free not to be personal" (167). Zoe's remark to her sister-in-law has the ring of bracing truth: women are socially mandated to be immured in the personal where, when we look at a character like George Eliot's Casaubon, we judge him for mastering books of learning while neglecting the personal. The women on the other hand must struggle to transcend the personal, which is why Anna's eventual realisation of her artistic muse through photography is so moving.

Anna may know "heroic types of both sexes" (167), but those are not especially in evidence in Harrower's most recent novel. Zoe's *choice* of Anna's brother Stephen, indeed,

---

36   Luce Irigaray, *Speculum of the Other Woman,* trans. Gilliam C. Gil (Ithaca, NY: Cornell University Press, 1985), 357.
37   Elizabeth Harrower, *In Certain Circles* (Melbourne: Text Publishing, 2014), 167. All subsequent references are to this edition and appear in parentheses in the text.

is made in a way and with a motivation reminiscent of Clemency's choice of Christian, Laura's choice of Felix, and Esther's choice of Stan: "Something in him took her from the pink marshmallow castle of her life to a high cliff over the ocean in the real world" (43). This search for escape from a sterile prison-like structure – notice the similarity of the pink marshmallow castle to the image of the watch tower – is what Harrower women tend to see in their men.[38] Nonetheless, this novel shows the old type of male crossing into the new. Stephen is honest with himself in a way that earlier analogues in Harrower's work – male working-class outsiders like Stan, Christian or Felix – are not. Stephen feels ill at ease among his upper-class in-laws, and this causes problems in his marriage to Zoe Howard, but Stephen is a gentle, thoughtful man, neither violent nor abusive. Zoe is attracted to him out of "the strangeness of his mind" (164), which might be said of Esther, Laura or Clemency. But unlike Stan, Felix or Christian, Stephen's mind, though at times vexatious and burdensome to Zoe, is not a monstrous one.

Reforming the Male?

One of the issues with *In Certain Circles* is that not only does it differ from Harrower's previous novels in taking place in the early years of contemporary feminism, but that there is a difference between its time of composition and its time of publication. By the time of the latter, the bloom had somewhat come off the rose of contemporary feminism. In the words of Madeleine Schwartz, "supposed feminist endorsement of harder work, put forth by well-meaning businesswomen, does not hold up to scrutiny: outside the home, women are encouraged to commit to a structure no more equal than the traditional family".[39] The strange circumstances of Harrower's career – respectful attention during the era of publication, a small but significant stream of feminist scholarship on the novels in the 1970s and 1980s, increasing obscurity as time went on, and then a flashy, media-led revival in the 2010s, while the writer, though of advanced age, is still alive – make her work's reception filled with astonishing transitions very different than the authorial norm. The transition that occurs within the pages of *In Certain Circles*, though, must be measured tentatively.

This is especially true with respect to the other major male character of *In Certain Circles*. Russell Howard, Zoe's brother and Stephen's brother-in-law, is a benevolent, broad-minded man. He seeks solace outside the moral paucity of his marriage to Lily, who invests so much of herself in her shallow daughters until that purely personal investment turns on her. Russell occupies himself far away in his printing firm, which, unlike Felix's chocolate factory, is not a vehicle to exercise authority and keep him solvent but is an essentially altruistic enterprise, which he values as a vehicle to advance leftist political causes.

Russell is a "new man", one who complements well the incipient new woman of contemporary feminism. He is good to old people and kind to strangers, not just to make

---

38 Even though in literal terms the watch tower refers to Clare's window, as Deirdre Coleman argues, the image of the castle/tower also applies to Laura's sense of confinement. Deirdre Coleman, "*The Watch Tower*: Bluebeard's Castle", in *(Un)common Ground*, ed. A. Taylor and R. McDougall (Adelaide: Centre for Research in the New Literatures in English, 1990), 97–107.

39 Madeleine Schwartz, "Kicking Back, Not Leaning In", review of *Fortunes of Feminism* by Nancy Fraser, *Dissent* (Summer 2013), http://bit.ly/1Tt0rxR.

himself feel good but because this is genuinely his character. He is valorous in quitting scientific work after the suicide of the bullied 22-year-old woman, "hounded" to death in "the interests of science" (121). But Russell fails until the very end to have a satisfying personal life; even if far more comfortable in his own skin than Max, he has similar problems in translating his moral goodness into a good life. For Russell, as for Max, benevolence is not enough. There is hope at the end of *In Certain Circles* that in marrying Anna Quayle, a woman who has developed herself as an artist the way other women in the books have not, Russell may, though, be on the road to redemption. The misplaced altruism of the benefactor male might be made whole through Anna who has weathered emotional stresses and matured through doing so. Anna is not a vulnerable, manipulable ingénue like the three classic Harrower women. Anna is not trapped in, to reuse Snitow's phrase, the force of her own gendered circumstances.

It is not just that Anna's friends think she has killed herself when she has not, but that the reader thinks so as well. This is perhaps symptomatic of the sense that Woman, as a Platonic category, must come near to suicide for men to reform, that the abyss of gender must be canvassed before the true behavioural and moral reform of the male can happen, which also means that the crisis of masculinity must be foregrounded and addressed in order to be solved. The withering away of crude, aggressive men can only come about when Woman nearly disappears. The "reformed men" of the novel, such as Russell and Stephen, are semi-promising portents, if still in early days. But *In Certain Circles* does not depict a utopian world where all previous gender problems are solved.

So it might be easy to say Harrower is negative about men and shows women as needing deliverance from them. But if we take this *tout court* it is easy to fall into thinking that men are better now: a too-comfortable temporal complacency. When Laura Vaizey is utterly shorn of faith in Felix she feels almost nihilistic, sensing that "there is no way of being right" (324), and this indicates that for her Felix had been an attempt at a substantive philosophy of life, albeit a misbegotten and disastrous attempt at such. Felix represents the wrong way of being right. He is a ghastly avatar of male domination. But it is Laura's quest for a right way of being right that is notable even though it disastrously fails. The crudeness of the classic Harrower man is something that should be jettisoned or transcended, but we should not discard the force in their posture. If we do so, we – in whatever gender configuration we inhabit or affirm – become merely, as Jodi Dean puts it, "quants and geeks" who "figure out how to value and put . . . to use" the "data banks on server farms". Dean argues that "perpetually engaged, we search and link" even as "Google claims the trace of its own".[40] Today's hyper-individuality may, according to Dean, be a masked corporatism, just as what Jeremy Gilbert describes as the "relatively stable and conformist culture of the welfare state" calls into being, by counterpoint, a curious individuality.[41] Laura feels comfortable in a deadlocked maw of containment and control which is at once what the mid-century welfare state sought to remedy and also an index of its tendency towards social control. With distributive justice comes stasis. The Harrower men try to break that stasis, even if they make it even worse.

The Harrower men, in their flailing, inchoate manner, are striving for a realm neither repressively egalitarian nor ruthlessly individualistic. And even the women who break free from their tyranny are also striving for that realm. Clare Vaizey in *The Watch Tower* has

---

40 Jodi Dean, *The Communist Horizon* (London: Verso, 2012), 121.
41 Jeremy Gilbert, *Anticapitalism and Culture* (Oxford: Berg, 2008), 170.

not just rebelled against Felix in her escaping with Bernard, taking the train up from the city into the interior. Clare has channelled Felix's force into her own, just as in the other direction, Stan in *Down in the City* took the anarchic potential Esther saw in Kings Cross and swept this energy into his masculine authority. But Clare is not *without* force; and that is her deliverance, which enables her to go off into the bush, unconstrained, out of the force of circumstances, and at least relatively free of the constraints of overly scripted gender scenarios. Force is transferable, and Clare achieves a more lucid and constructive version of Felix's. That can stand as the secret lesson of Harrower's tormented and conflicted men.

References

Blanton, C.D., Colleen Lye, and Kent Puckett. "Introduction: Financialization and the Culture Industry". *Representations* 126 (2014): 1-8.
Bordo, Susan. *The Male Body*. New York: Macmillan, 2000.
Brayshaw, Meg. "'No light, no land or sea': A Geocritical Reading of Elizabeth Harrower's *Down in the City* (1957)". http://bit.ly/2qCcnE7.
Byers, Jackie. *All That Hollywood Allows: Reenacting Gender in 1950s Melodrama*. Chapel Hill: University of North Carolina Press, 2011.
Coleman, Deirdre. "*The Watch Tower*: Bluebeard's Castle". In *(Un)common Ground*. Edited by A. Taylor and R. McDougall, 97-107. Adelaide: Centre for Research in the New Literatures in English, 1990.
Colmer, John. Review of *The Watch Tower* by Elizabeth Harrower. *Australian Book Review* 5, no. 11 (1966): 218.
Connell, Raewyn. *Gender: In World Perspective*. London: Polity, 2009.
Dean, Jodi. *The Communist Horizon*. London: Verso, 2012.
Dickens, Charles. *Hard Times*. (1854) New York: Dover Thrift Editions, 2013.
——. *Dombey and Son*. (1848) New York: Random House, 2003.
Ehrenreich, Barbara. *The Hearts of Men: American Dreams and the Flight from Commitment*. Garden City, NY: Doubleday, 1983.
Eliot, George. *Middlemarch*. (1872) Hertfordshire, UK: Wordsworth Classics, 2000.
Florida, Richard. *The Rise of the Creative Class, and How It's Transforming Work, Leisure, Community and Everyday Life*. New York: Basic Books, 2002.
Fraser, Nancy. *Fortunes of Feminism: From State-Managed Capitalism to Neoliberal Crisis*. New York: Verso, 2013.
Friedan, Betty. *The Feminine Mystique*. New York: Norton, 1963.
Galsworthy, John. *The Forsyte Saga*. (1922) Hertfordshire: Wordsworth Classics, 2001.
Gelder, Ken and Paul Salzman. *After the Celebration: Australian Fiction 1989-2007*. Melbourne: Melbourne University Press, 2009.
Gerster, Robin. "Travelling Is Victory: Australian Military Tourism and the Occupation of Japan". In *Occupying the "Other": Australia and Military Occupations from Japan to Iraq*. Edited by Christine de Matos and Robin Gerster, 107-22. Newcastle, UK: Cambridge Scholars Press, 2009.
Gilbert, James. *Men in the Middle: Searching for Masculinity in the 1950s*. Chicago: University of Chicago Press, 2005.
Gilbert, Jeremy. *Anticapitalism and Culture*. Oxford: Berg, 2008.
Hardy, Barbara. *The Appropriate Form*. London: Bloomsbury Academic, 2013.
Harrower, Elizabeth. *A Few Days in the Country and Other Stories*. Melbourne: Text Publishing, 2015.
——. *In Certain Circles*. Melbourne: Text Publishing, 2014.
——. *The Watch Tower*. (1966) Melbourne: Text Publishing, 2012.
——. *The Catherine Wheel*. (1960) Melbourne: Text Publishing, 2014.

——. *The Long Prospect*. (1958) Melbourne: Text Publishing, 2012.
——. *Down in the City*. (1957) Melbourne: Text Publishing, 2013.
Hochschild, Arlie Russell and Anne Manning. *The Second Shift: Working Parents and the Revolution at Home*. Revised Edition. New York: Viking Penguin, 2012.
Inness, Sherrie A. *Geek Chic: Smart Women in Popular Culture*. New York: Palgrave, 2008.
Irigaray, Luce. *Speculum of the other Woman*. Translated by Gilliam C. Gil. Ithaca, NY: Cornell University Press, 1985.
Jottkandt, Sigi. *Acting Beautifully: Henry James and the Ethical Aesthetic*. Albany, NY: SUNY Press, 2005.
Lawler, Ray. *Summer of the Seventeenth Doll*. (1957) New York: Samuel French, 2011.
Lusty, Natalya. "Introduction". In *Modernism and Masculinity*. Edited by Natalya Lusty and Julian Murphet, 1-18. Cambridge: Cambridge University Press, 2014.
McInherny, Frances. "'Deep into the destructive core'": Elizabeth Harrower's *The Watch Tower*". *Hecate* 9, nos 1 and 2 (1983): 123-34.
Riddle, Naomi. "'Turning inward on himself': Male Hysteria in Elizabeth Harrower's *The Watch Tower*".*Southerly* 72, no. 1 (2012): 204-13.
Roe, Jill. *Her Brilliant Career: The Life of Stella Miles Franklin*. Cambridge, Mass.: Harvard University Press, 2009.
Roiphe, Katie. "The Naked and the Conflicted". *New York Times Book Review*, 3 January 2010: 8.
Reid, Susan. "Idylls of Modernity: D.H. Lawrence's Subversive Pastoral". In *New Versions of Pastoral: Post-Romantic, Modern, and Postmodern Responses to the Tradition*. Edited by David James and Philip Tew, 95-116. Madison, NJ: Fairleigh Dickinson University Press, 2009.
Rohan, Criena. *The Delinquents*.(1962) Melbourne: Text Publishing, 2014.
Schwartz, Madeleine. "Kicking Back, Not Leaning In". Review of Nancy Fraser, *Fortunes of Feminism*. *Dissent* (Summer 2013). http://bit.ly/2qCCeMd.
Snitow, Ann. *The Feminism of Uncertainty: A Gender Diary*. Durham, NC: Duke University Press, 2015.
Summers, Anne. "Men Change, the Stereotypes Stay the Same". *Age*, 10 April 2011.
Weil, Simone. "The Iliad or the Poem of Force". Translated by Mary McCarthy. *Chicago Review* 18, no. 2 (1965): 5-30.
Williams, Tennessee. *A Streetcar Named Desire*. (1947) New York: Penguin, 2009.
Williamson, Geordie. *The Burning Library*. Melbourne: Text Publishing, 2012.
Wood, James. "No Time for Lies: Rediscovering Elizabeth Harrower". *New Yorker*. 20 October 2014. http://bit.ly/1Cqu4W0.
Wordsworth, William. *Selections from the Poetical Works of William Wordsworth*. Edited by Hawes Harrison Turner. Charleston, SC: Nabu Press, 2010.

6

"The wind from Siberia": Metageography and Ironic Nationality in the Novels of Elizabeth Harrower

Robert Dixon

Elizabeth Harrower's third novel, *The Catherine Wheel* (1960) – the only one set outside Australia – begins with an example of what Jon Hegglund terms modernist "metageography": that is, a use of maps and the conventions of cartographic representation in such a way as to defamiliarise the social production of space, and of national and personal identity.[1] Clemency James, a young Australian woman, has come to London in the late 1950s to study for the bar, and as she returns to her bedsitting room from a shopping trip to Notting Hill Gate, she takes her bearings from a weather report that locates London in relation to the landmass of hemispheric Europe: "The wind from Siberia as announced by the BBC came down Bayswater Road from the direction of Marble Arch somewhere in a straight line beyond which, half a world away, Siberia was taken to be".[2] Zooming in to a local scale, Clem locates her "centre of the universe" (3) in a boarding house just off Bayswater Road:

> Across the road the enigmatic façades of a row of semi-public buildings ended where the railings of Kensington Gardens began. Just opposite this corner of the gardens Miss Evans had her service-house, and it was here I had a room with a diagonal view of bare black avenues and paths and empty seats and grass. (4)

In this instance, the BBC weather map of Great Britain and the influence on the local weather of a distant location that is popularly understood as "Siberia" functions in much the same way that the idea of "Europe" does in Harrower's Australian novels, allowing her readers to understand that national and personal identity are formed through complex transnational circuits of exchange, by comparisons between national space and transnational or imperial space, and between the temporal dimensions of past, present and future. As an Australian girl in London, Clem understands that identity is subject to what Benedict Anderson calls "the spectre of comparisons".[3]

---

[1] Jon Hegglund, *World Views: Metageographies of Modernist Fiction* (Oxford: Oxford University Press, 2012), 6.
[2] Elizabeth Harrower, *The Catherine Wheel* (1960; Melbourne: Text Publishing, 2014), 3. All subsequent references are to this edition and appear in parentheses in the text.
[3] Benedict Anderson, *The Spectre of Comparisons: Nationalism, Southeast Asia and the World* (London: Verso, 1998).

The use of cartography to question rather than to ground national and communal identity is characteristic of a formal innovation in the modernist novel that Hegglund calls metageography. During the nineteenth century, the novel had evolved in an organic relation to the nation state in such a way that geographical space was depicted as a stable and coherent setting through the codes of narrative realism. In the early twentieth century, however, a new mode of "cartographic realism" laid bare the social production of space, subjecting geography to the processes of abstraction, defamiliarisation and self-consciousness that we associate with aesthetic modernism. Metageographical fiction exploits this formal innovation to mediate between the scale of the nation and perspectives associated with other scales both within and outside the nation. Perhaps the best-known example is Stephen Dedalus' meditation on the scales of belonging during a geography lesson in James Joyce's *A Portrait of the Artist as a Young Man* (1916): "Stephen Dedalus/Class of Elements/Clongowes Wood College/Sallins/County Kildare/Ireland/Europe/The World/The Universe".[4] Stephen's formulation locates him in a recursive series of geographical scales that apparently empties the nation of its natural priority. Yet modernist fiction did not simply transcend the national affiliations that were part of its formal evolution in the nineteenth century. Surveying the consequences of the global or transnational turn for the new modernism studies, Hegglund warns that some critics "have at times idealized the 'trans-' without fully considering the implications of the 'national'":

> Rather than posit another spatial scale that simply outflanks the nation-state . . . the turn to fictional metageography implies both identification with a "national" position while at the same time offering a perspective internal to the literary text that denaturalizes the perceived organicism and "givenness" of the nation. Irony, then, becomes the literary mode best suited to metageographical fiction; metageography, in other words, might be thought of as "ironic" geography. As Clare Colebrook has written, irony permits us to "discern the meaning or sense of a context without participating in, or being committed to, that context" . . . Metageographical fiction ironizes its "participation in and commitment to" a national community, but it also acknowledges that such communal attachments can and do remain strong and compelling reasons for the persistence of the nation-state.[5]

Like the Harvard geographer Neil Brenner, Hegglund therefore rejects those aspects of globalisation theory that insist on "a zero-sum game" between the nation and other scales,[6] recognising in the mode of "ironic nationality" a process of scalar mediation that operates through the "binocular gaze"[7] of transnational comparison. As Neal Alexander and James Moran also observe, "[s]uch a dual awareness is necessary because modernist texts are typically located within, and shuttle restlessly between, multiple and overlapping spatial frames: local, regional, national, and international".[8]

---

4 Quoted in Hegglund, *World Views*, 22.
5 Hegglund, *World Views*, 6–7.
6 Neil Brenner, *New State Spaces: Urban Governance and the Rescaling of Statehood* (Oxford and New York: Oxford University Press, 2004), 57.
7 Hegglund, *World Views*, 20.
8 Neal Alexander and James Moran, "Introduction: Regional Modernisms", in *Regional Modernisms*, ed. Neal Alexander and James Moran (Edinburgh: Edinburgh University Press, 2013), 1–21 (6–7).

In this essay, I argue that irony in Hegglund's and Colebrook's sense is the characteristic narrative point of view of Elizabeth Harrower's novels, the dominant tone that she adopts to questions of both personal and national identity. This is achieved through a persistent structure of narrative or dramatic irony, in which her narrators and readers, though not necessarily her characters, share access to "an external site of enunciation or observation",[9] often provided by the formal devices of metageographic or metatopographic description. Written between 1954 and 1971, Harrower's five novels provide a relentlessly ironic perspective by which the provinciality of Australian culture in the mid-twentieth century is not so much transcended as it is illuminated by an endemic habit of transnational comparison. In approximate chronological order, their immediate settings are Sydney and Newcastle in the 1940s and 1950s (*Down in the City* (1957), *The Long Prospect* (1958) and *The Watch Tower* (1966), postwar London in the late 1950s, on the cusp of its 1960s transformation (*The Catherine Wheel* (1960)), and Sydney again in the 1960s and 1970s (*In Certain Circles* (2014)). Harrower's "external sites of enunciation" are of two types. The first, usually associated with Europe, or the idea of Europe as it had become in the era of the Cold War and decolonisation, provides an ironic perspective on the provinciality and belatedness of Australia's postwar modernity. For those of her characters sensitive to this external point of reference – Thea, Max and Emily in *The Long Prospect*; Zoe Howard in *In Certain Circles* – that idea of Europe stands as a symbol for personal becoming, for the long prospect of being "translated into oneself".[10] As we will see, many of Harrower's characters do not share this ironic perspective, and so remain entrapped within their own and their provincial culture's world view, yet even those who are granted the spatial mobility of the "binocular gaze" also remain strongly embedded in communal and national attachments. The second point of external enunciation, associated with America or with the global export of American popular culture, also functions to confirm Australia's provinciality as an importer of that country's mass consumer goods in the era that Nicholas Birns identifies by the American term neoliberalism.[11] This is the external point of reference most often adopted by those of her characters who nonetheless remain encircled by inward-looking forms of communal and personal identity: Stan Peterson and Laura Maitland in *Down in the City*, Lilian Hulm in *The Long Prospect*, and Laura Vaizey in *The Watch Tower*. Harrower's "ironic nationality", in other words, illuminates and defamiliarises, but does not necessarily transcend, socially formed identities, including those of nation and gender.

In *The Spectre of Comparisons* (1998), Benedict Anderson recalls how, in 1963, after an extended period of fieldwork in Indonesia, he experienced "a kind of vertigo" caused by seeing European history for the first time from an Indonesian perspective: it was as if "I had been invited to see my Europe . . . through an inverted telescope", and the effect was to see it "simultaneously close up and from far away".[12] Elizabeth Harrower's initial decision to write about *her* Australia was prompted by a similar metageographical impulse, the "binocular gaze" of the expatriate Australian, through which she examined not only

---

9   Hegglund, *World Views*, 20.
10 Elizabeth Harrower, *The Long Prospect* (1958; Melbourne: Text Publishing, 2012), 119. All subsequent references are to this edition and appear in parentheses in the text.
11 Nicholas Birns, *Contemporary Australian Literature: A World Not Yet Dead* (Sydney: Sydney University Press, 2015), Chapter 3, "'Medium-sized Mortals': Elizabeth Harrower and the Crisis of Late Modernity", 45–66.
12 Anderson, *The Spectre of Comparisons*, 2.

London, but also London's antipodes, the now distant Sydney of her youth. Harrower was born in Sydney in 1928, and left for the United Kingdom in 1951 at the age of twenty-three: "Moving from Scotland to London in 1954, I decided to write novels. I was never homesick for Australia, but after years away I remembered Sydney with great affection and in great detail, and that was what I wanted to write about. I thought of the city in the years from 1945 till 1951, when I sailed away".[13] Patrick White's essay "The Prodigal Son", with its justly famous tirade against "the Great Australian Emptiness", was written in 1958, and exhibits the same structure of "ironic nationality", prompted, as he explains, by the critical gaze of the "returned expatriate".[14] In his autobiography, *Flaws in the Glass* (1981), White later recalled that on coming back to Australia, he felt like a "foreigner" in his own country.[15] White returned to Sydney to live in 1948, Harrower in 1959. As for White, and for her near contemporary Shirley Hazzard, Harrower's cycle of expatriation and repatriation produced an "ironic" relation to personal and national identity – an "ironic nationality".

Harrower's first novel, *Down in the City* (1957), is set in Sydney in the 1950s. It is the story of Esther Prescott, a young woman whose sheltered childhood in the wealthy harbourside suburb of Rose Bay has left her vulnerable to the rough charms of Stan Peterson, a self-made man with a smouldering resentment against his social superiors. The "fairytale" of Esther's childhood and her rude "awakening" to life is an epitome of Sydney's provinciality at mid-century, and while the narrative perspective identifies strongly with that setting, it also wields an ironic knowingness made possible by a more worldly experience of elsewhere: "Remote and unchanging, Esther spent her life in this way until she was thirty-three, when she married Stan Peterson, after having known him for two weeks" (16). The local culture has a claustrophobic, over-heated quality, inward-looking and isolated but at the same time adolescent and febrile, addicted to the melodrama and sensational excitement provided by the new mass-cultural entertainments imported from overseas: the cinema, the wireless, magazines, the mass-produced American consumer goods displayed in the new department stores: "[I]t was apparently unbearable that by contact with, and inevitably contamination from, the outside world, she would be spoilt" (11). Here, in this dialectical relationship between the inside and the outside of a provincial location, is the classic structure of narrative irony, which allows the reader to "discern the meaning or sense of a context without participating in, or being committed to, that context".[16] In Andreas Huyssen's cogent phrase, this is also to see provinciality "as Woman", as modernism's other.[17]

Stan Peterson's arrival, which disturbs Esther's prolonged childhood, is associated with the brash invasiveness of American popular culture: the "long, heavily nickelled, American Car" (18), the "garish sports jacket", the "loud tie" (19). In response to this "queer vulgar man", Esther experiences, almost against her will, "sensation" and "sparking, agitat[ion]" (21). She is "phrenetically excited" (27). Stan is the first in a series of Harrower's major characters – Brigid Rooney calls them her "antagonists"[18] – who live to exert power over

---

13   Elizabeth Harrower, *Down in the City* (1957; Melbourne: Text Publishing, 2013), xii.
14   Patrick White, "The Prodigal Son" (1958), in *Patrick White Speaks*, ed. Paul Brennan and Christine Flynn (Leichhardt, NSW: Primavera Press, 1989), 16.
15   Patrick White, *Flaws in the Glass* (London: Jonathan Cape, 1981), 46.
16   Colebrook, quoted in Hegglund, *World Views*, 7.
17   Andreas Huyssen, "Mass Culture as Woman", in *After the Great Divide: Modernism, Mass Culture, Postmodernism* (Bloomington: Indiana University Press, 1986): 44–62.

others in compensation for their own lack of power and self-confidence. This is partly a matter of social inferiority. Abandoned by his parents and brought up in a state orphanage, Stan is stricken by "fear and envy" when, for example, "shrill, confident, Oxford-Australian accents rang about him in the nightclubs and golf clubs" (33). The fact that Esther comes from that same, British-identified class makes her a target for his misogyny. These entangled class and gender identities are paralleled to Australia's ambiguous status at mid-century as a colonial and provincial society subject to fluid and conflicting modes of external cultural authority: the old high culture of Great Britain and the new popular culture of the United States. Behind the wheel of his streamlined Cadillac, Stan is like one of the boys on the North Shore who "dreamed of roaming the prairies of the Wild West" (32). Harrower registers these external sites of enunciation through her acute narrative focalisation. Stan's adoption of American modernity in compensation for his lack of social confidence is perfectly caught by the vernacular idiom of his thoughts: "He was afraid to touch her. He, Stan Peterson, of all people, was afraid to touch a dame" (33).

Like Esther, Sydney in the 1950s is in the grip of its "romance with modernity", which Jill Julius Matthews identifies as a transnational, especially trans-Pacific, commercial phenomenon:[19] "The wireless played all the time. Interspersed with advertisements for shaving cream and lawnmowers, on record after record, American voices proclaimed the invincibility of love . . . Stan joined the crooners" (258-9). When she agrees to drive with Stan in his Cadillac for the first time into the bush on the North Shore, Esther tells her brother that she is going to the Rialto (29), and after they have had sex Stan whistles an American dance hall tune, steering the Cadillac back over the Harbour Bridge late at night after the cinemas and theatres have closed. After their marriage, Stan and Esther Peterson live in a flat in Romney Court in Kings Cross, Sydney's most "cosmopolitan" suburb (4), that is replete with the trappings of transnational vernacular modernity. Stan here tortures Esther as a means to gain "confidence" in himself (137). As James Wood observes, Harrower's "staging of misogyny takes place alongside, as if in analogical relation to, other prejudices and presumptions of the era", including "English condescension".[20] Stan's misogyny and his adoption of American mannerisms are related aspects of his response to that "condescension". That is to say that in Harrower's novels, gender entrapment is spatialised as the subjection of a provincial to a metropolitan culture.

Rachel Demster, the teenage niece of a neighbour in Romney Court, appears destined to repeat Esther's subjection in the following generation, but her cultural affiliations are different to Esther's and give her a point of resistance, a site of external enunciation and observation. At seventeen, Rachel has lived the same "fairytale" as Esther, but she is immune to the attractions of the dance hall and the picture palace. Unlike the fashionable Laura Maitland, another neighbour, Rachel wanted "conversations like the ones in books", not "Hollywood shadows in a dark, disinfectant-smelling, air-conditioned cinema" (57). *That* escape from provincialism is associated with the fantasy of romantic love, and in turn with American popular culture, with which Stan and Laura Maitland both identify.

---

18   Brigid Rooney, "'White, fierce, shocked, tearless': *The Watch Tower* and Harrower's Electric Interiors", this volume, 86.
19   Jill Julius Matthews, *Dance Hall and Picture Palace: Sydney's Romance with Modernity* (Sydney: Currency Press, 2005).
20   James Wood, "No Time for Lies: Rediscovering Elizabeth Harrower", *New Yorker*, 20 October 2014. http://bit.ly/1Cqu4W0.

Rachel resists Sydney's romance with modernity by identifying, through her studies, with the history of classical Greece. While she washes the dishes she plays Crosby and Sinatra records (186), but at the same time she is reading Thucydides and Socrates, and her reading provides her with an alternative world view located in an idealised version of Europe: "Bright-eyed, olive skinned people filled her dreams. She was with them on an island that floated on an indigo sea. White marble columns shone against the sky" (188). Much to Laura's disapproval, Rachel is involved with a young Italian man, Luigi Roberto, a recent migrant from Milan, whom Laura refuses to acknowledge: "'But a foreigner! – I won't call him a new Australian – I don't suppose he's even naturalized'" (125-6). The presence of this minor, "foreign" character is a good example of the way Harrower uses external points of reference to create the classic structure of narrative irony. Rachel's resistance to the dominant provincial point of view is potentially available to the reader and narrator but not necessarily to other characters inside that culture, like Laura Maitland, the structure of knowingness generating Harrower's signature form of "ironic nationality".

Harrower's second novel, *The Long Prospect* (1958), is set in Ballowra, a provincial town based on the industrial city of Newcastle that is defined by its contrast to other, more "cosmopolitan" cities like Sydney and Melbourne, and in relation to Europe. Ballowra's economic dependency and cultural belatedness are epitomised by its toxic steelworks and the drab bungalows of Greenhills, a dormitory suburb. The people of Greenhills are powerless and inauthentic, their emotional lives subject to the machine-like modernity of the factory and the suburb. Lilian Hulm is another of Harrower's "antagonists". Her bungalow, where she lets rooms to employees of the steelworks, is a place of severe aesthetic and emotional constraint, but it is also a theatrical space for the display of an unregulated cruelty that powerless people like Lilian inflict upon others, including her granddaughter, Emily Lawrence: "[T]he house hovered round Emily with evil intent. She was trapped, encircled by it" (50). Lilian's affective life is explosive and unbalanced: her emotions have the volatile rhythms of popular song and cinematic melodrama; they are associated with " theatricality" and " electricity", with alcohol and the new mass media of cinema and radio. Harrower's fictional Ballowra is like the Middletown upon which F.R. Leavis based *Mass Civilization and Minority Culture* (1930), his own jeremiad against the "machine" culture of the automobile, the cinema, the wireless, advertising, and the popular press, with their "standardization" of living, and their "deliberate exploitation of the cheap response", a process of "Americanisation" he believed to be spreading from the Midwest of the United States to Great Britain and throughout "our British-speaking" world.[21] It is also a psychic space where those who are disempowered by their geopolitical location and the affective cage of "the cheap response" nevertheless exert power over others weaker than themselves.

Like Rachel Demster and Luigi Roberto in *Down in the City*, Lilian's granddaughter Emily, and her boarders Thea and Max, are at odds with this place and time, and have glimpses of their true or authentic selves through an optic of displacement, translation and decentring. This is the optic that Anderson calls "the spectre of comparisons", the view through the other end of the telescope that shows one's own culture at once from close up and from far away. Max finds his other self in the act of reading, where he encounters

---

21 F.R. Leavis, *Mass Civilization and Minority Culture* (Cambridge, UK: Minority Press, 1930), in *Cultural Theory and Popular Culture: A Reader*, ed. John Storey (London: Prentice Hall, 1998), 13–21 (14–15).

the idea of Europe, Greenhill's antipodes. This is not the actual postwar Europe, which Harrower, like Patrick White, knew at first hand for the ruin that it was, but is the spatial expression of another, better self to which some Australians aspire to be "translated" (119). It is this idea of Europe that gives people like Thea, Max and Emily the external point of reference with which an internal distance from their provincial context can be articulated:

> Adult, intelligent, feeling, the opposite of frivolous and yet not earnest, [Thea] was the opposite of the popular ideal of her place and time. Then and there, in the cities, great wealth masked a naïvety one would hesitate to call childlike. A contradictory stirring after perpetual adolescence, sophistication and accumulation of wealth were the motives of action. The chief conviction was one of superiority; this was brought about by the Pacific isolation of the continent, and, contrariwise, by trips to a Europe where all the famous treasures were old and frequently dirty, where there were peasants, and the city-dwellers were peculiarly poor. What the fuss was about Europe few Australians could imagine. Not all of them believed in its existence.
>
> To be one of the self-critical minority was to be not so much politically unsound . . . as thoroughly, disagreeably, un-Australian. (145)

As Leavis argued, "[i]n any period it is often upon a very small minority that the discerning appreciation of art and literature depends".[22] Thea and Max and Emily belong to that "self-critical minority" for whom the idea of "Europe" makes their own Australian nationality "ironic". When Lilian's alcoholic friend Billie Duncan tries to seduce Max, she enters his room to find him reading: "Abruptly deported from Europe, Max looked up from his book. His abstraction merged into impassivity when he saw what the situation was in the Antipodes, and was to be, according to Billie's plans" (189). When Lilian intrudes into Thea's flat, Thea "did not say that she had last night, with great pleasure, rediscovered Housman" (11). These are moments of "metageography", where the social production of gendered space in a provincial settler culture is materialised and nationality rendered opaque – though as Brenner points out, this is not a zero-sum game. Adopting an ironic stance to one's nationality and national culture does not mean that they cease to exist, still less that they cease to become the defining horizon of one's experience.

The novel has a recurring set of references to this optic of "the long prospect", of the temporal and spatial antipodes of its present location. In the reflection of herself in the mirror, for example, or in the view from the window of a distant horizon, Emily glimpses her "translation to a deeper level of reality, a translation to herself" (119). She is given her send-off from Ballowra at the aptly named Horizon Hotel (264), and she departs from there decisively into the region of her future self, in contrast to Stan Prescott, who at the end of *Down in the City* turns back from the Pacific Ocean at the Gap – a notorious suicide spot – only to resume the patterns of his old life at Romney Court. The eponymous space of *The Long Prospect* is at once socio- and geopolitical, and psychological or epistemological. Lilian's suburban bungalow in Greenhills is a real point in world space, a province of vernacular modernity, one of whose epicentres is Hollywood, and a dormitory suburb of regionalised industrial production and the globalised consumption of imported consumer goods in the era of neoliberalism. But it is also a psychic space where those disempowered by their geopolitical location exert power over others. Harrower's descriptions of Ballowra,

---

22 Leavis, *Mass Civilization and Minority Culture*, 13.

its steelworks, and the distant prospect of an alternative world, are metageographic in that they render the social production of space in postwar Australia visible, if only for those with eyes to see. For Harry Lawrence, Emily's father, the prospect of the city from Greenhills is claustrophobic, enclosed by the distant steelworks, and the only sense of an outside is provided by the false windows of "giant advertisement hoardings" (54). For Emily and Max, the same prospect seems more open, an abandoned monastery beyond the steelworks, which Harry does not notice, the symbol of an outside world: "To Emily the monastery's isolation was poetic . . . a concrete symbol of her aspirations" (124). The typical narrative perspective of Harrower's novels is therefore the "situated perspectivalism" that Hegglund calls "ironical nationality";[23] it is achieved by the pressure of the idea of elsewhere, a location "half a world away" that can place one's own nationality and provincial location in comparative perspective, illuminating what White calls "the Great Australian Emptiness".

In *The Catherine Wheel* (1960), Harrower's ironic gaze turns from Sydney to postwar London, yet far from providing a point of belonging, as it had seemed to promise for Max and Thea in *The Long Prospect*, London is unsettled by its relations with its own antipodes – continental Europe, the United States and even, ironically enough, Australia. Harrower's perspective, in other words, remains binocular, the idea of an antipodean "Siberia" or "Australia" – surely an ironic coupling – providing another external site of enunciation that defamiliarises both English and Australian identity in a transnational comparative optic. As she misrecognises her image reflected in the black gloss paint of Miss Evans' front door, Clemency James grasps the doubled or comparative nature of both personal and national identity, the feeling of not quite belonging to one's immediate time and place: "I turned the key in the lock wondering what it could be to fit so precisely into a mould. What *were* the legitimate trappings for an Australian . . . living alone in a bed-sitting-room [in London]?" (5). The Australian girl abroad is in "translation" across the layered chronotope of the novel's metageography, whose routes are both imperial and transnational.

The image of the BBC weather map which opens *The Catherine Wheel* is a visual reminder that conditions in one place or country are affected by conditions "half a world away" (3) – "[f]rom Mrs Slater's room downstairs the nine o'clock news rang out a gale warning to all shipping" (33) – in the same way that travellers from the dominions are translocated to Europe along various routes of transnational mobility: "Dora Carlton and her friend, Jean, had slumped over the table for two hours, laboriously exhorting each other to admire the beauties of the Louvre . . . Now they had gone" (33). Like Shirley Hazzard in her own life, and like Caro Bell in *The Transit of Venus* (1980), Clem James comes to London from Sydney at mid-century. It is an era defined, as Brigitta Olubas points out in relation to Hazzard, by the historical coexistence of the old geopolitics of Empire and the new geopolitics of the Cold War, the era of decolonisation, and the West's pivot to the Asia Pacific.[24] Great Britain is on the western edge of a divided Europe, as it is on the BBC weather map, yet it is now the terminus rather than the departure point for a series of routes that emanate from the Commonwealth countries, including Australia, New Zealand, Canada, South Africa, India and the Caribbean. The torsions between these two geographies produces a binocular vision, a recursive and unstable series

---

23 Hegglund, *World Views*, 20.
24 Brigitta Olubas, *Shirley Hazzard: Literary Expatriate and Cosmopolitan Humanist* (Amherst, NY: Cambria Press, 2012).

of perspectives that further defamiliarises both geopolitical space and national identity. As Alexander and Moran observe, modernist writing often has this "polytropic quality", whereby "radically different spaces and geographical scales are brought into relation with one another, creating distinctive effects of disorientation or displacement".[25] The people Clem meets in her Bayswater flat have distinctive national and personal identities, but they are also in transit along an extended transnational matrix: for Clem, it is between Sydney and London; for Christian Roland, the failed actor, it is between London and Paris; for her academic friend, Lewis, it is between London and New York: "I shall find myself in New York" (56). The very idea of these other places affects their being like "the wind from Siberia", or like the "sweetish dehydrated wind" that buffets their faces as they move through the London underground (55). For all that, Clem has a strong sense of her national identity as an Australian, of what it is to be "born Australian and free" (82).

These moments when personal and cultural identity are subject to ironic displacement are facilitated not only by the formal device of metatopographia – "the narrative instance of what is clearly marked as a representation of place – a description of a description"[26] – but also by a mode that Harrower repeatedly associates with the term " theatricality". This denotes a heightened awareness of the way in which the everyday domestic life that is an artefact of vernacular modernity is itself theatrical, artificial or performative – and therefore public. What I will call the *metatheatricality* of Harrower's style has an obvious affinity with Henry James' "melodramatic imagination": that is, the way in which the seemingly unremarkable domestic events of his novels take place against the background of an ethical code that has been occulted by secular modernity, but whose subterranean presence is registered as a heightened, ethically charged melodrama that enters deeply into the scenes of everyday life and into the form of the modern novel.[27] As Rooney observes, in Harrower's "electric interiors", "'moral shock' is a presiding affect, not only as a reaction felt by her characters, but . . . as a sensation that conditions narrative operations".[28] These metatheatrical moments are typically marked not only by an ironic use of theatrical language but also by theatrical devices, especially lighting: "'Here she is!', says the landlady, obviously referring to me, and the three of us stood almost theatrically still" (6). But in Harrower's world of late-colonial modernity, what is "she"? At such moments, the theatricality of everyday life and the melodrama of affect are subject to the same ironic distanciation as nationality.

A signal example is Christian Roland's command over others by means of domestic "melodrama" (85) and "sensationalism" (115). For ten years he has been an aspiring actor; his mother, Beatrice, was "a small-time actress" and his father Tony, "a popular idol in Europe and the United States" (95). His spiritual home is the *Comédie-Française* in Paris (52). This motif is echoed in the "theatricality" of his domestic scenes, which are "electric" (47) and "melodramatic" (164).[29] His "performance[s]" (84) echo, only slightly more professionally, those of Harrower's other "antagonists", such as Stan Prescott in *Down in the City* and Lilian Hulm in *The Long Prospect*. Christian avows, "I wasn't trying to

---

25 Alexander and Moran, "Introduction", 7.
26 Hegglund, *World Views*, 16.
27 Peter Brooks, *The Melodramatic Imagination: Balzac, Henry James, Melodrama, and the Mode of Excess* (New Haven, CT: Yale University Press, 1976).
28 Rooney, "*The Watch Tower* and Harrower's Electric Interiors", this volume, 84.
29 See Brigitta Olubas' discussion of theatrical motifs in the representation of Christian Roland in this volume, 104–6.

impress you by – sensationalism, you know that" (115). His protestations of love for Clem are described as "theatrical amorousness" (156), a *mise en-abyme* of irony and performance that might be described by the contemporary term "camp":[30] he "acts all the time", but "that doesn't mean that what he acts is false. It's just his way of *being*" (149). Harrower has an enduring suspicion of charisma, "magic" (84), and personal "electricity", which her metatheatrical descriptions of domestic interiors illuminate in the same way that her comparative metatopographies defamiliarise nationality.

Harrower's spatialisation of time in "the long prospect" of personal becoming recurs in *The Watch Tower* (1966), her fourth novel, which is set in Sydney during and immediately after the Second World War.[31] When Laura and Clare Vaizey's father dies suddenly, leaving them vulnerable to their mother Stella Vaizey's neglect, Harrower uses metageography and metatopographical description to distinguish between Laura, for whom the future appears to be as bounded as her nationality, and her sister Clare, who finds hope in thinking outside the apparent limits of personal and communal identity. For Laura, the problem of the future "rose on the horizon" (8), and what might happen "next year, or [in] five years' time" was "like the space off the edge of the world" (9). As their mother makes plans to return to England without them, Clare "broods" over an atlas, "her eyes roaming the coloured world" (13-14). For these two teenage girls from "the village" of Manly (31), the Pacific Ocean at the bottom of their street is "a boundary" (16) rather than a distant "horizon", as it was for Thea and Emily in Ballowra. The scales of local, communal, national and gender identity align in an opaque series of frames beyond which they cannot see. Yet when Clare remembers that their mother was born in India, foreign nationality seems to equate with choice, mobility and personal agency: "Clare wriggled her shoulders and grimaced at the map of the world. Old India!" (15). Stella Vaizey "sat in the faded canvas deck-chairs facing the ocean . . . and wrote to her brother Edward in India, and other distant relations in Somerset". "*They*", on the other hand – her daughters – "were Australian, medium-sized mortals, quite lacking in their mother's . . . exotic heritage" (17). In contrast to Clem James in *The Catherine Wheel*, for whom being born Australian means to be born "free", for Laura and Clare, like Esther Prescott, national identity seems to foreclose the prospect of their future lives. Stella Vaizey uses her overseas connections to escape to "the other side of the world" while she uses her daughters' nationality to bury them alive in the province: "This country's never been home to me. It's different for you two. You don't know any better" (53).

At Shaw's Box Factory, where Laura meets her future husband, Felix Shaw, the boxes manufactured by his female employees are another symbol of the containment and lack of external perspective in their young lives: "Four strokes of liquid cement and a moment's pressure completed a box. Towers of these colourless cubes were constructed daily" (22). Laura comes to work for Felix Shaw in 1939 and the events of *The Watch Tower* correspond with the duration of the war, during which a provincial, British-oriented Sydney is dramatically opened up by the change of perspective provided by the American troops. Here again, in charting the impact of "Americanisation" on Australia, Harrower is sensitive to what Leavis called "levelling down" and the aesthetics of the "cheap response", so that for some the opening up of a provincial culture can be another closing down. For the girls

---

30   Susan Sontag's essay "Notes on 'Camp'" first appeared in *Partisan Review* in 1964.
31   Elizabeth Harrower, *The Watch Tower* (1966; Melbourne: Text Publishing, 2012). All subsequent references are to this edition and appear in parentheses in the text.

who work at the box factory, who are the future "war brides", the scale of the war as they come to see it represented in the newsreels at the local cinema only makes their narrow experience and repetitive working lives seem all the more provincial: "They were pressed back on themselves and their few square inches of knowledge and experience" (37-8).

Clare Vaizey is unique in her capacity to find cause for optimism in the idea of an outside to their narrowly provincial lives. Constrained by the box-like spaces of Felix Shaw's immaculately white house at Neutral Bay, where they have come to live, and by the routines of factory and office work in Sydney, Clare experiences a strange sense of joy when a local shopkeeper gives her street directions: "'See that hill up there? Well, you go *up* there. You turn *left* at the second lot of cross-roads. You keep *straight on* for a block' . . . She herself had become a pinpoint astronomically distant" (41). This metatopographical description is proleptic, providing Clare with her first liberating glimpse of the " irony" of personal identity, the "binocular gaze" that allows her to see Sydney from the perspective of elsewhere: "An A.B.C. announcer was reading the world news. Clare tried to listen to it for the sake of her sanity" (227). In the house at Neutral Bay, she imagines the window of her bedroom to be a "look-out tower" (81), from which she sees the property's closed gate and the distant prospect beyond. The novel's title, *The Watch Tower*, is itself ironic: it can suggest either panoptic surveillance, like that which Felix exercises over his female employees in the factory and his female relatives at home – Laura and Clare, of course, are both – or the look-out tower of Clare's bedroom window, and the potential of those surveilled to plot their escape, to imagine an alternative point of view. In contrast to the domestic ferries on which Clare commutes from Manly to the city, the ocean liners that come into Sydney Harbour also herald the promise of that outside world: "Strolling through to the front of the house, Clare went on to the balcony. A big liner, lighted all over, was moving noiselessly across the dark harbour in the direction of the Heads" (250).

By contrast to Clare's intimations of the "irony" of identity, Laura's entrapment is also expressed through metatopographical description. When, after one of Felix's alcoholic outbursts, Laura flees from Neutral Bay by ferry to roam the streets of the inner city like a rat in a maze, her entrapment is visualised in a series of containers that includes the box, the house and the map:

> Laura walked down Pitt Street from the Quay to Central Station. She walked back down Elizabeth Street to Hunter Street, down Hunter Street to George Street, along that thoroughfare to Bathurst Street, up Bathurst to Castlereagh, along Castlereagh to King, down King to Pitt, along Pitt to Market, up Market and along Castlereagh to King, down King, along Pitt, up Market.
>
> She could not make her feet stop walking. She yearned to stop. (166-7)

As Birns argues, the city in Harrower's novels is typically "a Borgesian labyrinth", "an enclave as much as a metropolis", its spatial grid representing "containment" rather than "growth or progress".[32] Here, the idea of locality, visualised by the inner-city grid, the epicentre of Sydney's provinciality within the larger topography of Empire and global modernity, is also the site of Laura's gendered oppression as she seeks refuge from her abusive husband and employer. In this cartographic *mise en-abyme*, one scale of identity is contained inside another like Chinese boxes. Although she was born in the country, Laura

---

32 Birns, *Contemporary Australian Literature*, 58.

has lived all of her adult life in Sydney and has never been outside her own state, let alone overseas. Her husband taunts her, "'Never been out of New South Wales? . . . I'd been all over the world by the time I was your age'" (198).

Clare's final journey away from domestic entrapment is aided by the Dutchman, Bernard, the last in a succession of men brought home by Felix in an attempt to buy friendship, all of whom in the end act in some way against him, either by extorting money or, in Bernard's case, defeating him by escaping his influence and enabling Clare to escape with him. Like Luigi Roberto in *Down in the City*, Bernard is a "foreigner" who acts as a catalyst in helping Clare to find her own point of exit: "She and Bernard had traversed the same extreme country" (261). Yet Clare's escape, her own journey away, is no sooner spatialised in this way than it is denied any specific geographical location. When they meet on their outward journeys at Sydney's Central Railway Station, Bernard asks her to come with him to Europe, but she plans instead a more limited journey by train into the Australian inland. Clare realises that her escape from the subjection of gender and provincialism cannot literally be to "leave the country" for another actual place, because real freedom has to be personal rather than geopolitical:

> Every instinct rose even now to reject the idea of leaving the country, as though her course had still to be decided. A false gesture. As though pretending to believe what she did not: that the *real, significance*, existed in another country and might be found in a specific geographical position, like the Pyramids. (326)

The conclusion of *The Watch Tower* therefore complicates Harrower's persistent spatialisation of identity in terms of a dialectical relation between the inside and the outside, here and elsewhere. Harrower appears to associate personal becoming with the contemporary discourses of global travel and expatriatism, but the province of gender or nation cannot be left behind through physical expatriation. It has to be viewed from outside, or *as if* from the outside, through the internal distance of "ironic nationality". Laura makes this mistake, thinking that she and Felix can leave behind the habits in which they have become entrapped simply by travelling to South America: "'Felix and I are going away . . . We're going for a trip to America and South America. We might even live there. You see! Everything's different now'" (327). But everything cannot be made "different" through travel. Freedom can be anticipated in geographical terms but in the end it is as much epistemological as it is topographical.

The journey that Clare embarks upon is not so much a physical journey of expatriation as the discovery of an alternative way of being *inside* the internal space of gender and nation, by putting the inside into dialogue with the outside. When Bernard suggests that Clare's future will be far away from "that house", Clare corrects this too literal interpretation of her escape by insisting, "'No, no. That doesn't matter any more'" (333):

> "It made me recognize things as they were. And that – I was supported by a sort of faith. I'm not sure in what. But I thought I saw bits of the true, if not of the good and the beautiful. That made most things bearable. That was my retreat. There was the external world . . . And then there was home – so real it seemed to have six dimensions, fundamental as the floor of the world. Nothing at all from the outside could penetrate. The outside was a place of coloured tissue paper where people went about not knowing

about reality". She added, "So you see – it was all – as they say – in a way – pure gain." (334)

Clare's desire has persistently been expressed in spatial terms as a desire to escape from the entrapment of identity into an external space, but in the end she understands this as an epistemological rather than a physical alteration, the ability to see her immediate situation "inside" her identity from a situation "outside" it. This is not to transcend nationality but to see it from another optic, like that of Patrick White's "returned expatriate". Together with the externally identified sensibilities of Thea and Max in *The Long Prospect*, Clare's decision to remain within Australia anticipates what Rebecca L. Walkowitz calls "cosmopolitan style", in which "modernist writers troubled the distinction between local and global" that is so central to high modernist accounts of modernist internationalism, replacing relatively static models of exile and expatriation with more complex, more dynamic models of transnational circulation, internal distance and inverted or doubled perspectives.[33]

The titles of Harrower's first four novels had therefore signalled her recurring interest not only in patterns of self-destructive encirclement – *The Catherine Wheel* – but also in structures of ironic internal distanciation, often expressed through spatial and optical metaphors of doubling and inversion: *Down in the City*, *The Long Prospect*, *The Watch Tower*. In her last novel, *In Certain Circles*, which she completed in manuscript in 1971 but did not allow to be published until 2014, the title again suggests the idea of social "circles" or personal networks in which characters become trapped, as Russell and Zoe Howard do in their choice of marriage partners.[34] Yet this last novel, as James Wood points out, has a certain opening up or opening out.[35] In the end, Russell is released from his marriage to Lillian to be with Anne, Lillian is free to follow her children to London, and Zoe frees herself from her tortured marriage to Stephen Quayle, possibly to renew the career as a photographer and filmmaker that she had commenced as a younger woman in Paris. This last novel presents a different, less circumscribed Australia. It is apparently the difference between the Australia of the 1950s and that of the 1970s. Zoe's father expresses the older imperial spatiality by reference to the map and the idea of Europe, as Max does in *The Long Prospect*:

"When you're a child, the size of the continent on the map makes you proud of the place," Mr Howard said. "The space and the freedom to move about have a good effect on a young mind. But when you're older, it's a deprivation not to be in Europe. Your links with the human race are there".

His listeners, Zoe and Anna, gave each other a look, inclined to giggle.

"That's just snobbishness", his daughter said. Then, "Think of what they've done in Europe! What do you say, then?"

"Because, if you've had that childhood I mentioned, you're an outrider, willy-nilly. But, historically, we're so thin on the ground here that the life would be meagre if you didn't put up a struggle." (62-3)

---

33   Rebecca L. Walkowitz, *Cosmopolitan Style: Modernism Beyond the Nation* (New York: Columbia University Press, 2006), 6.
34   Elizabeth Harrower, *In Certain Circles* (Melbourne: Text Publishing, 2014). All subsequent references are to this edition and appear in parentheses in the text.
35   Wood, "No Time for Lies", 7.

When Zoe first returns to Sydney from Paris, Stephen dismisses her as a woman and a colonial artist by claiming that no internationally significant woman filmmaker is ever likely to "rise up *here*" (125). Yet he concedes in the end that things have changed, at least for his generation if not for Mr Howard's, and that Sydney is now a place where a woman might, after all, pursue a career in filmmaking (245) – the novel is set on the eve of the Australian film renaissance of the 1970s. Sydney is now an international city, and London, Paris and the United States are very much part of the lives of the characters, places to which they come and go, where ideals may be explored, loose ends tied up, or things put in perspective: "Winter here, summer in Paris" (83). We might think of this qualified opening out in Harrower's late work, again, in relation to Walkowitz's term "cosmopolitan style". Sydney feels now more like the Sydney of the 1970s than "the Great Australian Emptiness" of *The Long Prospect*, where Europe, or the idea of Europe, is the "antipodes", a distant ideal against which provincial lives are measured and found wanting.

In this essay I have argued that in her five novels, written between 1954 and 1971, Elizabeth Harrower repeatedly employs one of aesthetic modernism's distinctive formal innovations, cartographic realism or metageography, as part of her main fictional project, which is an extended aesthetic and ethical critique of Australian culture in the era of late modernity or neoliberalism. This suggests that her career in writing might usefully be thought of as belonging to an aesthetic formation of late-colonial, regional or provincial modernism. As Tom Lutz argues, such a "regional" awareness is defined precisely by its "cosmopolitan investments", its themes of "the relation of different groups to ongoing technological, economic, and social change, or, in other words, the relation of the region to the rest of the world".[36] The title of Lutz's book on American regional modernisms, *Cosmopolitan Vistas* (2004), might even be read as a gloss on Harrower's signature motif of "the long prospect".

The largest scale onto which Harrower projects her distinctive set of concerns is that of the world historical events of mid-century: the Nazi Holocaust, the Soviet gulags of Siberia, the Japanese labour camps, the Allied fire bombing of German cities, the nuclear bombing of Hiroshima. As Megan Nash observes, references to these events recur throughout the novels, often in the seemingly minute detail of Harrower's imagery; the moral conundrums they posed about human nature, about political power, and about private ethical behaviour were crystallised at mid-century by the capture and trial of Adolph Eichmann in 1961.[37] As Hannah Arendt argued in her seminal books *The Origins of Totalitarianism* (1951) and *Eichmann in Jerusalem* (1963), the syndrome that she famously called "the banality of evil" was epitomised by a single institution, "the camp", the most potent symbol of which, in turn, was the watch tower.[38] The smallest scale onto which Harrower projects these concerns, as if through a refractive lens, is the economy of the provincial, patriarchal household, with its wounded, cruel men – Stan Peterson, Christian Roland, Felix Shaw and Stephen Quayle – and its complicit, collaborating women, like Lilian Hulm and Laura Vaizey.

---

36 Tom Lutz, *Cosmopolitan Vistas: American Regionalism and Literary Value* (Ithaca, NY: Cornell University Press, 2004), 15.
37 Megan Nash, "Traversing 'the same extreme country' in *The Watch Tower* and *Daniel Deronda*", this volume, 120–1.
38 Hannah Arendt, *The Origins of Totalitarianism* (1951; London: Penguin, 2017) and *Eichmann in Jerusalem* (1963; London: Penguin, 2007).

Metageographical fiction is characterised by "the ironic use of geography as a way of mediating cosmopolitan desires and national attachments"; by "a stance that permits . . . writers to step outside a national homeland without sundering a meaningful, felt attachment to an imagined national community".[39] In Harrower's novels, as we have seen, the "external sites of enunciation" that generate this distinctive stance are of two types. The first, associated with the idea of Europe, provides an ironical perspective on the provinciality and belatedness of Australia's postwar modernity. The second, associated with America or the global export of American popular culture, also functions to confirm Australia's provinciality as an importer of mass consumer goods in the era of globalisation. This is the external point of reference most often favoured by those of her characters who are least able to distance themselves from destructive forms of identity: Stan Peterson, Laura Maitland, Lilian Hulm, Laura Vaizey. Harrower's own ironic nationality can be thought of as a double movement: a denial of the negative effects of provincialism accompanied by a surprising refusal of expatriation; a movement from provincialism to expatriation and then back again to repatriation. This is seen especially in Clare Vaizey's decision at the end of *The Watch Tower* to travel only within Australia. It can perhaps be understood as an early challenge, prompted by Harrower's strong local affiliation, to what Neal Alexander and James Moran describe as "the powerful and well-rehearsed narrative about modernism . . . as essentially metropolitan and internationalist in character".[40] Harrower's ironic nationality, her provincial modernism, is liberated epistemologically and aesthetically from provincial and local allegiances, though without necessarily claiming to transcend them altogether by adherence to some false ideal of exile, internationalism or transnationalism.

The relatively recent revival of interest in Harrower's work, from Text's republication of her novels, commencing in 2012, to the 2015 symposium from which the present volume of essays is drawn,[41] also corresponds with the transnational turn in Australian literature studies. While a critical movement of this kind can certainly contribute to the re-reading and reputational recovery of a novelist's body of work, its own founding premises must be subjected, in turn, to the kinds of aesthetic and political questions that are persistently asked by those works of fiction. Above all, Harrower's signature choice between expatriatism and ironic nationality sounds a timely warning about the purpose and methodology of a nationally identified discipline like Australian literary studies at the point of its encounter with what I have elsewhere described as "the problem of the world" – that is, the rescaling of literary analysis from national to world scale.[42] By analogy, Harrower's stance of ironic nationality suggests that *Australian* critics of Australian literature should be wary of that discipline's capitulation to transnational or world scales of analysis, adopting instead what Hegglund describes as the "dialectical relationship between a particularized place of identification and a detached space of enunciation that can put national identity in a larger, extranational context".[43] Such a binocular gaze is consistent with the social and narrative perspectives of some of Australia's

---

39 Hegglund, *World Views*, 20.
40 Alexander and Moran, "Introduction", 1.
41 "Rediscovering Again: Christina Stead / Elizabeth Harrower", University of New South Wales, 3–4 December 2015.
42 Robert Dixon, "National Literatures, Scale, and the Problem of the World", *JASAL: Journal of the Association for the Study of Australain Literature* 15, no. 3 (2015). http://bit.ly/2pWcWfD.
43 Hegglund, *World Views*, 20.

leading writers of the mid-twentieth century, including Christina Stead, Patrick White, Shirley Hazzard and Elizabeth Harrower.

References

Alexander, Neal and James Moran. "Introduction: Regional Modernisms". In *Regional Modernisms*. Edited by Neal Alexander and James Moran, 1-21. Edinburgh: Edinburgh University Press, 2013.
Anderson, Benedict. *The Spectre of Comparisons: Nationalism, Southeast Asia and the World*. London: Verso, 1998.
Arendt, Hannah. *Eichmann in Jerusalem: A Report on the Banality of Evil*. (1963) London: Penguin, 2007.
——. *The Origins of Totalitarianism*. (1951) London: Penguin, 2017.
Birns, Nicholas. *Contemporary Australian Literature: A World Not Yet Dead*. Sydney: Sydney University Press, 2015.
Brenner, Neil. *New State Spaces: Urban Governance and the Rescaling of Statehood*. Oxford and New York: Oxford University Press, 2004.
Brooks, Peter. *The Melodramatic Imagination: Balzac, Henry James, Melodrama, and the Mode of Excess*. New Haven, CT: Yale University Press, 1976.
Dixon, Robert. "National Literatures, Scale, and the Problem of the World", *JASAL: Journal of the Association for the Study of Australian Literature* 15, no. 3 (2015). http://bit.ly/2pWcWfD.
Harrower, Elizabeth. *In Certain Circles*. Melbourne: Text Publishing, 2014.
——. *The Watch Tower*. (1966) Melbourne: Text Publishing, 2012.
——. *The Catherine Wheel*. (1960) Melbourne: Text Publishing, 2014.
——. *The Long Prospect*. (1958) Melbourne: Text Publishing, 2012.
——. *Down in the City*. (1957) Melbourne: Text Publishing, 2013.
Hegglund, Jon. *World Views: Metageographies of Modernist Fiction*. Oxford: Oxford University Press, 2012.
Huyssen, Andreas. "Mass Culture as Woman". In *After the Great Divide: Modernism, Mass Culture, Postmodernism*, 44-62. Bloomington: Indiana University Press, 1986.
Leavis, F.R. *Mass Civilization and Minority Culture* (1930). In *Cultural Theory and Popular Culture: A Reader*. Edited by John Storey,13-21. London: Prentice Hall, 1998.
Lutz, Tom. *Cosmopolitan Vistas: American Regionalism and Literary Value*. Ithaca, NY: Cornell University Press, 2004.
Matthews, Jill Julius. *Dance Hall and Picture Palace: Sydney's Romance with Modernity*. Sydney: Currency Press, 2005.
Nash, Megan. "Traversing 'the same extreme country' in *The Watch Tower* and *Daniel Deronda*". In *Elizabeth Harrower: Critical Essays*. Edited by Elizabeth McMahon and Brigitta Olubas, 119-132. Sydney: Sydney University Press, 2017.
Olubas, Brigitta. *Shirley Hazzard: Literary Expatriate and Cosmopolitan Humanist*. Amherst, NY: Cambria Press, 2012.
Rooney, Brigid. "'White, fierce, shocked, tearless': *The Watch Tower* and Harrower's Electric Interiors". In *Elizabeth Harrower: Critical Essays*. Edited by Elizabeth McMahon and Brigitta Olubas, 81-95. Sydney: Sydney University Press, 2017.
Sontag, Susan. "Notes on 'Camp'. *Partisan Review* (Fall 1964): 515-30.
Walkowitz, Rebecca L. *Cosmopolitan Style: Modernism Beyond the Nation*. New York: Columbia University Press, 2006.
White, Patrick. *Flaws in the Glass*. London: Jonathan Cape, 1981.
——. "The Prodigal Son". (1958) In *Patrick White Speaks*. Edited by Paul Brennan and Christine Flynn. Leichhardt, NSW: Primavera Press, 1989.
Wood, James. "No Time for Lies: Rediscovering Elizabeth Harrower". *New Yorker*, 20 October 2014. http://bit.ly/1Cqu4W0.

7
Weather and Temperature, the Will to Power, and the Female Subject in Harrower's Fiction

Kate Livett

> And the weather seems menacing.
> —Elizabeth Harrower, "The Cost of Things"[1]

> I want to teach men the sense of their existence, which is the Superman, the lightning out of the dark cloud - man.
> —Friedrich Nietzsche, *Thus Spake Zarathustra*[2]

The opening sentence of the first short story Elizabeth Harrower ever completed[3] plunges the reader into a dramatic meteorological event:

> And then, as if the lightning that ripped the sky apart wasn't enough, the lights round the edge of the swimming pool, and even the three big ones sunk into it on cement piles, went out. At once the solid blackness rang with shrieks and laughter; only Janet was struck dumb to find that she had been obliterated. It was like nothing so much as that astronomical darkness into which she had been plunged last year when they took out her tonsils.[4]

This *Ur*-passage encapsulates many of the ongoing dilemmas and figurations of Harrower's fiction, particularly the female subject at risk of obliteration in a tumultuous universe in which the earth is wired to the heavens, the weather and physics, but not to God. Tellingly also, Harrower begins and ends this story in mid-event, in a literary imaginary devoid of telos but preoccupied with experience. This essay will turn a microscope to

---

1   Elizabeth Harrower, "The Cost of Things", in *A Few Days in the Country and Other Stories* (Melbourne: Text Publishing, 2015), 145.
2   Friedrich Nietzsche, *Thus Spake Zarathustra: A Book for All and None*, trans. Thomas Common (1909). Project Gutenberg ebook, http://bit.ly/2qfgcDi.
3   Harrower explained to Elizabeth McMahon that although she had done other writing before, "The Fun of the Fair" was the first story to be completed. Elizabeth Harrower to Elizabeth McMahon, 3 June 2016.
4   Elizabeth Harrower, "The Fun of the Fair", in *A Few Days in the Country and Other Stories* (Melbourne: Text Publishing, 2015), 1–14. All subsequent references are to this edition and appear in parentheses in the text.

the basal elements of Harrower's work as they are introduced in this story and replayed across her oeuvre. For the godless cosmos in Harrower is characterised by the ineluctable connections between human dynamics and the broader physics of the natural world.

The weather in the godless late-modern world of Harrower's fiction is an atmospheric and thermodynamic symbol of the conflict between individuals and the assertion of self and the will to power. This contest of wills occurs with most force between humans who are attracted to each other for romantic or sympathetic reasons, or who are part of a family group by accident of birth. This analysis will identify how these human dynamics and interactions connect to the meteorological fluctuations within and without the human person. Specifically, this essay will show how the contest of wills generates heat in attraction and in clash. Alternatively, it produces chilling coldness when the struggle results in separation, akin to entropic death. Most particularly, the thwarting of individual identity results in extremes of coldness for the women subjugated within a relationship, despite the initial heat of their attraction to their male tyrant. These thermodynamics work on multiple levels, incorporating but exceeding conventional metaphorics of heat and cold and the human passions.[5] Meteorological conditions of seasonal heat and cold and their manifestations in daily weather are integral indices of world and self in Harrower's oeuvre, most oppressively in the first three novels, where they operate as the literal and metaphorical atmosphere in and against which the characters strive. In Harrower's late-modernist writing, I argue, the fundamental paradox of not only character, but each discrete text, and the oeuvre as a whole, is that the entropic movement from heat to cold is also the movement of the female's necessary removal from tyrannical power dynamics.[6]

Since the publication of Harrower's full oeuvre in 2015, it is possible to chart a progressive development of ideas across her entire body of work. This essay takes up this opportunity, and in doing so repositions "The Fun of the Fair", published in 2015, as Harrower's first publication, to recognise the potency of its original position and charge. Ultimately, I will suggest that the conclusion of Harrower's final novel, *In Certain Circles* (2014), resolves the struggle of the female subject against the obliterating universe. In the character of Zoe, Harrower's oeuvre concludes with a female subject who can assert the self without succumbing to the hypothermic death of entropy.

Meteorological and internal thermodynamic heat indicate life in Harrower's fictional universe, though it is a figuration of life as a cosmic but godless "will to power" in the Nietzschean sense. Nietzsche argues that God is dead and the primary drive of the human is the "will to power", namely the urge to express and assert the self, as the self is felt only

---

5 In his essay on "Katherine Mansfield's Modernist Thermodynamics", Alex Moffett summarises the standard correspondences of human emotions to thermodynamic temperatures: "Heat has been used for centuries in English to describe emotional valences: we are hot when we are filled with passion, warm when we demonstrate affection, cold when we lack any sympathy". Alex Moffett, "Hot Sparks and Cold Devils: Katherine Mansfield and Modernist Thermodynamics", *Journal of Modern Literature* 37, no. 2 (2014): 59-75 (63). Passion, rage, fear, dread, loneliness and despair are all tied to temperature adjectives in Harrower.

6 Robyn Claremont identifies the crucial negotiation of Harrower's characters between independence and intersubjectivity: however, Claremont argues for the possibility that the characters might achieve independence *within* a relationship: "The paradox [in her work] then is that success within these relationships depends primarily upon the individual's ability to stand alone, to attain and hold on to an integrity which is not solely defined *by* the relationship." Robyn Claremont, "The Novels of Elizabeth Harrower", *Quadrant*, November 1979, 16.

through its assertion: "A living thing seeks above all to DISCHARGE its strength – life itself is WILL TO POWER".[7] Seen directly in Harrower's fiction, the will to power sees the assertion of the self always, inherently, at the expense of an other upon whom authority is effected, whether good or bad.[8] For Harrower, however, it is the negative, destructive effects of the will to power – especially in their gendered formations – that are of interest. In each Harrower novel there is a range of encounters between multiple pairings of characters who are striving to assert their will to power over each other. In *Down in the City* (1957) for instance, the dominant power dynamics are between Esther and Stan, with Stan constantly striving to assert his will to power over Esther. However, such struggles are also evident in the interactions between the majority of characters, and every one of her novels is riddled with this contestatory form, figured through and in thermodynamic heat and cold. The use of temperature metaphorics connects Harrower, in some ways, to earlier modernist investigations in the wake of Einstein and the "new science", as Alex Moffett has identified in relation to Katherine Mansfield, Virginia Woolf and T.S. Eliot.[9] However, this connection also underscores Harrower's departure from these earlier modernists in her distinctive inter-figuration of thermodynamics with a Nietzschean will to power.

Her first novel, *Down in the City*, inaugurates Harrower's novelistic preoccupation with the elements debuted in "The Fun of the Fair": a narrative immersion in the thermodynamics of the will to power that threatens to obliterate the female subject. The wealthy but inexperienced, emotionally neglected protagonist Esther is defined by thermodynamic extremes. She experiences the world almost entirely through degrees of heat and cold and their correspondences to her relationship with her husband, the charlatan businessman Stan Peterson. This is not the conventional trope of the "heat of desire" – Esther is figured as a lover of heat, even before she meets Stan: "This was, in fact, her greatest pleasure – to be hot, to be alone in the sun".[10] Esther's love of heat and warmth is equated with independent life, what critic Rosie Yeo describes as the "intense engagement with life which Esther finds in her marriage".[11] This desire to assert a self is defined against her family. Esther sees a match for herself in conflating her own sense of heat as life with the life energy that animates Stan's will to power: "This day she flourished, breathed, felt the heat, and waited for Stan. And with him, she lived" (133). In choosing to marry Stan, Esther chooses the vascillation of thermodynamics their relationship becomes: a struggle in which both heat and cold become painful. As

---

7   Friedrich Nietzsche, "Prejudices of Philosophers, No. 13", in *Beyond Good and Evil*, trans. Helen Zimmern. Project Gutenberg ebook, http://bit.ly/2pAnAaI.
8   Nietzsche expert Galen Strawson explicates the inherent nature of the will to power as an effect on others: "The only way to exist without being potent, without being disposed to have an effect on other existing things, is not to exist!" Galen Strawson, "Nietzsche's Metaphysics?" in *Nietzsche on Mind and Nature*, ed. Manuel Dries and P.J.E. Jail (Oxford: Oxford University Press Online, 2015), doi 10.1093/acprof:oso/9780198722236.001.0001.
9   Moffett argues that Woolf and Mansfield, who corresponded in letters and discussed their work, were committed to a "warm" modernism, which they deliberately distinguished from the "cold" modernism that they felt was being created by modernists such as T.S Eliot. Alex Moffett, "Hot Sparks and Cold Devils: Katherine Mansfield and Modernist Thermodynamics", *Journal of Modern Literature* 37, no. 2 (2014): 60–1.
10 Elizabeth Harrower, *Down in the City* (1957; Melbourne: Text Publishing, 2012), 14. All subsequent references are to this edition and appear in parentheses in the text.
11 Rosie Yeo, "*Down in the City*: Elizabeth Harrower's 'Lost' Novel", *Southerly* 50, no. 4 (December 1990): 491–8.

Jasmin Kelaita has argued, "Esther's subjectivity [shifts] from seemingly self-composed and solitary, to porous and utterly emotionally co-dependent".[12] Heat is the suffering of their life together, and their life is his subjugation of her. Stan finds pleasurable heat and warmth in asserting his will to power over Esther: "And whether it was because Esther had sounded heartsick at the news, or because he had proved to himself that he had some control over his life, Stan felt the warmth of rising confidence" (137).

Cold is also experienced as a negative, threatening to obliterate Esther in a metaphorical cosmic entropy of cosmological death: humans as isolated chunks of matter drifting further and further apart from one another. Esther is described as "crouching over a thimbleful of sand, in a world that was colder and less bright" (92). This "sense of cosmic loneliness, and of her own incapacity" is figured in terms of weather and temperature, as it "swe[eps] over her chillily" (146). *Down in the City* ends, as does "The Fun of the Fair", mid-event, in this case from within their tumultuous marriage, with no indication that Esther has any intention of separating from Stan. The very last chapter observes Esther alone in the apartment, waiting for Stan to return. Esther is figured here as thermodynamically cooling, entropically dying, when she is not with Stan. Her love of heat is still evident, even though it is the destructive heat of their relationship that is the cause of her encoldening when she is alone:

> After a time, with a movement, stiff, somehow burdened, she rose . . . It was hot [on the balcony]. She felt the heat strike her body and the heat rise in her to meet it . . .
> The slow realisation that a postponement of decision was, after all, possible, brought with it a sensation of relief that made her lean against the sink for support . . . With cold curiosity she listened to the screech-screech of [the telephone] bell . . . until at length it stopped . . .
> By no moisture of eye, or trembling of hands, by no frown did she betray the blankness of her spirit, the exhaustion of her heart. That she was she, that this was her one life, her past and future, she most tiredly knew . . .
> Straightening, as he could be heard in the hall, she gave a sigh, and turned on the empty room, into which he was about to come, a look that changed at last to one of calm. Going forward to meet him, she said, "Hello, Stan." (290)

Heat, and life, her life as the subjugated in the conflict with Stan, is the only form of identity she has. When he is absent from the room in this final scene, Esther's heat dissipates, she becomes slow and cold, cosmically "blank", her heart too tired to beat. She "straightens" and becomes "calm" and achieves the capacity to move again as he arrives, and her movement is towards him. Having merged her previously independent love of heat in the choice to be with Stan, this heat is now the life that animates her, and she cannot withdraw from him without losing her own thermodynamic warmth and life.

In Harrower's second novel, *The Long Prospect* (1958), the female protagonist Emily is another neglected child who, like Esther, experiences heat and warmth as life and love, in her relationships with Thea and Max. Unlike in *Down in the City*, this warmth is reciprocal and mutually productive. However, it is doomed to be replaced with entropic coldness. As

---

12 Jasmin Kelaita, "'If someone knocks at the door tonight, don't answer it': Penetrating Walls in *Down in the City*", paper presented at "Rediscovering Again: Christina Stead / Elizabeth Harrower", University of New South Wales, 3–4 December 2015.

with "The Fun of the Fair", *The Long Prospect* immerses the reader in a proximal narrative perspective; like *Down in the City*, it ends with a female subject caught in the process of cosmic obliteration. The obliteration of the teenage Emily is caused by the combined wills to power of her monstrous grandmother Lilian and Lilian's lover Rosen. Heat and warmth are the temperature of Max and Emily's relationship: symbolic (in their case in opposition to that of Stan and Esther's) of their mutual regard and sympathetic wills. In this case it is not Max whose will to power sucks the heat from Emily's existence but Lilian's assertion of power which effects Max's complete removal from Emily's life and thereby causes her loss of warmth. The jealous Rosen recruits Lilian into a suspicion that Max is sexually preying on Emily. Affected by a chain of will-to-power struggles, Emily is the one subjugated by Rosen's will to power over Max, and Lilian's over both Max and Emily. Lilian is described explicitly in Nietzschean terms from both her own and Max's focalised perspectives. Her cruelty to others is described as an unanchored discharging of the strength of her will in the absence of a Superman who can control and civilise her:

> the lack of [a man with a] hard hand and will inspired Lilian to ride over her own and other lives with the mindless destructiveness of a hurricane. Whoever the superman was, or was to be, it was not Rosen.[13]

Max thinks that Lilian's "underlying motive" "could often be placed no higher than sadism. In microcosm Lilian was the world . . . Living with her was practice in bloodless warfare" (179). The combined and malicious wills of Lilian and Rosen against the combined and happy sympathies of Emily and Max are evident in a scene in which their respective wills to power are given symbolic expression. Lilian and Rosen are physically present in the scene, while Emily and Max are physically absent but are engaged in the contest through an atmospheric heat that symbolises their relationship. On an extremely hot summer's day, Max and Emily are the only characters not described as inordinately suffering in the heat (in contrast to Lilian, Rosen and the dog, all of whom are described as heavily oppressed by it) (175). Under this heat, symbolic of Emily and Max's happiness, Lilian and Rosen pantingly strive to assert their conjoined wills to power, discussing their request to Thea to visit as part of the entrapment of Max:

> [Emily's] arms rose like wings, she cast the swiftest smile over her shoulder at the car as if to say, "Rejoice!" before she cut noiselessly away, running to meet Max who had appeared at the top of the hill.
> "What is it? What's the matter? Where's she off to?" Lilian asked, assuming a testy air of mystification.
> "Him," he said, without turning his head to look. "I wish I had her energy" . . .

---

13   Elizabeth Harrower, *The Long Prospect* (1958; Melbourne: Text Publishing, 2012), 167–8. All subsequent references are to this edition and appear in parentheses in the text. Lilian's self-conception in contentiously (and ironically) gendered terms reflects Nietzsche's explicit categorisation of the Superman (*der Übermensch*) as male only, in *Thus Spake Zarathustra*. Further direct reference to Nietzsche occurs when, at a moment of her own feeling of cosmic isolation, Lilian thinks to herself, "And there was no God" (174), her thoughts echoing the cry in *Thus Spake Zarathustra*: "DEAD ARE ALL THE GODS: NOW DO WE DESIRE THE SUPERMAN TO LIVE" ("XXII, Bestowing Virtue"). Nietzsche, *Thus Spake Zarathustra*, http://bit.ly/2qfgcDi.

> Lilian held before her eyes for a moment that expression of Emily's. She tapped the letter in her lap with moist fingers. Gusts of dusty air beat against her flushed face and added to the chaos begun by the melting of her makeup. "Energy?" she repeated vaguely.
> "Anyway, this is from Thea" . . .
> ". . . she's coming to see me. She will. I know she will!"
> And momentarily forgetful of their discomfort, Lilian and Rosen beamed through the shimmering air . . . (176)

Ally to Max and Emily's relationship and symbolic of Emily's will to power as temporarily in ascendance, the oppressive heat is accordingly detrimental to Lilian and Rosen, whom it drains. The narrative switches scenes here to a conversation between Max and Emily, still outdoors in the heat, and the atmosphere inversely symbolises Lilian and Rosen through a meteorological coldness in the midst of the heat:

> There appeared at that moment in the glaring deserts of the sky a single cloud – a small untidy mass inconceivably composed of moisture and coolness, inconceivably designed to shade and dampen. Watching it, they were forced to sigh. (180)

This little cloud foretells the end of the warmth and heat that her relationship with Max and her own will to power brings to Emily. When Lilian and Rosen's dominance over Max has finally been achieved at the expense of Emily, the temperature of Emily's life is figured as drained of its heat and fundamentally cold, separating her, as it does, from the only other human who makes life warm for her.

> [Emily] trod deliberately on an ant and looked up, looked suddenly round as if to identify the nature of her own murderer. And it was everything and everywhere. Polished pale-blue sky, white streaky clouds, grey smoke – relentless. Painted wooden houses overlaid with grime; gutters, telegraph poles, insensate wood and brick – relentless: all part of what was opposed to her, what was cold, implacable. And the pale-skinned people in the house behind her, to whom she was, she felt, no more than a troublesome force to be held in check by will . . . (234-5)

Emily here enacts over the ant the obliterating will to power that has been symbolically enacted upon her by Lilian, bearing out the point from Nietzsche that all life is will to power that affects others.[14] Emily rightly identifies that to her parents and grandparent she is "a troublesome force to be held in check by will". Such is the struggle for identity and power in the godless world of modernity, and as Emily sees here, it is located in the weather of the sky ("white streaky clouds") and the temperature of reality ("what was opposed to her, what was cold, implacable").

The ending of *The Long Prospect* leaves the reader amidst a scene of Emily's (and her mother Paula's) subjugation to the will of their new tyrant, Harry, in the cold cosmic loneliness 1concentrated in a suburban kitchen. After Max has left, Emily has been removed to live with her mother and father, Paula and Harry, in a new house in a new

---

14   Galen Strawson, "Nietzsche's Metaphysics?" in *Nietzsche on Mind and Nature*, ed. Manuel Dries and P.J.E. Kail (Oxford: Oxford University Press Online, 2015), doi 10.1093/acprof:oso/ 9780198722236.001.0001.

suburb. Emily digs in the garden at sunset, and "soon it would be dark, but meantime the earth gave up earthy evening scents, dampness in spite of heat" (268).[15] Having written Max a letter from her new life, she receives an answer, out of the cosmos:

> And what had he said in all that space? She could hardly remember. With a slow, incredulous chilling of her blood, she had read, and seen only what he did not say. No promises. No declarations. (275)

Emily's blood has been chilled by her – perhaps permanent – separation from Max and all he represents, and by the triumph of her philistine relatives' wills to power. Emily's cosmic alienation is then reiterated immediately within the seemingly oppositional female space of the domestic interior, the kitchen of the family's new home. In this interior the line between will to power and cosmic entropy is symbolically drawn: the last sentence of the novel leaves her conflated with her mother, together deliberately abasing themselves for Harry's self-congratulation.

The issues of thermodynamic correspondence and conflict and the dilemmas of merged identity and alienation are reimagined and intensified in Harrower's third novel, *The Catherine Wheel* (1960), set in London. Harrower refigures Esther and Emily's deliberate "choosing" of a male by a female protagonist in *The Catherine Wheel*, and the novel's ending follows the pattern, established by the first two novels, of the resultant hypothermic entropy of the female subject. As Clem (Clemency),[16] the female protagonist, tries to extricate herself from the heat of her relationship with Christian,[17] her inverse chilling is represented by Harrower as a literal illness and pseudo-death. Imagined by both Clem and Christian in an idealistic form as a partnership of warmth and mutual nurturing, their relationship quickly moves into the same will-to-power struggle for assertion of the self against the other seen in *Down in the City* and *The Long Prospect*. Over and over again Clem relinquishes her own painstakingly achieved selfhood in order to allow Christian to assert his identity at her expense – a deliberate move that she believes she has control of and that will ultimately feed her own sense of self by making her his saviour. But as Brigitta Olubas contends, the quality of will is a characteristic of both Clem and Christian. Olubas argues that Clem's devotion to Christian "works to compromise her independent life, her very will".[18] While Esther in *Down in the City* has no aspiration in regards to Stan, and Emily in *The Long Prospect* has only the amorphous dreams of any adolescent for a future involving Max, Clem is presented as acting in relation to Christian with deliberate martyrish intention, and from an initial position of independence. The level of

---

15 Megan Nash argues that despite the standard assertion that Harrower's fiction takes place in and is concerned with the constrained interiority of the domestic sphere, Harrower "mobilises world events inside the otherwise intimate or domestic narrative spaces of her novels". Megan Nash, "Traversing 'the same extreme country' in *The Watch Tower* and *Daniel Deronda*", this volume, 119.
16 The fascinating etymology of Clem's name is researched by Olubas as part of her argument for the theological significations in *The Catherine Wheel*. Brigitta Olubas, "Addiction, Fire and the Face in *The Catherine Wheel*", this volume, 100–1.
17 Christian's name introduces a complexity of meanings from theology, as Olubas unpacks in "Addiction, Fire and the Face". When read in the context of Harrower's oeuvre as partaking in a post- Nietzschean godlessness, his name functions ironically.
18 Olubas, "Addiction Fire and the Face", 101.

her diminishment is commensurate with that of her hubris. This perverse and doomed battle plays out through metaphorics of temperature.

Taken as a unit, like Emily and Max in *The Long Prospect*, Clem and Christian's internal heat and warmth characterises their initial attraction and sense of harmonious happiness, and casts them as striving against the literal and metaphorical atmospheric coldness of the world. The novel is set in London in winter, and opens with a description of the wind from Siberia:

> The wind from Siberia as announced by the BBC came down Bayswater Road from the direction of Marble Arch somewhere in a straight line beyond which, half a world away, Siberia was taken to be. Searing skin, and petrifying metal and wood, it took possession of London and this early day of the new year.[19]

This movement of coldness from Siberia "in a straight line" to London is the linear movement of all the universe towards entropy and cold-death.[20] Artificial warmth and light – barheaters and the always-on-the-fritz electric lighting in the boarding house in which the main characters live, and the heat of alcohol that frequently fills Christian – are the very human attempts to maintain life in this cosmic coldness. Christian is to some extent the heat and warmth and cellular agitation that brings warmth and light to the Australian, Clem, who is perhaps missing the heat of Australia, and who is certainly represented as battling not only the figurative coldness of the capitalist class structure (in her autodidactic studies in law) but also the literal coldness of the Mother Country.

Personal thermodynamic heat and atmospheric cold are set up as oppositional in *The Catherine Wheel*, and both are indicators of degrees between the poles of independent identity and intersubjective loss of individual selfhood. Clem suffers from a loss of warmth and heat whenever Christian's will to power is manifested as an insistence on his separateness from her. His deliberate absence from three French lessons in a row with Clem turns her cold with rage: "And the next appointment was ignored. No word at all. I'd waited with chilly calm . . . a frozen raging anger made me useless for work" (111). After they have become (virtually) inseparable,[21] when they are about to elope to Dublin, Christian ruins the plan and reasserts his independence from Clem by getting extremely drunk. As she realises what he has done, it is a "clammy cold" that spreads through her (256).

---

19 Elizabeth Harrower, *The Catherine Wheel* (1960; Melbourne: Text Publishing, 2014), 3. All subsequent references are to this edition and appear in parentheses in the text.
20 Robert Dixon reads this weather in London by way of Siberia through Jon Hegglund's notion of "metageography", and argues that it points to Harrower's representation of personal and national identity as formed through "circuits of transnational exchange". Robert Dixon, "'The wind from Siberia': Metageography and Ironic Nationality in the Novels of Elizabeth Harrower", this volume. Alongside the political, cultural and economic significations of the proper noun, "Siberia", however, is its function as a place of extreme and hostile weather, both literally and symbolically affecting the weather in London.
21 Julian Murphet argues that "[Christian's] effective seduction of [Clem] is coterminous with the period they spend physically separated, during which they can only converse by phone. His purely electronic presence as a disembodied telephone voice is what triggers her deepest desire for him." Julian Murphet, "Projecting the Sixties: Mediation and Characterology in *The Catherine Wheel*", this volume, 109. From here on in, however, whether physically together or not, Clem's consciousness is represented as at all times charged with his hovering presence.

The literal atmospheric coldness of the novel, and the coldness experienced by Clem when her existential isolation is felt, both symbolise the modern scientific understanding of the literal entropy of the universe: the inexorable freezing in which all life and planets are slowing growing colder, drifting outwards away from each other, and dying.[22] Clem enacts this dying, entropic movement away from Christian at the end of *The Catherine Wheel* from inside her own body. She falls ill with a sickness caused by her attempt to extricate herself from Christian. Even her temperature is cold, rather than hot:

"Flu," I told [the doctor].
   He said, "Your temperature's below normal."
   Dully I tried to understand.
   "How?" I asked at last. When you had this awful new flu you deserved at least the compensation of a high temperature. (313)

Her low temperature is the hypothermia of approaching death: "My arms were bony. I had no flesh. I smelled like someone dying. Through scented skin, and fresh linen and laundered nighties, I smelled like death, and decomposing matter" (315). This ending is strangely ambiguous. Her illness – which she comes down with immediately after organising a job and flat for Christian and Olive to take in Paris and signifying her separation – is a form of "come down" or "withdrawal" from the addiction to Christian that has overrun her body and mind, as Olubas argues. Clem's physical and mental "curing" of Christian, then, would seem to be a clear achievement of her reassertion of selfhood. However, this is convalescence rather than complete recovery, as the narrative timespan does not extend long enough to record Olive and Christian's actual departure to Paris. Given Christian's past failure to do what he has promised (as with the elopement to Dublin), there is an equal possibility that he will not go to Paris, and his relationship with Clem will continue. The ending of Harrower's third novel, *The Catherine Wheel*, then, repeats the ongoing will-to-power dynamic seen in her first two novels, when Esther is caught and left mid-obliteration in the first novel, *Down in the City*, as well as in the loss and chilling of Emily through the removal of Max at the end of *The Long Prospect*.

Crucially different in this third iteration, however, is that Clem *chooses* to leave Christian, and actively organises their separation. The intensity of her illness and hypothermic dying reflects the force of the decision – a decision which neither Esther nor Emily in the first two novels is able to make (Esther is described as "relieved" at "postponement of the decision"(290), and Emily has no say at all in Max's leaving). Clem's recovery from "dying", then, is potentially an assertion of an independent self, although the reader is not given the certainty of this. In its insistence on the possibility or otherwise of escape and independence for the female subject, the ending of *The Catherine Wheel* prefigures the subsequent fourth and five novels, however.

Harrower's fourth novel, *The Watch Tower* (1966), is often cited as the culmination of her literary investigations.[23] However, when we view *In Certain Circles* (2014) as the

---

22   Kevin Pimbblet, "The Fate of the Universe: Heat Death, Big Rip, or Cosmic Consciousness?" *The Conversation*, 2 September 2015, http://bit.ly/2pGsovu.
23   D.R. Burns, for example, reads *The Watch Tower* against *Down in the City*, and calls the former "a considerable advance forward along the same path". *The Directions of Australian Fiction* (Melbourne, Sydney: Cassell Australia Limited, 1975), 150. R.G. Geering reads *The Long Prospect*

last novel, the now penultimate *The Watch Tower* can be read as a turning point as much as a culmination. This fourth novel begins to chart the modes by which female escape is made possible. It both is and is *not* the female protagonist of *The Watch Tower* who "escapes" from the terrible (thermo)dynamics of the will to power in Harrower's fourth novel, in which the same preoccupations of the first three are reiterated. There are two protagonists in *The Watch Tower*, the sisters Laura and Clare, enabling Harrower to present the female in both her entrapped and escaped forms. In this novel, Harrower replays many of the dynamics seen in the first three. But *The Watch Tower* deploys a more distant spatiotemporal perspective, profoundly affecting the interfiguration of weather, temperature and will to power in the novel. Unlike the female protagonists in Harrower's first three novels – all of whom have made an active "choice" of the other (male) subject on whom their will to power becomes interdependent – Laura in *The Watch Tower* has never made this choice. It is not mutual attraction that brings them together; rather, it is Felix's identification of Laura as an easily subjugated victim. Laura acquiesces to the marriage because she is young and ignorant of the world, and has been living in a bubble of isolation in which no other options have arisen.[24] In a structural sense, she suffers from a lack of opportunities based on class and economic dependence tied to patriarchal public/private structures, as Carole Ferrier has argued.[25] The novel begins and ends amidst Laura's subjugation of self because she has already, before the novel's beginning, been made subordinate by the will to power of her mother, Stella Vaizey, who is an iteration of the other tyrants of Harrower's oeuvre. Her mother arranges the transferral of Laura as a pre-subjugated object to Felix, before disappearing from the novel almost entirely. Naomi Riddle reads Felix as a male hysteric who "brings authority and instability, power and incoherence into the feminine domain of the suburban house".[26] In his achievement of this, Laura is therefore a profoundly obliterated subject who lives only as an echo of Felix's subjectivity. This is demonstrated in her pathetic brandishing of Felix's will to power as a pretence of her own opinion/will to power, over Clare (94-6). Frances McInherny has described this operation – "Laura's attempts to enslave Clare to Felix" – as "the blighted history of female-procuring-female".[27] Laura is lost to herself and becomes lost to the

---

against *The Watch Tower*, and argues that "the exploration of evil in ordinary suburban surroundings is conducted with greater intensity and insight" in the latter. *Recent Fiction* (Melbourne, London, New York: Oxford University Press, 1973), 36. Bernadette Brennan is more emphatic: "Arguably, Harrower's first three novels operated as a kind of extended case study in which she developed her characters and her style in preparation for the devastating, brilliant *The Watch Tower*". "Ideas of Certainty: Elizabeth Harrower's Last Novel Is Finally Published", *Australian Book Review*, May 2014: 19–21 (21). Geordie Williamson calls *Down in the City* "a template for what would follow" and suggests that across her novels Harrower's investigations are "exhausted or refined down to their essence". *The Burning Library: Our Great Novelists Lost and Found* (Melbourne: Text Publishing, 2012), 158–9. Harrower's resolution of these investigations with *In Certain Circles* is, perhaps, the answer to the question of "why novelist Elizabeth Harrower abandoned writing", which Helen Trinca calls "one of the great puzzles of Australian letters". Helen Trinca, "Living Dangerously", *Weekend Australian*, 27 October 2012, 8.

24 Elizabeth Harrower, *The Watch Tower* (London: Macmillan, 1966), 16. All subsequent references are to this edition and appear in parentheses in the text.
25 Carole Ferrier, "Is an 'Images of Woman' Methodology Adequate for Reading Elizabeth Harrower's *The Watch Tower*?" in *Who Is She? Images of Woman in Australian Fiction*, ed. Shirley Walker (St Lucia: University of Queensland Press, 1983), 197.
26 Naomi Riddle, "'Turning inward on himself': Male Hysteria in Elizabeth Harrower's *The Watch Tower*", *Southerly* 72, no. 1 (2012): 208.

narrative, which shifts focalisation from her to her sister Clare after the first fifty pages of the novel (52).

Clare is the second protagonist of *The Watch Tower* – an observer who is both proximal and distant, and who experiences the coldness of existential loneliness and universal entropy but is not subsumed by it. Her position as the third wheel and the fact that she has never been (similarly to Laura, in fact) attracted to Felix by thermodynamic heat, makes her different from the women of the first three novels in relation to thermodynamic influence as an integral part of the will-to-power struggle. Clare has been part of this closed family unit from her birth, and is subjected to first her mother's unloving tyrannical will and then the will of Felix, undergoing extreme emotional trauma when she is victimised by their relationship: "Tears, anger, sheer incredulity at the madness and stupidity of their lives choked her" (96). However, there is something special about Clare, and despite suffering this turmoil some part of her is distant rather than proximal – her selfhood can never be truly affected by the others' attempts to dominate her: "The level of her spirits was not to be assailed" (192). In the scene in which Clare is told to strip naked by a sexually exploitative doctor, Clare complies and then stares with calm composure out of the window while he voyeuristically gazes on her naked body (71-3). Brigid Rooney identifies the importance of this scene, arguing that when the doctor and Clare exchange eye contact, the "moment of shock, of enlightenment and reanimation, arises from and disrupts, like an electrical charge, the en-framing social and physical matrix within which Harrower's protagonists are held captive".[28] The scene also demonstrates Clare's profound detachment from her own physical, psychological and emotional responses in the face of oppression by others' wills to power. Nicholas Mansfield contends that Clare is a character who represents the literary mode of realism itself, "[making] her aware of the vacancy or unreality of the life around her".[29] She is able to see the power struggles and dynamics of the relationship between Felix and Laura, and articulates it to Laura:

> "What about us? What are we? I mean – are we both supposed to exist just as a sort of hobby for Felix? All these years! Maybe you don't want a life for yourself. I do. I'm a person, too ... Why is my life so much less important than Felix's? How can you let him talk to you the way he does? Oh, Laura." (96)

Clare's capacity to resist, to assert an objective truth of tyrannical oppression, is tied to her paradoxical proximity and distance.[30] When she first tries to leave – resulting in an

---

27 Frances McInherny, "'Deep into the destructive core': Elizabeth Harrower's *The Watch Tower*", *Hecate* 9, nos 1 and 2 (1983): 125.
28 Brigid Rooney, "'White, fierce, shocked, tearless'": *The Watch Tower* and the electric interior", this volume, 82.
29 Nicholas Mansfield, "'The only Russian in Sydney': Modernism and Realism in *The Watch Tower*", *Australian Literary Studies* 15, no. 3 (1992): 137.
30 This is not to suggest, however, that Clare is the only character in the first four novels who gives thought to, and has understanding of, the psychological and other reasons for the situation they are in. Elizabeth McMahon examines both the epiphanies had by protagonists in Harrower's fiction, and the subsequent impacts and playing out of such epiphanies. Such modernist epiphanies do not, McMahon argues, tend to be gathered into resultant narrative force for the rearrangement of the world by those who have undergone self-revelation. McMahon notes this specifically in relation to the ending of *Down in the City*, quoted also in this essay, in which Esther "most tiredly knows" her situation, but this knowledge has no impact on the situation. "The heroines have gained truths of

argument with Laura, viciousness from Felix and her own exasperated tears – Clare is represented as standing alone in a cosmic darkness. Unlike Clem in *The Catherine Wheel*, however, this darkness cannot obliterate Clare:

> Clare stared up into the cold blackness and heard the wind rising and felt its bombardment against her head and arms and chest. Blackness all about and above. The night existed, forbidding, unfeeling. Anything was bearable. The wind was clean and undemanding. Blotted out in the tremendous night, in the midst of it, she was at home. In a way, all she had was herself and the sky. (98-9)

"Bombarded" but still there, "blotted out" but "in the midst of it" "at home", Clare is paradoxically living despite the nothingness that surrounds her. This image of Clare depicts anew the end of *The Long Prospect*, in the portrayal of Emily alone in the garden as night falls.[31] Having been in a sense born into the dynamic with Laura and Felix (and never having had a comparison to warmth, as Emily has with Thea and Max), Clare can survive in the existential, cosmic, godless coldness of the universe. Her sense of self maintains an equilibrium, "her spirits" a "level", even as she goes through the emotional torments of immersion in Laura and Felix's will-to-power attempts to subjugate her.

Clare's final escape at the end of *The Watch Tower*, counterposing Laura's ongoing imprisonment, is effected through temporal and perspectival dislocation. The division and transferral of the narrative perspective – caused by and symptomatic of Clare's proximal/distant sense of self – is joined at the end of the novel with a sense that Clare's entire life has been a temporal dislocation. In the final scene Clare is travelling away from Felix and Laura, away from Sydney, into the bushland, and a temporal inversion brings her into a present of a real reality that she has been locked away from in the house with the others: "Whatever [the smell of the bush air] is, I remember it, she thought, breathing in. Her eyes paused here on a line of willows as they glided past, and the willows were familiar, too. She remembered it all. Yet it was funny that she should think so; for it did occur to her that she had only just arrived" (219).

In Certain Circles, published belatedly in 2014, is the culmination and point of resolution of the basal elements of Harrower's oeuvre. This final novel re-enacts the structural operations of dislocated time and narrative perspective in *The Watch Tower*, to realise the reconsolidation of a female subject's selfhood. As in *The Watch Tower* – which figures female escape through Clare's temporal re-meeting with a parallel reality she has never known but "remembers" – the achievement of spatio-temporal distance from dynamics and events is key to the resolution of *In Certain Circles*. The protagonist of *In Certain Circles*, Zoe,[32] chooses her tyrant, Stephen Quayle, in a repetition of Esther's, Emily's and Clem's choice of a thermodynamic, cosmic "matching". In a perhaps ironic gesture to the interfiguration of thermodynamics and relationships in her earlier novels,

---

self and others but this understanding does not lead to change." Elizabeth McMahon, "Moments of Being in the Fiction of Elizabeth Harrower", this volume, 139.

31 The use of light and dark permeates Harrower's oeuvre and is too enormous an operation to consider even in summary in this essay. McMahon points to one of its key aspects: "the interplay of diurnal and noctural contexts and experiences". "Moments of Being", this volume, 134.

32 The name "Zoe" comes from the Greek word for "life". Beginning, as it does, with the final letter of the English alphabet, her naming suggests that she is both the end and the beginning, the last female subject and the only one who still lives.

Harrower uses a condensed form of this for Zoe's impassioned attraction to Stephen with whom her will to power will be tested: "'Oh, Anna! Oh, Anna! It's so hot. Or is it cold?'"[33]

Clare's rejoining of a parallel reality at the end of *The Watch Tower* is enacted in a definitive form at the end of *In Certain Circles*. It is this temporal paradox that gives the final novel's protagonist, Zoe, the distance necessary to end their will-to-power struggle and extricate herself from it without being destroyed. As Elizabeth Webby identifies, "the final outcomes for [Zoe], Lily and Anna are positive when compared to the situations of female characters at the end of Harrower's earlier novels".[34] When Russell and Zoe both receive a suicide letter from Anna in the mail, for a while neither the main characters nor the reader knows whether Anna is alive or dead. She is therefore temporarily "both", as with the "cat in a box" thought-experiment that is often taken as a symbol of the nexus of modern physics/philosophical thought.[35] As a result of this literal demonstration of the potentiality for multiple pasts/futures/presents that Einstein identified as a logical possibility of relativity, a "different ending" than all the other novels is made possible.[36] From this disruption Zoe gains a distance from the event of herself and her husband's intersubjective thermodynamics to be able to articulate and explain, to him, the physics of their relationship. In doing so, Zoe expresses their relationship in thermodynamic and will-to-power terms:

"It's as if you only lived to suppress me – as if I were a fire out of control. It doesn't seem very constructive. . . . What do you hold against me, apart from the fact that I've loved you?" (144)

In this conversation Zoe still feels the coldness, the cosmological entropy that indicates separation of the two individuals otherwise engaged in the will-to-power struggle: "Cold, at an astronomical distance, his eyes made her feel" (145).

She sees the fundamental cellular arrangements of the universe and their symmetries at the same moment that she speaks "the truth" of their relationship to Stephen:

Pressing her eyes shut with her fingers, Zoe saw a myriad geometrical shapes symmetrical as snowflakes magnified. ". . . You're afraid of me . . . And the funny thing is – if it strikes you as funny – I'm afraid of you."

All of Stephen's senses listened as though to the voice of an oracle. What Zoe so dispassionately said, without reflection or hesitation, had the authority of absolute truth. . . . She thought: I cannot solve you. You must solve yourself. (145)

---

33 Elizabeth Harrower, *In Certain Circles* (Melbourne: Text Publishing, 2014), 34. All subsequent references are to this edition and appear in parentheses in the text.
34 Elizabeth Webby, "Review: *In Certain Circles* by Elizabeth Harrower", *The Conversation*, 17 April 2014, http://bit.ly/2pb63r2.
35 Jim Shelton, "Doubling Down on Schrödinger's Cat", *Science Daily*, 26 May 2016, http://bit.ly/1TIgubB.
36 Michael Emanuel Goldberg's doctoral thesis on Einstein's relativity and the "new science" in James Joyce's *Ulysses* points to the inspiration that Einstein provided for some Modernist writers such as James Joyce. "Moving Bodies: James Joyce and the 'New Physics'", doctoral thesis, University of Illinois at Urbana-Champaign, 1999. Goldberg argues that Joyce's knowledge of Einstein's discoveries as they were being heavily reported in the contemporary media gave him a popularist understanding of concepts such as relativity, which can be seen in the narrative perspectives of *Ulysses*.

The final line of *In Certain Circles* depicts a neutral, atmospherically mild, even tepid, day, neither hot nor cold. In an assertion of Zoe's survival of her will-to-power struggle with Stephen, the ending of Harrower's swansong repeats but overreaches the endings of the previous four novels. Zoe achieves the resolution of the dynamics in which the other women of Harrower's fiction remain trapped, proximally immersed in their relationships and at the mercy of the godless weather and entropic thermodynamics. In the final line of this final novel there is an acknowledgement that it is time that has enabled Zoe's escape, and that freedom is always a movement away from:

> What a slow learner, she thought, slowly rising. Still, the day was lovely. And now she could move on. (155)

References

Brennan, Bernadette. "Ideas of Certainty: Elizabeth Harrower's Last Novel Is Finally Published". *Australian Book Review*. May 2014: 19-21.

Burns, D.R. *The Directions of Australian Fiction 1920–1974*. Melbourne, Sydney: Cassell Australia Limited, 1975.

Claremont, Robyn. "The Novels of Elizabeth Harrower". *Quadrant*, November 1979, 16-21.

Dixon, Robert. "'The Wind from Siberia': Metageography and Ironic Nationality in the Novels of Elizabeth Harrower". In *Elizabeth Harrower: Critical Essays*. Edited by Elizabeth McMahon and Brigitta Olubas, 49-64. Sydney: Sydney University Press, 2017.

Ferrier, Carole. "Is an 'Images of Woman' Methodology Adequate for Reading Elizabeth Harrower's *The Watch Tower*?" In *Who Is She? Images of Woman in Australian Fiction*. Edited by Shirley Walker. St Lucia: University of Queensland, 1983.

Geering, R.G. *Recent Fiction*. Melbourne, London, New York: Oxford University Press, 1973.

Goldberg, Michael Emanuel. "Moving Bodies: James Joyce and the 'New Physics'". Doctoral thesis. University of Illinois at Urbana-Champaign, 1999.

Harrower, Elizabeth. "The Fun of the Fair". In *A Few Days in the Country and Other Stories*, 1-14. Melbourne: Text Publishing, 2015.

———. *In Certain Circles*. Melbourne: Text Publishing, 2015.

———. *The Watch Tower*. London; Melbourne; Toronto: Macmillan, 1966.

———. *The Catherine Wheel*. (1960) Melbourne: Text Publishing, 2014.

———. *The Long Prospect*. (1958) Melbourne: Text Publishing, 2012.

———. *Down in the City*. (1957) Melbourne: Text Publishing, 2013.

Kelaita, Jasmin. "'If someone knocks at the door tonight, don't answer it': Penetrating Walls in *Down in the City*". Paper presented at "Rediscovering Again: Christina Stead / Elizabeth Harrower", University of New South Wales, 3-4 December 2015.

McInherny, Frances. "'Deep into the destructive core': Elizabeth Harrower's *The Watch Tower*". *Hecate* 9, nos 1 and 2 (1983): 123-34.

McMahon, Elizabeth. "Moments of Being in the Fiction of Elizabeth Harrower". In *Elizabeth Harrower: Critical Essays*. Edited by Elizabeth McMahon and Brigitta Olubas, 133-143. Sydney: Sydney University Press, 2017.

Mansfield, Nicholas. "'The Only Russian in Sydney': Modernism and Realism in *The Watch Tower*". *Australian Literary Studies* 15, no. 3 (1992): 131-40.

Moffett, Alex. "Hot Sparks and Cold Devils: Katherine Mansfield and Modernist Thermodynamics". *Journal of Modern Literature* 37, no. 2 (2014): 59-75.

Murphet, Julian. "Projecting the Sixties: Mediation and Characterology in *The Catherine Wheel*". In *Elizabeth Harrower: Critical Essays*. Edited by Elizabeth McMahon and Brigitta Olubas, 107-117. Sydney: Sydney University Press, 2017.

Nash, Megan. "Traversing 'the same extreme country' in *The Watch Tower* and *Daniel Deronda*". In *Elizabeth Harrower: Critical Essays*. Edited by Elizabeth McMahon and Brigitta Olubas, 119-132. Sydney: Sydney University Press, 2017.

Nietzsche, Friedrich. *Thus Spake Zarathustra: A Book for All and None*. (1896) Translated by Thomas Common. Project Gutenberg ebook. http://bit.ly/2qfgcDi.

——. *Beyond Good and Evil*. (1886) Translated by Helen Zimmern. Project Gutenberg ebook. http://bit.ly/2pAnAaI.

Olubas, Brigitta. "Addiction, Fire and the Face in *The Catherine Wheel*". In *Elizabeth Harrower: Critical Essays*. Edited by Elizabeth McMahon and Brigitta Olubas, 97-106. Sydney: Sydney University Press, 2017.

Pimbblet, Kevin. "The Fate of the Universe: Heat Death, Big Rip, or Cosmic Consciousness?" *The Conversation*, 2 September, 2015. http://bit.ly/2q14FY5.

Riddle, Naomi. "'Turning inward on himself': Male Hysteria in Elizabeth Harrower's *The Watch Tower*". *Southerly* 72, no. 1 (2012): 204-13.

Rooney, Brigid. "'White, fierce, shocked, tearless': *The Watch Tower* and the electric interior". In *Elizabeth Harrower: Critical Essays*. Edited by Elizabeth McMahon and Brigitta Olubas, 81-95. Sydney: Sydney University Press, 2017.

Shelton, Jim. "Doubling Down on Schrödinger's Cat". *Science Daily*, 26 May 2016. http://bit.ly/1TIgubB.

Strawson, Galen. "Nietzsche's Metaphysics?" In *Nietzsche on Mind and Nature*. Edited by Manuel Dries and P.J.E. Kail. Oxford: Oxford University Press Online, 2015. doi 10.1093/acprof:oso/9780198722236.001.0001.

Trinca, Helen. "Living Dangerously". *Weekend Australian*, 27 October 2012: 8.

Webby, Elizabeth. "Review: *In Certain Circles* by Elizabeth Harrower". *The Conversation*, 17 April 2014. http://bit.ly/2pb63r2.

Williamson, Geordie. *The Burning Library: Our Great Novelists Lost and Found*. Melbourne: Text Publishing, 2012.

Yeo, Rosie. "*Down in the City*: Elizabeth Harrower's 'Lost' Novel". *Southerly* 50, no. 4 (December 1990): 491-8.

8

"White, fierce, shocked, tearless": *The Watch Tower* and the Electric Interior

Brigid Rooney

> the truth of a text is not the truth of what that text says;
> it is – paradoxical notion – *the truth of its form*
> —Roland Barthes[1]

In Elizabeth Harrower's *The Watch Tower* (1966), Clare Vaizey visits a doctor in Sydney's Macquarie Street to see about an allergic rash on her neck. She assures the doctor that the rash appears nowhere else on her body and yet – ominously – he requires her to take off all her clothes. She obeys. The doctor's motives are opaque, his expression impassive, his manner clinical. His tenth-floor surgery sits high in a cliff-like row of buildings, its windows staring down on the harbour and the "barbered greenness" of the Botanical Gardens.[2] The doctor's office resembles, it seems, a "watch tower". It is uncertain whether the surgery is a malignant space of punishing surveillance or benign, illuminating perspective. The view the surgery commands recalls the watch tower that is Clare's own suburban bedroom in the Neutral Bay house where she lives with her sister Laura, and with Laura's husband, Felix Shaw, the novel's Bluebeard. With its view of the world outside, of glittering blue harbour and suburban streets, Clare's bedroom is, on the one hand, a space of retreat from the more threatening communal areas of the Shaw house. On the other hand, the bedroom is uneasy, occupied territory; it is cheerless, blank and exposed, clinical and impersonal like a doctor's surgery. In both locations Clare must submit to the intrusive gaze of a dominant male figure. Naked but for her high heels, Clare gazes upon the dazzling landscape of garden and harbour while the doctor circles her body. She practises detachment, shielding her private self as her pearly white flesh is exposed. She maintains composure under inspection. But at the moment of parting, an intense, wordless exchange takes place, the import of which is not directly stated: the doctor looks at Clare deeply and she returns his gaze. In that moment, "an invisible rocket sped between them,

---

1 Roland Barthes, *The Preparation of the Novel: Lecture Courses and Seminars at the Collège de France (1978–1979 and 1979–1980)*, trans. Kate Briggs (New York: Columbia University Press, 2011), 276–7.
2 Elizabeth Harrower, *The Watch Tower* (1966; North Ryde, NSW: Angus & Robertson, 1991), 71. All subsequent references are to this edition and appear in parentheses in the text.

rocked the room, shocking and enlightening her to the very tips of her high-heeled shoes" (72).

This enigmatic scene only *seems* tangential to the main action. But in microcosm it replays both the core dynamic and the affect that pervades not only *The Watch Tower* but Harrower's fiction overall. The moment of shock, of enlightenment and reanimation, arises from and disrupts, like an electrical charge, the en-framing social and physical matrix within which Harrower's protagonists are held captive. This social matrix, aligned with the urban grid, dominates and oppresses. It both contains and flattens out the different locations in the novel, foreclosing clear distinctions between the urban and the suburban. So, for instance, the narrative doubling of the tenth-floor surgery with the house in Neutral Bay conflates the verticals of the urban core with the horizontals of suburban terrain. The affective interchangeability of these usually opposing sites – the feeling that they both serve equally as conduits of an unbearably oppressive insularity – aligns with Nicholas Birns' observation that Harrower's "city does not represent possibility . . . but boundedness . . . it is rectilinear, spatial; not yielding any sort of growth or progress. It is enclave as much as metropolis, representing immurement as much as potential".[3] Collapsing core and periphery, Harrower's novels form a fictive topography in which city and suburb are subsumed within and governed by the grid. Birns points out that Harrower's fiction is all about "constriction", arguing that the enclosure of her suburban worlds, their system-oriented, welfare-statist rigidity, speaks to the sense in her narratives of being hemmed in, confined by the past, and unable to move forward: "too late to be euphoric about nationalism" but "too early or too prescient to be euphoric about globalisation".[4] In narratives that seamlessly pivot between the scales of self, house, suburb, city and globe, characters beat against the bars of an entrapping system – one sensed and felt, rather than visualised or pinpointed.

Yet it is despite – or even because of – the grid-like system within which Harrower's subjects are immobilised that moments of moral shock and enlightenment acquire their powerfully disruptive, indeed electric charge. For Marshall McLuhan, electricity gives rise to media that disrupt traditional hierarchies of place:

> Obsession with the older patterns of mechanical, one-way expansion from centres to margins is no longer relevant to our electric world . . . Electricity does not centralize but decentralizes . . . Electric power . . . permits any place to be a centre, and does not require large aggregations.[5]

McLuhan's account coheres with Harrower's rendering of the urban-suburban continuum. The arrival of the electric age disrupts the form of the novel itself, as Julian Murphet argues in his reading of Harrower's *The Catherine Wheel* (1960). The latter, her third novel, is set in London, with its strangely decentred antagonist, Christian Roland, whose composite, contradictory attributes Murphet likens to a radio signal. The novel's internalisation of the character-as-radio-signal performs a reflexive negotiation of the

---

3   Nicholas Birns, *Contemporary Australian Literature: A World Not Yet Dead* (Sydney: Sydney University Press, 2015), 57–8.
4   Birns, *Contemporary Australian Literature*, 52.
5   Marshall McLuhan, *Understanding Media: The Extensions of Man* (1964; London: Sphere Books, 1967), 45.

form and status of the novel itself (as long-form narrative in the medium of print) at this late-modern juncture and in response to the emergent electric-media ecology of postmodernity.[6]

In Harrower's electric interiors, "shock" is the presiding affect. "Shock" is not only a sensation felt by her characters but also, I argue, something that conditions narrative operations and the reading experience. Around the word "shock", cognate terms cluster to form the contours of Harrower's moral and psychological landscape: "electric", "nerves", "neurosis", "factory", "machine", "mechanical", "light switch", "wireless", "house", "room", "war". This set of terms coheres with the concentration in Harrower's fiction, as Robert Dixon notes, of electrified domestic interiors.[7] They build a distinctive affect that works as a kind of *punctum* – Barthes' word for the accidentally poignant or arresting detail in a photograph that seizes, punctures or wounds its viewer.[8] In *Cruel Optimism* (2011), Lauren Berlant discusses the "sense of the historical" that historical fiction provides. She makes the argument that history *per se* exists "neither in footnotes, nor in the representation of historical figures or events, nor in style as such, as in the period piece, but *in atmospheres* (an aesthetic genre)" [my emphasis].[9] She draws attention to the workings of affect as a kind of *punctum*. Like Barthes' *punctum*, affect in fiction "unites disparate detail and acts as the relay through which the historical is sensed before it can be redacted".[10] Arresting and wounding, a sense of electrical charge, sometimes shocking, breaks through the conventional, referential detailing of place and time in Harrower's fiction to produce its unmistakable tone. It is this affective quality, this atmosphere, that works to reanimate lost time and place. Producing an intensely affective, sense-laden field, Harrower's "electric interiors" and uses of "shock" go beyond metaphor: they relay late modernity's suburban terrain through narrative form and style. Shock is simulated in the syntactical composition of Harrower's writing, delivered by means of her style, through tightly wound sentences, shifting perspectives and ever-tightening plots. These elements produce Harrower's poetics of constriction, of captivity and immobilisation. Her repetitions produce confined and confining scenes; her narrative forms pulse with the electric charge of desire.

Disenchanted Night (1989), by Wolfgang Schivelbusch, offers a social history of industrial electrification, which saw the gradual division of homogenous electrified light into outside and inside, close or distant, a development that coheres with the increasing bourgeois distinction between public and private spheres; in addition, he says, unease attended the industrialisation of light which so intimately connected the bourgeois interior with distant, centralised "big industry", with gas-works and electricity stations.[11] For McLuhan, the electric light needs to be understood as the paradigmatic social medium that inaugurates the electric age. This cultural continuum with its positive and negative values is suggested in the way that Harrower's fictional houses are malevolently, electrically lit, and

---

6   Julian Murphet, "Projecting the Sixties: Mediation and Characterology in *The Catherine Wheel*", this volume.
7   Robert Dixon, "'The wind from Siberia': Metageography and Ironic Nationality in the Novels of Elizabeth Harrower", this volume, 57.
8   See also Roland Barthes, *Camera Lucida: Reflections on Photography* [*Le Chambre Claire*, 1980], trans. Richard Howard (London: Vintage, 1993), 27.
9   Lauren Berlant, *Cruel Optimism* (Durham and London: Duke University Press, 2011), 66.
10 Berlant, *Cruel Optimism*, 66.
11 See Wolfgang Schivelbusch, *Disenchanted Night: The Industrialization of Light in the Nineteenth Century*, trans. Angela Davis (1988; Berkeley: University of California Press, 1989), 185–6.

the frequency with which she gestures to other electric media – such as wireless, telephone and cinema – all media that "extend", as McLuhan says, the human sensorium, collapsing space-time coordinates and physical distances.[12] Electricity connects the private interior to the global exterior; it interiorises the global and the industrial within the house. But it is Schivelbusch's brief history of the meanings of "shock", in *The Railway Journey* (1977), that proves especially salient for the affective contours of Harrower's fiction. "Shock" first denoted a stack of sheaves bunched and standing upright but from the sixteenth century this meaning crossed into military discourse. Today, a phrase like "shock and awe" still carries the sense of machine-like, industrialised approaches to battle such as the massed onslaught of soldiers (bunched like shocks of wheat) or the simultaneous delivery of firepower. This military usage was then extended to the after-effects of battle, as in "shell shock". As a result, "shock *describes the kind of sudden and powerful event of violence that disrupts the continuity of an artificially/mechanically created motion or situation, and also the state of derangement*".[13] This is important to Schivelbusch's argument that railway technology was not just something created for modern subjects to use but a technology that in turn creates or shapes its users. Passengers form protective shields against technological stimuli, protecting themselves from awareness of the always-present potential for catastrophic accident. Railway accidents are "shocking" because they shatter the subject's stimulus shield. Analogously, the interiorised stimulus shield of social convention is shattered and deranged by shock and trauma.

Talking in 1980 with Jim Davidson about the moral charge of truth, Harrower cites a favourite phrase from Saul Bellow's *Henderson The Rain King*: "'the shock that wakes the spirit's sleep'".[14] Bellow borrows the phrase from Shelley's "The Revolt of Islam". The phrase must be important to Harrower because some thirty years later, in conversation with Ramona Koval, she repeats it verbatim.[15] Unless it first came to her via Shelley's poem, Harrower could not have encountered the quote until after writing *The Long Prospect* (1958) since Bellow's novel was not published until 1959. More important here is the way Harrower misremembers the wording. In Shelley's lines, repeated almost verbatim in Bellow's novel, the operative phrase is "hour that burst": "I do remember well the hour which burst / My spirit's sleep".[16] Harrower substitutes the phrase "shock that wakes" for the "hour that burst", however, and this signals her orientation to the poetics of the electric age. Shock is the moment of arrest, of reaction to the discharge of invisible, electrical currents into the body. Such a moment interrupts the smooth current of electricity itself as the invisible circuiting force that artificially regulates modernity's night and day, that ceaselessly travels the grid it supplies, that

---

12   McLuhan, *Understanding Media*, 11–14 and 15ff.
13   See Wolfgang Schivelbusch, *The Railway Journey: The Industrialization of Time and Space in the Nineteenth Century* (1977; Berkeley: University of California Press, 1986), 151.
14   Elizabeth Harrower interviewed by Jim Davidson, *Meanjin* 39, no. 2 (July 1980): 163–74.
15   Harrower glosses for Koval – "It just means what it means, doesn't it? I think life is just one long shock. We are constantly waking the spirit" – also mentioning she had recently given her friend, the painter Salvatore Zofrea, a copy of Bellow's novel. Ramona Koval, interview with Elizabeth Harrower, *The Monthly Video*, October 2014. Transcript at http://bit.ly/2pGhjKU.
16   In Bellow's *Henderson the Rain King* (1959) the words are: "They went like this: 'I do remember well the hour which burst my spirit's sleep'". In Bellow's novel the key word is "burst", which recurs twenty-six times, whereas "shock" recurs eight times as indexed in the Kindle ebook. The word "burst" recurs twenty-eight times in Shelley's "The Revolt of Islam". Saul Bellow, *Henderson the Rain King* (London: Penguin, 2007), Kindle edition, loc. 1033.

envisages private interiors as already plugged in to public, global forces to which they are implicitly, inexorably exposed.

As the signal affect in Harrower's fiction, shock does not simply designate the after-effect of characters' sudden contact with these invisible, shaping forces. Rather, I suggest, shock forms a continuing dramatic pulse in Harrower's narratives. Electrifying moments transpire between characters, shattering stimulus shields and rocking social conventions. Moreover, the power of Harrower's fiction is built through an insistent *shielding* or *veiling* of something traumatic sourced in the autobiographical scene. Harrower has not disclosed much about her childhood but it forms an absent presence that haunts her novels and is felt in her fiction's persistent reconfiguration of certain abusive and traumatic patterns. Her settings, moreover, hew closely to autobiographical locations. *The Catherine Wheel* speaks to Harrower's sojourn in 1950s London, while *Down in the City* (1957), *The Watch Tower* and *In Certain Circles* (2014) summon Sydney's North Shore harbourside suburbs where she lived during the 1940s and after her return from London in 1959. *The Long Prospect* triangulates the Sydney-London nexus by returning to a fictive version of the industrial suburb of Mayfield near Newcastle, where Harrower lived for the first twelve years of her life. Asked if *The Long Prospect* mirrored her childhood circumstances, Harrower replied that "the emotional truth is there in all of the books, but none of the facts. It's like putting real electricity into a dream palace".[17]

While her conceit of the novel as "dream palace" recognises that fiction always transmutes the primal house, Harrower's analogy for the emotional truth in her fiction – "real electricity" – thoroughly implicates the techno-industrial suburb. Since the early twentieth century sub/urban forms have thrived on the instant delivery of cheap energy through systems at once ubiquitous and banal. In Harrower's suburban interiors, over-bright electrical illumination brings menacing exposure to invisible forces. Exposure within these electrified interiors is not to be mistaken for illumination. Moral illumination awaits shock of the kind that occurs in the doctor's surgery when Clare's inner self is rocked and enlightened by unspoken, mutual recognition. Clarity arrives in the end for the aptly named Clare, but moral truths do not quite contain the affective charge that galvanises Harrower's fictional works. The tensions at work in these novels between concealment and exposure are analogous to the operations of the invisible grid. Emotions blindly circuit within the dream palace until the moment of shock.

Electricity recurs across Harrower's novels as a physical force that contours urban and suburban terrain. Identifying Harrower's reflexive use of "metageography" as an immanent modernist critique of an insular national culture, Dixon notes the irony with which her novels register the Australian adoption of postwar American consumer culture. Some characters, like the suburban Lilian Hulm, are phrenetic sensation-seekers pursuing the "cheap response"; they are enthralled and animated by "the volatile rhythms of popular song and cinematic melodrama; they are associated with 'theatricality' and 'electricity', with alcohol and the new mass media of cinema and radio".[18] For Dixon, Harrower's "self-consciously metatheatrical descriptions of domestic interiors illuminate in the same way that her comparative metatopographies defamiliarise nationality", conveying her "enduring suspicion of charisma, 'magic' (84), and personal 'electricity'".[19]

---

17 Davidson, interview with Elizabeth Harrower, 173–4.
18 Dixon, "'The wind from Siberia'", this volume, 54.
19 Dixon, "'The wind from Siberia'", this volume, 58.

As that which interconnects domestic interiors with industrial exteriors, electricity both tropes and defamiliarises postwar consumerist culture. But "electricity" functions in these novels in more layered and paradoxical terms than first appears, serving as a metaphor for psychic forces that are dangerous but also, sometimes, revelatory and re-animating. Electricity is not only associated with Harrower's antagonists – Stan Peterson, Lilian Hulm, Christian Roland, Felix Shaw and Stephen Quayle – with their dehumanised artificiality, wicked energy or life-sapping negativity, but also with her female protagonists who are shocked into wakeful activity, awareness or action. There is a progression towards a shocked awakening that is enacted across the series, in the movement from Esther Prescott, Emily Lawrence and Clemency James to Clare Vaizey and Zoe Howard. Within the electric interior, these characters are nervously sensitised, electrically attracted to opposites and (at least initially) disoriented and immobilised by their antagonists. The persistent problem, the thing that keeps Harrower's protagonists hooked and bound for so long, is the difficulty of pinpointing, and therefore responding to, the source or origin of the malaise. Like young Emily in *The Long Prospect*, they are unable, at least for a time, to "localise the intense disquiet of [their] being".[20] The inability to localise (to earth or materialise) the source of disquiet is the puzzle to which Harrower's metaphorics of electricity speaks in the play between an invisible currency and embodied moral shock.

The puzzle of what sustains the dynamics of persecutor and victim is at the heart of all Harrower's fiction: how and why do women become captive to the narrow demands of the family or male-female coupledom? Such neat reduction of the core "puzzle" to one of persecutor and victim, however, remains inadequate to the affective load of queasy fascination generated by Harrower's repeated scenarios of electric attraction. *The Watch Tower* may be Harrower's most piercing rendition of this puzzle, a culminating reconfiguration and rehearsal of scenes that play out across her fiction. The recently widowed Stella Vaizey, a vain and self-absorbed woman, shrugs off her maternal duty of care for her two young daughters, Laura and Clare. Her casual indifference and narcissism strongly recall Emily's grandmother Lilian in *The Long Prospect*. Stella's rejection of Australian suburban culture in favour of her social set in England replays in reverse Lilian's valorisation of the suburban milieu of Greenhills. This particular inversion signals the novel's ultimately decisive refusal of those cultural binaries that privilege the cosmopolitan, expatriate traveller over those who stay at home. Even so, home is the site of narrow insularity and parochial oppression, an "extreme country" that must be traversed. The older daughter Laura learns early to appease and excuse her mother, to survive by suppressing the bitter reality of heartless parental neglect. Her sister Clare, seven years younger, is less biddable but because attached to her sister is recruited for a time into compliancy. Wanting a secure future for both herself and Clare, Laura acquiesces to her employer Felix Shaw's marriage proposal, seduced by his show of financial support and the prospect of a comfortable home. Their mother, Stella, leaves, fading out of the narrative, and Felix thereafter looms as the displaced, amplified repetition of the mother's powerful, brutal indifference.

The novel's time period is at once focused and elastic. Its opening domestic hostilities – as Megan Nash observes – parallel the onset of World War Two, but ambiguously. As Nash

---

20   Elizabeth Harrower, *The Long Prospect* (1958; North Ryde, NSW: Angus & Robertson, 1988), 191. All subsequent references are to this edition and appear in parentheses in the text.

argues, this parallel intensifies with references to bombardment and imprisonment that invoke the Holocaust.[21] Yet the implied chronology of the narrative disrupts parallels with World War Two given that Clare is around twelve years old when the action begins but twenty-three in the novel's final scenes. Stretching across a full decade, the temporal frame elongates the mid-century moment in which open hostilities converge with Cold War. This elongation is set against narrative rhythms that tighten and press. The novel is structured in three tightly-written parts reminiscent of theatrical naturalism, like an Ibsen play. In part one the trap is set. In part two, the trap acquires its monstrous, labyrinthine character and the malignance of the domestic interior meshes with the wider urban environment. Part three sees the arrival of Bernard – a Dutch immigrant working as a presser in Felix's clothing factory, a survivor of wartime trauma. The arrival of the stranger within the home, a refugee from war, defamiliarises the interior and yields the thread by which Clare, alone of her family, makes her escape.

The sisters, Laura and Clare, struggle with the puzzle of Felix. What does he want? What's wrong with him? Can he be changed? The hope for change that these questions imply drives Laura's efforts to anticipate, placate and understand Felix in his various moods. Laura therefore *watches* Felix. Her constant watchfulness – her extreme vigilance – becomes itself pathological. Laura's watchful solicitude is directed entirely at Felix, a project into which she continually seeks to recruit Clare. Increasingly, however, the orientation of each sister's watchfulness diverges. Clare watches Laura, seeing her sister's supplications as both futile and complicit. By part three, Clare's growing awareness of Laura's numb complicity in her own bondage marks a shift in attention away from Felix's aberrant psychology towards the wider social context within which his behaviour, fuelled by alcohol, is overlooked, condoned and even fostered. Clare shifts from playing the family "game" of placating Felix to searching for signs of goodness in the world. The problem for Clare is now redefined: is it possible to balance conflicting demands of loyalty, pity and freedom? Can, or should, one be loyal to another if it requires the sacrifice of freedom or self-worth?

The novel's domestic, suburban and urban spaces reflect and configure wider social forces that discipline, contain and entrap. *The Watch Tower* opens where *The Long Prospect* ends, in an apartment by the water in which the reluctant child protagonist is recruited into a game of marital appeasement. In *The Long Prospect*'s concluding sentence, Paula signals to her daughter Emily "in the hope that she would respond and join her in the fascinating, necessary game of teasing Harry" (208). In *The Watch Tower*, we are told that Stella Vaizey and her daughters live in an apartment on the ridgeline above Manly, on a height that commands a view of the ocean. The "semicircle of pines and fine yellow sand beyond which there was only the Pacific" forms a boundary both physical and psychological, hinting at the spatial limit and the cultural isolation of settler Australian experience.[22] In a reversal of the movement from house to harbourside apartment in *The Long Prospect*, the characters in *The Watch Tower* move from seaside apartment to Felix's Neutral Bay house. In both novels, this transfer undermines any obvious privileging of urban verticals over suburban horizontals, making all spaces equally claustrophobic and insular.

---

21 Megan Nash, "Traversing 'the same extreme country' in *The Watch Tower* and *Daniel Deronda*", this volume, 119.

22 Narrative coordinates suggest the apartment is located on the ridgeline above the historic Presbyterian church, St Andrews, on Raglan Street in Manly.

The name of the suburb that forms the chief setting, Neutral Bay, stems from its early colonial designation as a docking bay for foreign vessels. But the Shaw house and its environs are only outwardly neutral. In psychological terms it is a war zone, refracting the trauma of mid-century global events: enemy invasion, persecution, terror, bombardment and holocaust and even, as suggested above, the Cold War fear of nuclear annihilation. The beautiful house purchased by Felix to lure Laura into loveless marriage harbours these malignant energies in its domestic interior. A sense of local and colonial history becomes seamlessly continuous with the transnational lineaments of settler-suburban forms. The description of the Shaw house suggests this North Shore suburb's gracious ease, its colonial, Victorian and Arts and Crafts Californian bungalows having been built in the nineteenth and early twentieth century by wealthy professionals and businessmen:

> It was a lovely single-storeyed colonial house painted white, with a roof of grey slate and long shady verandahs decorated with old wrought iron. There were lawns. There were daphne and camellia and gardenia bushes with dark shiny leaves. In the garden behind the house there were fruit trees, two of which were hung with enormous lemons, sweetly scented. (31-2)

The Shaw house bears a resemblance to the gothic villa "Honda", in Neutral Bay's prestigious Shellcove Road. Built in an "isolated position at the head of Shell Cove" in 1858 by architect Francis H. Grundy, "Honda" is one of the oldest surviving colonial houses in this exclusive suburb.[23] Harrower's description breathes with the light, grace and tranquillity of an architect-designed bourgeois house in its genteel garden suburb. With its prospect across harbour and city, the house promises ease, comfort and social command. Its spatial properties naturalise the casual affluence, poise and complacency of an established bourgeoisie:

> Inside, the rooms were large and cool, and stood awaiting furniture and embellishment at the hands of their new owner. A pattern of leaves, criss-crossed and winking light, blew and shivered on the empty white wall of the sitting-room as the poplars at the side of the house shook and sent shadows indoors.
> She glanced through the bare French windows, over the greenness of grass and flowering hedges to the blue ship-laden harbour, and the city beyond it. She had no idea what she was thinking. (32)

The blank interior awaits the imprint of its new owner. This blankness suggests an amnesic relation to self and history: the subtle shadows and shivering emptiness of the house suggest the aftermath of suppressed violence. The Neutral Bay house is a fairytale house, a "dream palace" charged with no less hidden malevolence and disfiguring psychic force than Lilian Hulm's hideous red brick bungalow in *The Long Prospect*'s Greenhills. Felix soon stocks this empty, waiting house with fine goods and furnishings, with silverware and expensive dinner plate calculated to impress the guests who almost never come. Its

---

23   Details about "Honda", 55 Shellcove Road, Kurraba Point (near Neutral Bay), are from the "Federation House" Wikispace, http://bit.ly/2qHjUBz. "Honda" is one of a cluster of heritage listed homes in this precinct. See also the NSW Office of Environment and Heritage website at http://bit.ly/2qHlbIW.

white-painted interiors and its brocade upholstery signal elegance and charm. Among its furnishings and objects, the most spectacularly loaded with significance is Felix's prize possession, the fifteen-inch red and blue china statue of Bluebeard with its swarthy, leering face and curving assassin's knife. This piece of orientalist bric-a-brac recalls the first description of Felix himself as "a swarthy, nuggety man of forty-four" (12). Occupying the mantelpiece, the statue directs its ever-present joke against the women of the house. Felix's self-declared, mocking performance as Bluebeard enacts a characteristic shuttle between cruel, narcissistic amusement and unhinged, alcohol-fuelled violence. The portrait of Felix, argues Naomi Riddle, is suggestive of the male hysteric who "*deliberately turns inward into the domestic space*", competing with and seeking to destroy emerging female agency, producing an ambiguous and unstable male subjectivity.[24] Felix not only appropriates the feminine other but also, it seems, the oriental other, a figure from deep in the white European imaginary. As an oriental monster within the self-made, over-bright domestic interior, he forms an opaque, impenetrable element in Harrower's narrative labyrinth.

The narrative synthesises commodity culture, fable and psychological realism in its fevered animation of the neurotic domestic interior. Fragments of nursery rhymes and fairytales are interwoven with popular cultural texts and everyday suburban discourse. This textures the narrative's persistent critique of the cruelty that attends conventional promises of happiness and the good life. Cruel optimism is an affective condition theorised by Lauren Berlant who describes the "good life" as an ideal – a "moral-intimate-economic thing" – that impels the subject to invest in and strive optimistically after an object or scene that in fact works to thwart the conditions under which the self can thrive (2). Under the spell of the good life embodied in the beautiful house, Laura binds herself to Felix – or rather binds herself to the fantasy of what he represents; they simulate the happy marriage. The affective condition of cruel optimism is nowhere more perfectly signalled than in the novel's implied homophonic slide between "Bluebeard" and "Bluebird". In the novel, the popular song "The Bluebird of Happiness" plays intermittently on the radio, its refrain haunting both Laura and Clare, its lyric sincere yet its sound strangely "lugubrious" (18).[25] The conjunction of Bluebird with Bluebeard is achieved in "Felix", a name that means "lucky" or "happy". Laura is trapped by cruel optimism, by her adherence to a conventional, fantasy ideal of the good life grasped in the absence of other possibilities and pursued so long that – even in crisis – it cannot be relinquished. The interior of the beautiful, comfortable modern home occupied by its home-maker-cum-destroyer is thus furnished with the continual interlacing of optimism with cruelty.

The natural and cultural features of the setting load the narrative with significance, drawing on the idea of North Shore suburbia as a zone that displays the tastes and desires of a genteel social class. The novel's delineation of this well-heeled, professional or entrepreneurial class suggests the residual trace of the settler-colonial history that its beneficiaries must erase and forget. At the same time, through the novel's specific

---

24 Naomi Riddle, "'Turning inward on himself': Male Hysteria in Elizabeth Harrower's *The Watch Tower*", *Southerly* 72, no. 1 (2012): 206.

25 According to its Wikipedia entry, the song, "The Bluebird of Happiness", was first composed in 1934 by Sandor Harmati and Edward Heyman for singer Jan Peerce but did not gain worldwide commercial popularity until 1945. This detail corresponds with the ambiguous stretch across wartime and early postwar periods in the novel's timeframe. The conceit of the bluebird of happiness travelled through popular culture thereafter, as exemplified in the song "Over the Rainbow" from *The Wizard of Oz* (1939).

correlation with real terrain, the mythic potential of place is amplified. Extreme moral and physical danger is omnipresent despite the neutral tones of the beautiful house. The sinister curve of Bluebeard's knife echoes the curving green of lawn against harbour. The whiteness of the Shaws' house – reflecting, as previously stated, the attributes of the real suburb – mirrors the false "neutrality" of Neutral Bay. The word "white" occurs more than fifty times in the novel. "Blue", with forty-five mentions, is the only other hue so often repeated. Around this white-blue colour palette gathers an array of sensations and emotions that texture the novel's affective terrain. Signifying purity, "white" is culturally associated with the bridal and the regal, with nobility, and so favoured by the wealthier bourgeoisie. "White" things are hard to keep clean and so the choice of white décor or white clothing bespeaks leisure because it relies on invisible domestic labour – of the housewife or a service (or servant) class. The fact that Laura spends a great deal of time assiduously cleaning the white surfaces of the Shaw interior not only emphasises her own entrapment in the domestic sphere but also her constant maintenance of the fiction of Felix's (in fact dubious) social status and upward mobility. Felix's lacklustre career in business, his self-destructive decisions, his dwindling reputation, his continual churn through a series of enterprises (box, chocolate and clothing factories) indicate an unstable masculinity linked to failed socio-economic aspirations. First Felix's factories and then his house become sweatshops, spaces of mechanised female servitude. The white of the Shaws' domestic interior highlights the vulnerability of female flesh to predation, as evident in phrases like "white and weak", "small white teeth", "white-hot", "white citadel", "white fiery surface", "bloodless white", "white, fierce, shocked, tearless" (125), and the image of Laura's veins as they "rose in blue welts from the milk-white skin" (128). Whiteness is both the refractive veneer of endlessly cleaned surfaces and the searing white of feared nuclear blast. When Laura loses track of her expensive diamond ring (secreted by Felix to torment her), she flinches as he returns in a hyperbolic convergence of domestic interior with atomic warfare: "Fright exploded in her, and her flesh fell from her bones" (206).

The combination of white and blue also describes the ionised glow of lightning, of the electric spark or shock that produces on the one hand violent arrest and on the other revivification. In the latter half of the novel, Laura and Felix are "shocked wide awake" in the night by a mysterious "ghastly noise", "extraordinary wind", and the sense that their solid house has been shaken to its foundations. Despite "the uneasiness of the house under the bombardment", neither then nor in the morning are they able to locate the cause (192–5). They entertain but cannot quite voice the fear of apocalypse. This fear of catastrophe, sensed but unable to be pinpointed or localised, refers back to the wartime 1942 incursion of Japanese midget submarines into Sydney Harbour and also to the collective mid-century fear of nuclear annihilation during such Cold War crises as the 1961 Bay of Pigs. For Slavoj Žižek, global catastrophe constitutes the nightmare to which the comfortable, cushioned classes of the Western world are prone. Buffered by the illusion of the everyday "real", Western consumerist "reality" rests upon a fantasy structure threatened by the Real, by the prospect of having to relinquish a fantasy at once "pacifying, disarming . . . and shattering".[26] The togetherness of Laura and Felix in this moment of terror projects their dysfunction from interior to exterior, enacting anxieties about invisible threats to these collective fantasies.

---

26 Slavoj Žižek, *Welcome to the Desert of the Real! Five Essays on September 11 and Related Dates* (London and New York: Verso, 2002), 16–18.

8 "White, fierce, shocked, tearless": *The Watch Tower* and the Electric Interior

The Shaw house is only apparently neutral. War is dismissed from the everyday, an unreal spectre pertaining to distant elsewheres. Yet it is embedded, as others have observed, in the novel's imagery and language, intimately shaping the domestic interior. Harrower's novel is at its most modernist, its most Woolfian, in its simultaneity, its rescaling of the house to encompass global terror. Dixon argues that this is achieved through Harrower's ironic metageography, her conjoining of distant with local coordinates.[27] The affective rescaling to contain the globe within the prosaic interior effects a chiastic crossing of outside and inside, microcosm and macrocosm. Citing Gaston Bachelard, Susan Stewart describes how perspectives generated by scalar switching between the miniature space of the doll's house and the scale of the gigantic materialises the abstract apparatus of historic global forces and class relations.[28] That the miniature can contain and eclipse the gigantic poses an ethical challenge. As Nash writes, this parallel risks collapsing differences between the individual trauma of two white Australian women and the historical trauma brought by the Holocaust, or closer to home, by genocide. Yet scalar switching may be less about making simple equations than prompting reverberations that suggest a shared, structural logic of violence.

Rescaling makes distant events proximate, the private public, the invisible visible. The city grid is scaled down to a tightly bounded space within which Laura, in crisis, paces under a mad clockwork spell: "She yearned to stop. She had walked for hours. But her feet bore her on past every terminus" (108). Laura's comportment, recalling Schivelbusch's definition, is "deranged": she moves in shock, mechanically. This is the displaced physical manifestation at the scale of the city of the Shaws' domestic interior, projecting that interior onto public space and collapsing distinctions between them. Laura soon represses her recognition all the more thoroughly as she resumes her place in the domestic trap, returning as though from a long illness, "shriven and strange" (111). The re-staging in city space of the domestic interior is also, however, witnessed by Clare. On Castlereagh Street amid the "motionless crowd", she watches as two policemen hold between them the limp body of a young man and drag him across the street (135). This horror is compounded by the sight of a shop window full of china ornaments – creatures in poses of predation and captivity – and finally by the reified vision of an uncaring metropolis with its hideous buildings and vapid faces. Everywhere Clare sees signs of cleverness and avidity rather than the goodness she yearns to see (136).

At one point the narrative enters into Clare's bedroom, an elegantly furnished space lacking homely comfort: "a pretty, sterile room carpeted in pale green", its walls white, its furniture of rosewood, with a small chair "in which no one ever sat" (74). Despite its "coupon free" loveliness, Clare's bedroom is not a dwelling place: there is "nowhere in particular to *be* in it" (74). Nonetheless, it affords at least the possibility of retreat into solitude even though Felix construes this as evasion of his control. The room is under surveillance but – like the doctor's surgery – it also serves as Clare's watch tower, a spatial correlative to her own inner watchfulness, the vigilant interior she cultivates. Self, room, house and suburb are framing, nested coordinates, contiguous, echoing and in tension. As Clare looks out of her window, she apprehends the illusion of the garden suburb, its grace

---

27 Dixon, "'The wind from Siberia'", this volume.
28 Susan Stewart, *On Longing: Narratives of the Miniature, the Gigantic, the Souvenir, the Collection* (Durham, NC: Duke University Press, 1993), 85–6.

and beauty drained away. The vision projects her own situation and targets the settler-suburban possessiveness that flattens and degrades place:

> there were asphalt streets, cement footpaths, tight little bungalows, ripe gardens, and scratchy ones, hovels, crowded reverberating streets in the city, advertising, dust, nothing wonderful, no work of genius, only the monotonous harbour, dead from being over-admired by its suburban landlords. (99)

This image meshes the dynamics of the Shaw family with the built suburban environment, economic world and social milieu. It makes a concerted allusion to the paradoxical self-defeat of the suburban idyll or pastoral (beautiful places now "dead from being over-admired by suburban landlords"). Various nested scales, of house, suburb, city and world, are all captive to the grid of capitalist modernity. This vacuous community is figured in the idle conversation of the Shaws' self-satisfied neighbours Blanche and Richard Parkes who, overhearing Felix's rages, are not moved to assist but merely scandalised and titivated. This ethos extends to Felix's business associates and factory co-workers who seem oblivious to the plight of the Vaizey women, and to doctors and psychiatrists who unquestioningly defer to the male alcoholic over the abused housewife. The perfectly beautiful interior of the Shaw house may seem to offer sanctuary but in fact serves as a conductor for the dehumanising social grid. The Shaws' fetishistic display of the good life barely forestalls recognition of the brutalising system on which their domestic space not only depends but reproduces with electric intensity.

In her quest to escape the malignant interior, Clare desperately seeks the "good" (137). She reads novels populated by characters who model virtues lacking in the real world: Tolstoy's *The Cossacks*, Stendhal's *The Red and the Black*, and Bowen's *The Heat of the Day*. She contrives encounters with goodness, bestowing a daily shilling on a Salvation Army officer at Circular Quay in order that she may receive his blessing (152). Then Bernard – a refugee from war-torn Holland who sends his earnings home to his family and who collapses from malnutrition – arrives in the Shaws' house to convalesce. Clare seizes the opportunity he presents to rehearse goodness. She marshals resources and avenues for Bernard's future study so he can support his family and achieve an independent life. Indeed, she bestows on Bernard precisely what has been denied to her. Seeking to subvert Clare's efforts, Felix knows she is eluding his grasp. At one point he remarks that she looks "radioactive", that she appears "electric, electrifying, like a fiery avenger or angel, like someone alive twice over, and it had nothing to do with the colour of her dress" (174-5). Bernard is not, as one might otherwise have expected, a love interest for Clare; rather, he materialises the distant war zone within the Australian house. Producing an electric charge of the kind prefigured in the doctor's surgery, Bernard is an enlivening, awakening force. Galvanising Clare into action, Bernard shocks her awake, electrifies her, precipitating her act of salvation – his salvation and her own, by proxy.

Negotiating the blockage presented not only by her mother Stella and Felix but also – importantly – by her sister Laura, Clare works her way through and beyond the malignant interior towards an (electrically) transformed prospect that is mostly withheld from the protagonists of Harrower's earlier novels. Elements of *The Long Prospect*, as I suggest above, are repeated and inverted in *The Watch Tower*. This intensification seems significant given that *The Watch Tower* was written after Harrower's return to Sydney, during the 1960s; it thus coincided with an important time of cultural change both in Australia and abroad. Considered in relation to her previous writings, *The Watch Tower* is both a reconfiguration and culmination of a series of shocking interiors in which suburban forms incorporate, extend and encompass an emerging global modernity. Harrower's suburban interiors are thus multi-layered. They both evoke the sense-memory of place and critique the claustrophobic insularity that is brought by a technologically modernising world. *The Long Prospect*'s industrial Newcastle not only finds its echo in *The Watch Tower*'s working harbour, with its traffic of cruise ships and rusty oil tankers, but takes shape in Laura's recognition that "the circumstances of her life" were now "as rigid as a steel foundry" (202). Recalling and reversing the scene of Emily's vulnerability to hidden watchers in *The Long Prospect*, as she stands within that "hideous lighted tomb", Clare stands in the dark garden outside the illuminated house, listening in fear to the sounds of escalating violence issuing from its brightly lit but opaque interior (189ff).

How is the polarity between the enclosed domestic realm and the exterior world – a polarity that feminists argue signals the co-dependency of separate spheres – to be negotiated? In *The Watch Tower*, the threat brought by the oppressive, disciplinary division of the world into separate compartments is not just fended off but ultimately transformed by means of the exercise of interior watchfulness, of a vigilance ultimately directed not towards defensive self-protection and the maintenance of tight boundaries, but outwards, in an active search for the good. The episode in the doctor's surgery with which my discussion began dramatises what may be yielded by moments of exposure. It suggests what happens when the boundary between interior and exterior perspectives is breached, when habits of passivity and self-abnegation are relinquished, when malignant surveillance is superseded by the strength of the good. At such moments, the electric disruption of boundaries shifts from fear to reanimation and life-giving connection.

The wrench involved in changing course inscribes itself within Harrower's prose. Her fiction not only generates images of electrified interiors but also carries the electric age in its narrative operations: in its compressed and shifting perspectives, in the sometimes tortured compression and pivoting of its sentences, and the careful orchestration of scenes and plot. Harrower's use of the novel may represent an effort to recalibrate the medium of print in an engagement with and transformative resistance to the electric media of twentieth-century suburban modernity. The novel is not just a machine for thinking with but for harnessing reader affect and desire. This aesthetic is borne out in Clare's final journey, her choice to travel inland by train rather than away from Australia. This direction – as Dixon points out – registers the novel's resistance to the easy solution of literary expatriation – the overseas holiday plans of Laura and Felix demonstrate that escape does not lie in that direction. But there is more going on here. Clare's movement into the interior, by train, also reminds us of the railway journal in the nineteenth-century English novel. Steam engine and railway technology accompany and speak to the form of the novel in works by Dickens, Eliot, Hardy and Henry James.[29] As long-form narrative in the medium of the printed, portable book, the novel carries its readers on an interior journey

---

29 As a young woman Harrower frequented the City Library in the Queen Victoria Building, Sydney, and reports having read there voraciously in fiction, philosophy and politics: Elizabeth Harrower in conversation with Text publisher Michael Heyward, Mosman Library, 4 November 2015. Elsewhere in this volume, Dixon discusses striking correspondence between Harrower's fictional interiors and those of Henry James, while Nash draws attention to intriguing parallels between George Eliot's *Daniel Deronda* and Harrower's *The Watch Tower*.

in linear fashion towards an anticipated destination. As well as modernity's experience of speed and shock, the train journey serves to figure the novel-reading experience itself. Clare's journey away from Sydney, away from the suburban interior, towards the bush interior, affords the narrative's last, retrospective sweep of an already receding suburban chronotope, a figure of time-space, as Clare travels forward:

> The outer suburbs marched up, crowded, formal and hard as nineteenth-century cemeteries.
> More outer suburbs and more time: hills and valleys of roofs, grey-blue gravelled streets, blue-black tarred roads, square miles of brick, corrugated iron, gravel, concrete, hard dry substances, hard shapes, graveyard architecture and landscape. Still time and suburbs passed. (219)

Beyond this receding panorama with its harsh surfaces, Clare jerks the train window up and looks forward. Travelling towards a yet-unknown interior as though into the past of her childhood when her father was still alive, Clare leans out to sense the shapes and scents of the bush interior; she revels in wonderful light, in waves of air and the "smell of grass, or clover, or honey" (219). A nostalgic summoning of lost place, of sensations associated with primal experience and interior memory, with a deeper past that Clare travels to meet, also – it seems to me – enacts an elegiac affirmation of the remembered forms of the novel even as this novel closes.

Clare's physical crossing in space and time effects a novelistic suspension between acts of remembering and actual return to beginnings – performing an aesthetics of repetition and circularity in tension with narrative progress. If this gesture suggests Harrower's late-modernist aesthetic, then it also affirms Barthes' observation that the truth of a novel inheres finally not in its subject matter or content but in its formal and aesthetic properties.[30] Harrower's shock tactics are not only the subject matter, therefore, but integral to the form of her fiction, bearing the sensation and affective load that charges and makes real her electric interiors.

References

Barthes, Roland. *The Preparation of the Novel: Lecture Courses and Seminars at the Collège de France (1978–1979 and 1979–1980)*. Translated by Kate Briggs. New York: Columbia University Press, 2011.
——. *Camera Lucida: Reflections on Photography* [*Le Chambre Claire*]. (1980) Translated by Richard Howard. London: Vintage, 1993.
Bellow, Saul. *Henderson the Rain King*. (1959) London: Penguin, 2007. Kindle Edition.
Berlant, Lauren. *Cruel Optimism*. Durham, NC: Duke University Press, 2011.
Birns, Nicholas. *Contemporary Australian Literature: A World Not Yet Dead*. Sydney: Sydney University Press, 2015.
Davidson, Jim. Interview with Elizabeth Harrower. *Meanjin* 39, no. 2 (July 1980): 163–74.
Dixon, Robert. "'The wind from Siberia': Metageography and Ironic Nationality in the Novels of Elizabeth Harrower". In *Elizabeth Harrower: Critical Essays*. Edited by Elizabeth McMahon and Brigitta Olubas, 49–64. Sydney: Sydney University Press, 2017.

---

30 Barthes, *Preparation of the Novel*, 276–7.

Harrower, Elizabeth. *The Watch Tower*. (1966) North Ryde, NSW: Angus & Robertson, 1991.

———. *The Long Prospect*. (1958) North Ryde, NSW: Angus & Robertson, 1988.

Koval, Ramona. Interview with Elizabeth Harrower. *The Monthly Video*. October 2014. http://bit.ly/2pGhjKU.

McLuhan, Marshall. *Understanding Media: The Extensions of Man*. (1964) London: Sphere Books, 1967.

Murphet, Julian. "Projecting the Sixties: Mediation and Characterology in *The Catherine Wheel*". In *Elizabeth Harrower: Critical Essays*. Edited by Elizabeth McMahon and Brigitta Olubas, 107–117. Sydney: Sydney University Press, 2017.

Nash, Megan. "Traversing 'the same extreme country' in *The Watch Tower* and *Daniel Deronda*". In *Elizabeth Harrower: Critical Essays*. Edited by Elizabeth McMahon and Brigitta Olubas, 119–132. Sydney: Sydney University Press, 2017.

Riddle, Naomi. "'Turning inward on himself': Male Hysteria in Elizabeth Harrower's *The Watch Tower*". *Southerly* 72, no. 1 (2012): 204–13.

Schivelbusch, Wolfgang. *Disenchanted Night: The Industrialization of Light in the Nineteenth Century*. (1987) Translated by Angela Davis. Berkeley: University of California Press, 1989.

———. *The Railway Journey: The Industrialization of Time and Space in the Nineteenth Century*. (1977) Berkeley: University of California Press, 1986.

Shelley, Percy Bysshe. "The Revolt of Islam". (1818) The Literature Network. http://bit.ly/2vcYSAl.

Stewart, Susan. *On Longing: Narratives of the Miniature, the Gigantic, the Souvenir, the Collection*. Durham, NC: Duke University Press, 1993.

Žižek, Slavoj. *Welcome to the Desert of the Real! Five Essays on September 11 and Related Dates*. London and New York: Verso, 2002.

9
Addiction, Fire and the Face in *The Catherine Wheel*

Brigitta Olubas

My point of departure for this discussion of *The Catherine Wheel* is the connection (observed, in passing, by D.R. Burns)[1] between Elizabeth Harrower's 1960 novel and Henry Handel Richardson's *Maurice Guest*, published nearly half a century earlier (1908). The points of similarity between the two novels are instructive: both trace the inexorable decline of moderate talent and ambition in the face of searing obsession; both treat the question of performance, musical or theatrical, which trumps the force of words and language; both displace their narratives away from Australia to northern cities, reflecting in a further shift their authors' own departures from Australia; and both focus narrative attention on the impossible, liminal promise of youth and talent, on student life, life without parents or family, pursuing a mode of living where adult maturity is barely imaginable. But while both are heavily invested in melodramatic incident, the dramas of *The Catherine Wheel* are largely internal, unvoiced, or they take place off-stage, or in the novel's unimaginable future. And Harrower's characters are remarkable not for their external acts so much as for their interactions; it is in their relationships rather than their individual personalities that we find the crackle and hum, the pyrotechnics promised by the novel's title. There is also a dramatic scaling back of narrative scope in Harrower's mid-century setting compared to Richardson's: we move from Wagner's Leipzig to Clemency James' London bedsit, and much of *The Catherine Wheel*'s action takes place over the telephone, a mediation working as a further and technologically specific kind of displacement. And while *Maurice Guest* resolves tempestuously with the suicide of its protagonist, Clem's narrative (as always with Harrower) concludes bleakly, with the opaque, inconclusive conviction that it is "too late".[2]

The narrative slightness of *The Catherine Wheel* is balanced by and organised around an intense and melodramatic interest in addiction: specifically, alcoholic obsession. The novel traces the fraught options remaining for those – Clemency and patient Olive – caught up in circuits of devotion as well as the determining desire of the alcoholic Christian, in the unyielding face of such obsession. As theorist of addiction Jason Lee

---

1 D.R. Burns, "Australian Fiction Since 1960", *World Literature Written in English* 11, no. 2 (1972): 53–63.
2 Elizabeth Harrower, *The Catherine Wheel* (Melbourne: Text Publishing, 2014), 325. All subsequent references are to this edition and appear in parentheses in the text.

notes: "The word addicted originated in the Latin verb *addicere*, meaning 'to declare', and an obsolete sixteenth-century English adjective meaning 'bound or devoted to someone'. Etymologically and at its core, addiction concerns devotion, worship and ritual".[3] The declarative capacity of addiction, the occasions it provides for speaking around the truth are tied, through this etymology, to the circuits and connectivities of electricity, which Brigid Rooney describes as an "analogy for the emotional truth" in Harrower's work.[4] Following this logic, in *The Catherine Wheel*, the flickering light and heating, fed by shillings in the meter, of Clem's London bedsit are part of a grid that reconnects addiction as connectivity, a flow, like the telephone; declarative but distracting, misleading, unreliable. The emotional terrain of Christian's alignment with electricity is as mendacious as it is compelling: he tells Clem: "'I may stay in London after all if I land this contract. The money's good in electronics'" but then the following day exposes the deceit:

> "Good God! There'd be a nationwide blackout if they let me near any apparatus. That was my first fuse – the one I mended for you in Miss Evans's. What did I tell you?" he asked, still laughing . . . I told him and he roared with delight . . . "I was plastered, darling. But electronics! How in hell did I think that up?" (147)

Through such halting circuitries, *The Catherine Wheel* works to amplify and animate those addictive obsessions which are shared by Christian and Clem (and for that matter, Olive) beyond the concept, simply, of cure, of remediation or redemption, thus bringing Lee's categories of devotion and ritual, but also Rooney's insights around electricity and emotional truth, into play. Within the drug discourse of the late twentieth century, Clem (and again, also Olive) might have been classified as "co-dependent", and in some ways the concept of co-dependence, with its capacity to highlight the complications of selfhood, the flickering, unstable to-and-fro between subjects caught in the addictive spin, is a useful way into thinking about what addiction might mean in Harrower's novel. It also allows us to prise *The Catherine Wheel* away from the rest of Harrower's oeuvre for a moment, freeing it from readings that see the drama between Clem, Christian and Olive simply as a less accomplished version of the extraordinary psychic violence of, for instance, *The Watch Tower*.[5] More particularly, the concept of co-dependence carries an inherent looseness: Lennard Davis observes its historical and cultural specificity, but also its links to broader and looser traditions of obsession, devotion and addiction, arguing that "[c]odependence is . . . a variation on the addiction scenario added in the 1990s . . . [and it comes] directly out of Alcoholics Anonymous".[6] Applying the concept to Harrower's novel from three decades earlier adds an anachronistic gloss to the conflicted tracery of comings and goings, of pairings and ruptures, between Clem, Christian and Olive as well as providing an added perspective on the dire belatedness that Christian

---

3   Jason Lee, "Introduction", *Cultures of Addiction*, ed. by Jason Lee (New York, NY: Cambria Press, 2012), 4.
4   See Brigid Rooney, "'White, fierce, shocked, tearless': *The Watch Tower* and the Electric Interior", this volume, 85–6.
5   See for instance John Colmer: "While the third novel, *The Catherine Wheel*, laudably attempts to extend the range of the fictional world by having its setting in London bed-sitter-land, it is a somewhat disappointing work that hardly prepares the reader for the splendid fourth novel, *The Watch Tower*." John Colmer, "Elizabeth Harrower", Brief Biographies, http://bit.ly/2pbfrXA.
6   Lennard Davis, *Obsession: A History* (Chicago: University of Chicago Press, 2009), 178.

identifies within their relations: "'I hurt her. Poor Olive. I mustn't do it again . . . She'll be my nurse and housekeeper, and I'll be unfaithful and abuse her, but she'll stick to me.' And he smiled at me grimly. 'I'm not for you. We're too late for each other'" (259). This belatedness is traced minutely across the lives of the three protagonists in the course of the novel, coming to define their relations and their shared fates, so that Clem and Christian's early meetings are predicated on telephone messages from her delayed students, and their classes or the starting dates of his jobs repeatedly postponed while he is out drinking. Throughout, he endlessly replays lamentations to Clem about his life being over – "'Thirty! I'm nine hundred. I should be dead'" (140) – an insight echoed decisively by his friend Rollo, who tells a disbelieving Clem: "'For some people . . . it's too late.' Too *late*, he said. My heart emptied at the finality of his tone. Too *late*?" (297), in a chain leading inevitably to the novel's ultimate acknowledgement of the present as a site of the belated in the novel's final line: "And now, anyway, it was too late".

In their consideration of co-dependency in popular culture, Matilda Hellman and Varpu Rantala note the capacity of this dimension of addiction to "[blur] the boundaries between normal and pathological, self and other, life and death, and male and female in the cultural imagination of second-order modernity",[7] and I want to propose that this spatial instability mirrors the mismatches across time just noted. The absence of fast and sure boundaries comes in the course of the novel to dominate Clem's relationship with Christian, drastically compromising other aspects of her life. Indeed, her devotion to him works to compromise her independent life, her very will. She neglects her law studies to make way for his study of French – she was to be his unpaid tutor, he her sole student; replacing the income she had previously earned as a tutor, to fund her own law studies, with his charm, his beauty, and the promise of his future brilliant return to the stage. Clem's encounter with Christian, her co-dependent fixation on his alcoholism, is framed throughout around the decline of her will: her loss of autonomy, of financial independence, the gradual depletion of her physical self as she declines to eat, and ultimately the shattering of her psychic integrity, caught as she is in the stasis of obsessive care for Christian and carelessness for herself.

Eve Sedgwick argues that with the late-twentieth-century expansiveness of the concept of addiction (to include both ingestion and refusal of a given substance), "the locus of addictiveness cannot be the substance itself and can scarcely even be the body itself, but must be some overarching abstraction that governs the narrative relations between them". Further, the addict is propelled "into a narrative of inexorable decline and fatality", the only alternative to which is not to consume.[8] And this is precisely what is played out between Clem and Christian, relentlessly structuring the main narrative, but also darkening smaller moments of connection and transmission as elements within just such an "overarching abstraction". In the novel, addiction – Christian's to alcohol, and Clem's to him – presents itself as a condition of modern selfhood; it is at once an abstraction and a problematic of the will. Carol Davidson notes "addiction's role as a cultural pathology, its location at the crossroads of desire and anxiety, and the possibilities it opens up for exploring human consciousness *in extremis*", observing

---

7   Matilda Hellman and Varpu Rantala, "Codependence, Madness and Glamour: Narratives of Women Celebrity Addicts in Internet Tabloids", in *Cultures of Addiction*, 176.
8   Eve Sedgwick, "Epidemics of the Will", in *Tendencies* (Durham, NC: Duke University Press, 1993), 131.

further that while "religious groups generally promoted the notion of addiction as a moral pathology . . . medical professionals have advanced the idea of addiction as 'a disease which afflicted the individual's will'".[9] In Harrower's novel, it is viewed from both perspectives – although the medical discourse dominates; for instance at one point, halfway through the novel, after a bender, Christian says: "'But why do I do these things? Could anyone straighten me out? Perhaps Helen – you said she was a doctor – perhaps she would get me an appointment with a psychologist?'" (178). And later that day, Clem reflects: "Out of nowhere the understanding had sprung up that it was my turn to do what I could with him. He would go through his paces, and we would see who won. He *would* break free, grow up, I was certain" (191). Her own decline and rescue are likewise viewed through a medical lens.

Addiction is also to be understood as a temporality; not just a point of persistent belatedness, but more profoundly "a condition of conformity and repetition that resists change".[10] David Punter is expansive on this point, describing addiction as "the very mechanics of the same":

> Under conditions of addiction, the supposedly exciting possibility of every day being a different day, of there being endlessly new things under the sun, is dissolved, resolved, absolved under the condition of sameness: each different morning succumbing to the "long, empty noon", each hope of a new beginning cancelled by the repetition of the past. Some commentators . . . posit a terminus for addiction; but the terminus is really, almost literally, beside the point: the point is "more of the same" . . . [W]hat is at stake is the replacement of myths of human progress, of individuation, of development, by the brute facts of the absence of escape, the tying down to the wheel – not, in this case, the "wheel of desire" with its many, if painful, points and spokes, but the more bitter wheel, which perhaps Saint Catherine knew, the wheel which endlessly reproduces the same point of stasis while the body is being torn apart and demonstrating an endless but in the end unfriendly, resilience.[11]

Punter's metaphor is of course beautifully apposite for my reading of this novel, adding texture to the understanding of addiction as brutal and outward looking, tearing the body apart and in the process condemning the self to endlessly centrifugal movement at the cost of individual singularity and development. It also presses the language and iconology of addiction resolutely, and in quite literal terms, towards the domain of the Christological, where we see Clemency's relation to Christian shift from addictive obsession to understanding and forgiveness, even as she loses her own grasp on selfhood. At the same time, Clemency's name connects (or reconnects) her to the basis of the law, her primary object of study, suggesting another body of stability that is progressively weakened as the narrative proceeds. According to Austin Sarat and Nasser Hussain, in Aristotle's *Nicomachean Ethics*, what translates into "clemency" is "*epieikeia*", not so much sympathy or pity, as the capacity within judgement for indeterminacy and interpretation. Clemency is thus in Aristotelian

---

9   Carol Margaret Davidson, "The Gothic and Addiction: A Mad Tango", *Gothic Studies* 11, no. 2 (2009): 1, 2.
10 Davidson, 5.
11 David Punter, "William Burroughs: The Scene of Addiction", *Gothic Studies* 11, no. 2 (2009): 80.

terms both the basis of law and the movement away from its rigid or thoughtless application.[12] Within Christian doctrine, clemency is brought to the Trinity through the action of the Holy Spirit in the wake of Christ's death. Without pushing this point too far, I want to draw attention to the way the history of Clemency's name inflects the sense of narrative decline with more complex relations and understandings – the repetition and stasis of her compulsion come to be parsed with insight and compassion, as, for instance when she observes that she feels "charmed and indulgent" towards Christian: "Christian's protestations only proved the truth of his face. He was good. Not only that, [his] preoccupation with his condition, the consciousness of sin – in spite of his histrionics – spoke of sensibility and insight" (54). Clem's error, which will determine the novel's central narrative, is based in this misrecognition of Christian, which is, at the same time, a capacity to see the truth of him, that is, "the truth of his face".

Of course, Christian himself, not least by virtue of his name, is at the heart of the novel's Christological metaphorical chain, which renders his intoxication, in part at least, sacramental. And within this rubric, Clemency's error is part of a necessary wandering in the process of redemption. Marty Roth argues for the inextricability of spiritual and physical intoxication within the Christian tradition, in terms that resonate for this novel:

> Christianity is a drink religion with a great drink or drunk, the Eucharist, at its center, since the purpose of the Eucharist is to produce spiritual intoxication (notice that in this case one attains not by unspeakable or transcendent means but by *drinking wine*).[13]

Christian's frequent literal elevation through the novel – mostly on ladders, attending to the electrics – invokes this connection and in particular the larger investment in and weight of loss itself. It literalises the threat of falling, the always inevitable failing of the addict, as does the narrative's intense focus on Christian's face and his physical beauty.

The novel returns over and over to figures of devotion which draw explicitly on Christological iconography, for instance in this exchange from chapter two where Olive, Christian's much older lover, recalls the devotion and endless loss of the mother of Christ, as she cradles his head in a tableau scene with touches of the Pietà:

> Olive went to stand behind him now, her hands lightly touching his hair. He looked round at her quizzically. She said, "Did you know he almost fell yesterday?"
>
> "On my head. On my head," he grinned. "Would it have made much difference do you think?"
>
> "That beautiful head," Olive said in a heavy yearning voice, and we all fell into a respectful silence . . .
>
> Christian lowered his eyelids in a travesty of modesty, then raised them to look directly at me, his expression grave, deliberate and full of meaning. Behind him Olive held his massive head between her hands. (46)

---

12 Austin Sarat and Nasser Hussain, *Forgiveness, Mercy, and Clemency* (Palo Alto, CA: Stanford University Press, 2007), 197.
13 Marty Roth, *Drunk the Night Before: An Anatomy of Intoxication* (Minneapolis: University of Minnesota Press, 2005), 91.

Olive's "heavy" voice impels the falling into silence of all three characters, binding them together in the vain support of Christian's "beautiful head", suggesting the immobility of marble. The weight of Christian's fall and the monumental devotion it demands from the women around him are tied metaphorically, albeit through the defiles of "travesty", to the Christian notion of sacrament and sacramental loss; however, at the same time they are also bound up with the novel's complex and fraught negotiation of questions of display, representation, and even mediation. The figure represented here is classical as much as Christian, but above all static and, of course, broken into pieces. What animation there is comes from the interaction between the three, relations above all of displaying and of looking. The scene comes at the end of an extended narrative negotiation of the ethics of representation, the problematics of "artifice", and false display – Christian is, after all, an actor. Not long before this scene, Clem, musing on her developing relationships in the boarding house, has repudiated conventional sociality as inadequate to the demands of personal authenticity:

> For artifice destroyed me, and even in this house I'd witness horrifying charades entitled "Friendship" performed by people who had known each other for years. Arch and brittle as creations of Congreve's: that they refrained from the use of wigs, fans, snuff, titles and Restoration cries, seemed odd. (34)

Her invocation of the stage is an oblique way of naming Christian, of setting him at the centre of the circle of deception. Christian, nonetheless, is such an accomplished performer that he is able to convince her of his own veracity – "He had the look of a truthful person, and in a quite impersonal way this look was tonic to me, gave me a momentary sensation of having been translated from sickness to health" – so that she responds, against her own better judgement, to his physical presence in an aesthetic register, which allows her to overlook the ethical threat he poses:

> He was leaning against the wall, arms folded, head down, held by his thoughts. He had a large head, a broad head, with lines that might please a sculptor: it seemed eminently a head to be hewn, chiselled. This feeling surprised me, for I had, in no sense, an artist's eye. (35)

These moments of sculptural connection and what passes for mutual recognition, at least in Clem's eye, are extended in a series of scenes involving a framed exchange of glances centred on Christian's face,[14] which work against any possibility of a stable or healthful relationship developing, according to David Punter's logic whereby "myths of human progress, of individuation, of development" are replaced "by the brute facts of the absence of escape". The narrative focus is on Clem and Christian's nascent mutual attraction, desperately attentive but patently misbegotten, which enacts a kind of displaced or delayed erotic charge. Leaving his "massive" head to Olive, and compelled by what she later calls "his habitual air of electric immobility", Clem thrills to the *life* of Christian's face:

---

14 See Elizabeth McMahon's essay in this volume for a more substantial discussion of this figure across Harrower's work.

> Behind this glittering projection of personality, he sat, seeming confident to the very last degree in his fresh youthful skin. Even now, in the third week of our acquaintance, I was still startled by the variety of his tones and expressions. Without a wrinkle of the smooth forehead or the slightest distortion of cheek or jaw, he was recreated constantly, at will. (44)

Christian's face, even broken down into its components (forehead, cheek, jaw, skin, eyes) is the site of his will, and increasingly, of Clem's. It is a point of two-way relay between them. Reflecting on his beauty, she thinks:

> How wrong Jan had been . . . to describe him as some sort of celluloid hero. He seemed the very opposite of all that was implicit and derogatory in the phrase. Watching his face one hazily apprehended that his flesh had intelligence. I realised with the slow and earth-turning sensation of a revelation the difference that existed between that stereotype and this – a face as finely proportioned and outwardly pleasing that possessed the astonishing gift of reflecting thought, transparently, like magic. (84)

Clem here struggles to articulate beauty itself – its life and liveliness, its "intelligence", and its function in the relaying of thought itself. Although this transfer is built around a rejection of the cinematic face, there is nonetheless something here of Norma Desmond's triumphant claim from a decade earlier: "We didn't need dialogue. We had faces".[15] If the energy of Christian's face is beauty itself as a form of thought, it holds out the promise of some new kind of connectedness or transmission between the lovers, predicated on their loss of individual will. Clem observes this in their French lessons:

> Intense concentration made it seem that syntax and vocabulary flowed automatically from my head to his, suffering no loss or confusion. We became complementary machines. A switch had been touched and a current of knowledge passed between us. (200)

There is another instructive comparison here with *Maurice Guest*. Richardson's romance narrative and its central, obsessive relation is configured as a form of *prosopopeia* or face-making, with the hero Maurice repeatedly seen in the highly conventionalised act of gazing at the face of his unresponsive and resistant lover, Louise Dufrayer:

> [H]is thought wandered as he gazed. How he loved it! – this face of hers. He was invariably worked on afresh by the blackness of the lustreless hair; by the pale, imperious mouth; by the dead white pallor of the skin, which shaded to a dusky cream in the curves of neck and throat, and in the lines beneath the eyes, was of a bluish brown. Now the lashes lay in these encircling rings. Without doubt, it was the eyes that supplied life to the face: only when they were open, and the lips parted over the strong teeth, was it possible to realize how intense a vitality was latent in her. (401)

---

15 Norma Desmond, played by Gloria Swanson, in *Sunset Boulevard*, directed by Billy Wilder, Paramount Pictures, 1950.

The trope of *prosopopeia* – literally *poeien* (to make) and *prosopon* (face) – through the art of rhetoric – opens up a fundamental undecidability between subject and object; it works to bring life to something inanimate, as we see in the above passage, and at the same time to sign it with death. *Prosopopeia*'s labour is the labour of representation, of art, and it works in the service of beauty. Louise's face is linked through the trope of beauty to the the face of the hapless Avery Hill, caught in her own obsessive relation to Heinz Krafft, himself bound obsessively to the genius Schilsky, object of Louise's endless desiring. Avery's face speaks to the circuits of desire as the very ground of *prosopopeia*: "Seen like this, it now became evident that this face was one of those which are all along intended for death – intended, that is, to lie waxen and immobile, to show to best advantage" (578). More particularly, *prosopopeia* harnesses the power of speech, of "oratorical performance, of role-playing" to "counterfeit" presence,[16] and in this it draws literary construction alongside theatrical performance into the ambit of metaphor, rendering the achievement, however truthful, to be always a form of deception. Maurice Guest approaches self-knowledge through a final, extended recounting of the details of Louise's face, this time as she sleeps, observing, finally: "This, then, was love? – this morbid possession by a woman's face?" (610). Earlier, he has struggled to find the truth of her being in her face, just as Clem noted "the truth of [Christian's] face" in the form of a declaration: "He was good". So too Maurice, in trying to understand how Louise could contemplate marrying for wealth, wonders:

> [W]as there something in her nature that he could not, would not understand? He denied it fiercely, almost before he had formulated the question: no matter what her actions were, or what words she said, deep down in her was an intense will for good, a spring of noble impulse. It was merely that she had never had a proper chance. But he denied it to a vision of her face: the haunting eyes which, at first sight, had destroyed his peace of mind; the dead black hair against the ivory-coloured skin. It was in these things that the truth lay, not in what she was prompted by impulse to do: these were elemental facts on which he was prepared to stake his faith. (364-5)

Maurice confuses the truth of Louise's face with goodness; the "elemental facts" he discerns there are a form of error, and in this moment it is clear that he has drawn over Louise's face a vision of his own death.

Prosopopeia is at once animating and death-driven. It cannot secure life, despite the hum of Christian's animus and the escalation of Clem's fascination with it. Further, the face of obsessive devotion is a point not only of *propsopopeia* but also of mis- or non-recognition, of *prosopagnosia*: the former constrained by the intimate circles of love; the latter facing or failing a demand of the social world, where self collapses. The two tropes are often twinned: on the one hand, the capacity or compulsion to give a name and face through love's acts of devotion; on the other, the failure to recognise another, or possibly oneself. Narcissus is the point of connection for the two (in falling in love with his own reflection, Narcissus does not recognise that it is his own face). Scott Wilson observes that the poetry of courtly love, that of Dante and Petrarch in particular, oscillates between the two.[17] While *prosopopeia* calls to mind the face of the beloved, it is also highly

---

16 Elizabeth M. Sturgeon, "Prosopopoeia", in *The Literary Encyclopedia*, 14 July 2007, http://bit.ly/2q10Ul9.

conventionalised or generic, and thus elides the beloved's individual specificity in a certain failure of recall. For Wilson:

> [The] fixation on certain isolated aspects of the face [is] both the condition and the means of the production of poetic subjectivity as an effect of the interminable amorous commentary on its own anxiety concerning the desire of the beloved that it generates.[18]

This is precisely the condition of agonised devotion. On the other hand, "the *prosopagnosia* of courtly passion in which a 'discrete number of physical attributes'" – for instance Christian's fragmented body parts, the forehead, cheek, jaw, skin, eyes noted earlier – becomes the focus of rapt attention, yet the face itself "never comes together as a portrait".[19]

Wilson further notes that alongside and bound together with this tradition of face-making and forgetting in erotic poetry is its religious iteration: "Was God's face part of the Creation? God produces himself for himself in an act of divine *prosopopeia*. Behold, I am".[20] In part, Christian embodies just such an act of displaced divinity, in his "electric immobility" (47), with the face of a god. He first appears in the novel as a god, golden, bringing light; that is to say, in his yellow jumper, replacing light bulbs around Clem's boarding house. In this divinity he is bound to the world of electricity, to "the fire-world", which, as Northrop Frye notes in his introduction to Bachelard's *Psychoanalysis of Fire*, "was most significantly the world of heavenly bodies between heaven proper and the earth".[21] Christian's electric divinity and propensities operate under the sign of elemental fire. Bachelard observes that "electrical fire . . . was a sexualized fire. Since it is mysterious, it is clearly sexual. Concerning the idea of friction, of which we have just pointed out the obvious primary sexuality, we shall again find applied to electricity all that we have said about fire".[22] But, Bachelard also reminds us that fire is to be found in the novel's preoccupation with alcohol. He describes alcohol (actually brandy – alcohol in its therapeutic guise, perhaps) as "fire-water", "a water which burns the tongue and flames up at the slightest spark. It does not limit itself to dissolving and destroying as does *aqua fortis*. It disappears with what it burns. It is the communion of life and of fire".[23] Further, "[s]ince brandy burns before our entranced eyes, since, from the pit of the stomach, it radiates heat to the whole person, it affords proof of the convergence of inner experience and objective experiment".[24] Here, I am suggesting, is where we find the animation and energy of this novel – what it offers us, perhaps, in place of a secure and resolved narrative. Clemency's entrancement in the face of Christian is precisely this self-consumption, this meeting of water and fire – Christian changes his yellow jumper for a borrowed blue one at one point (84) – and the irresistible connection that Christian provides between her inner self – the stomach that Clem declines to feed – and his outer light.

---

17 Scott Wilson, "Prosopopeia to Prosopagnosia: Dante on Facebook". In *Glossator: Practice and Theory of the Commentary, Vol. 5: On the Love of Commentary*: 19–56. http://bit.ly/2qRmAfX.
18 Wilson, "Prosopopeia to Prosopagnosia", 29.
19 Wilson, "Prosopopeia to Prosopagnosia", 38.
20 Wilson, "Prosopopeia to Prosopagnosia", 51.
21 Northrop Frye, "Preface", in Gaston Bachelard, *The Psychoanalysis of Fire*, trans. Alan C.M. Ross (Boston: Beacon Press, 1964), vii.
22 Bachelard, *The Psychoanalysis of Fire*, 26.
23 Bachelard, *The Psychoanalysis of Fire*, 83.
24 Bachelard, *The Psychoanalysis of Fire*, 83.

Finally, then, this novel draws on the fire and force of alcohol, which drive passion if not desire, and swing attention wildly away from the paths of health, coherence and stability. In its account of the exigencies of addiction and addicted devotion, this novel strives to imagine the lineaments of art and creativity as well as the costs they exert. To turn again to Bachelard:

> It appears evident that alcohol is a creator of language. It enriches the vocabulary and frees the syntax . . . [It is] the reverie which in the final analysis best prepares us for engaging in rational thought. Bacchus is a beneficent god; by causing our reason to wander he prevents the anchylosis of logic and prepares the way for rational inventiveness.[25]

In other words, fire in the form of alcohol works against stasis, just as clemency opens out judgement. Within the flickering circuits of mid-century modernity, Harrower's protagonists remind us that there is still, or always, the possibility of movement, of flow, of thought itself.

References

Bachelard, Gaston. *The Psychoanalysis of Fire*. Translated by Alan C.M. Ross. Boston: Beacon Press, 1964.
Burns, D.R. "Australian Fiction Since 1960". *World Literature Written in English* 11, no. 2 (1972): 53–63.
Colmer, John. "Elizabeth Harrower". Brief Biographies. http://bit.ly/2pbfrXA.
Davidson, Carol Margaret. "The Gothic and Addiction: A Mad Tango". *Gothic Studies* 11, no. 2 (2009): 1–8.
Davis, Lennard. *Obsession: A History*. Chicago: University of Chicago Press, 2009.
Harrower, Elizabeth. *The Catherine Wheel*. (1960) Melbourne: Text Publishing, 2014.
Hellman, Matilda and Varpu Rantala. "Codependence, Madness and Glamour: Narratives of Women Celebrity Addicts in Internet Tabloids". In *Cultures of Addiction*. Edited by Jason Lee, 175–206. New York: Cambria Press, 2012.
Lee, Jason. "Introduction". In *Cultures of Addiction*. Edited by Jason Lee. New York: Cambria Press, 2012.
McMahon, Elizabeth. "Moments of Being in the Fiction of Elizabeth Harrower". In *Elizabeth Harrower: Critical Essays*. Edited by Elizabeth McMahon and Brigitta Olubas, 133–143. Sydney: Sydney University Press, 2017.
Punter, David. "William Burroughs: The Scene of Addiction". *Gothic Studies* 11, no. 2 (2009): 74–82.
Richardson, Henry Handel. *Maurice Guest*. (1908) Melbourne: Text Publishing, 2012.
Rooney, Brigid. "'White, fierce, shocked, tearless': *The Watch Tower* and the Electric Interior". In *Elizabeth Harrower: Critical Essays*. Edited by Elizabeth McMahon and Brigitta Olubas, 81–95. Sydney: Sydney University Press, 2017.
Roth, Marty. *Drunk the Night Before: An Anatomy of Intoxication*. Minneapolis: University of Minnesota Press, 2005.
Sarat, Austin and Nasser Hussain. *Forgiveness, Mercy, and Clemency*. Palo Alto, CA: Stanford University Press, 2007.
Sturgeon, Elizabeth M. "Prosopopoeia". In *The Literary Encyclopedia*. 14 July 2007. http://bit.ly/2q10Ul9.
Wilder, Billy, director. *Sunset Boulevard*. Paramount Pictures, 1950.
Wilson, Scott. "Prosopopeia to Prosopagnosia: Dante on Facebook". In *Glossator: Practice and Theory of the Commentary, Volume 5: On the Love of Commentary*: 23–56. http://bit.ly/2qRmAfX.

---

25   Bachelard, *The Psychoanalysis of Fire*, 87.

10
Projecting the Sixties: Mediation and Characterology in *The Catherine Wheel*

Julian Murphet

One of the indelible moving images of the postwar era is Marlon Brando's screen-and-T-shirt-ripping realisation of Stanley Kowalski in the screen version of Elia Kazan's *A Streetcar Named Desire*, in 1951.[1] It is worth dwelling for a moment on that date, because there is something extraordinary and almost uncanny about it. This is a film whose visual style (noir-ish chiaroscuro and heavy set design) associates it with the late 1940s, but whose acting style lifts it into the 1950s thanks to Karl Malden and Kim Hunter, both engaged in a new naturalism cribbed from Stella Adler. But then, on top of that palimpsest, another layer is added: for somehow, Brando's performance belongs neither to the 1940s nor the 1950s, but is projected ahead into the future, and – in its hulking, electric, infantile combustibility – manages to incarnate something essential and true about the 1960s to come. And this is an anomaly that cannot be said to inhere in Tennessee Williams' play text either, since it only emerged, fully fledged on the New York stage, through Brando's muscular interpretation of the role, which shocked Williams and turned audiences into unwitting supporters of a character that he had intended mainly as an unsympathetic brute.

What I want to draw from the paradoxical *contretemps* between this iconic screen image and the play text in which it originated is the general observation that certain aesthetic elements inherent to a work of art seem to be "projected" out beyond their immediate historical coordinates and into a speculative future – they somehow manage to deform the "natural" continuum of history in which they take root and anticipate results merely latent on the sociological horizon. This under-theorised, future-oriented dimension of aesthetic texts is something I take to be equally indispensable in understanding Elizabeth Harrower's second novel, *The Catherine Wheel* (1960), that emotionally grim London book about a very ill-advised love affair between an Australian student abroad and a moody charismatic British man about four years her senior. And this not only because of the way that Christian Roland (his name plucked straight from the wellsprings of romance) is presented to us: he too, climactically, is to be found yelling "Stella! Stella!" (to his absent dead sister),[2] wearing a wife-beater, being compared with "something from Hollywood . . . one of the Method boys

---

1   Elia Kazan, director, *A Streetcar Named Desire*, Warner Brothers, 1951.
2   Elizabeth Harrower, *The Catherine Wheel* (1960; Melbourne: Text Publishing, 2014), 299. All subsequent references are to this edition and appear in parentheses in the text.

from the New York Theatre Workshop" (31), and even explicitly to "Marlon Brando" himself (32). This dangerously attractive, animalistic character is sprung, it would seem, direct from the silver screen, into a novel that doesn't quite know what to do with him, for the simple reason that he doesn't properly fit the novel as a form. Christian is not a creature of the book; he nonchalantly "borrows" a library book from Clem, our narrator (198), and at one point even reads a bit of Villon to her (288–9), but it's all acting, stagecraft, a matter of props, vocalisation and prefabricated gestures. Inasmuch as he has, in fact, been "projected" laterally from a media ecology that has already outstripped many of the formal resources of the novel for refracting contemporaneity, Christian is therefore doubly a cipher of the coming future, of the "1960s-to-come". Just as Brando's cinematic Stanley Kowalski belongs neither to the war-torn decade that precipitated his writing nor to the nascent Cold War decade that undergirded his initial staging, Harrower's Kowalski wannabe Christian Roland belongs neither to the venerable romance forms that furnish his name nor the novel form in which he appears to be positioned, but to a speculative cultural future woven of electronics, mass mediation, and an utterly transformed public sphere – to "the 1960s" as an idea that can only be articulated as a tissue of textual incongruities and formal lapses, projected on the basis of a deliberately courted aesthetic failure, which is what *The Catherine Wheel* assuredly is.

The Catherine Wheel elaborates a pattern of generic interference and with it an openly inconsistent character system – a characterology – with strong allegorical overtones. Specifically, it pits the standard marriage plot of inter- and postwar British fiction (a range of suitors, one of whom must be chosen by the eligible and available narrator) against an emergent form associated with the "Kitchen Sink" school of playwrights and novelists and which generally involves the threat of pregnancy across class lines in the context of proletarian "embourgeoisement" in the 1950s. And within this space of generic torsion, Harrower constructs a range of fairly standard "novelistic" characters (their names are Helen, Bertrand and Lewis, and with them the background people: Rollo, Jan, Miss Evans, Lucy Turner and so on), against which to feel more starkly the anomaly of this ill-fitting and unstable construct "Christian Roland", who on first inspection belongs to the "Kitchen Sink" order of things, but even more tellingly is presented to us through a thick representational filter of media technologies, all powered by that underlying grid of electricity that Brigid Rooney has clarified elsewhere in this volume.[3] And this is done in order that the "narrating instance" of Clemency James can transcend the tired role cast for her by the marriage plot (as deliberator among suitors) and make a final determination of an altogether more striking kind; namely, to use the electrified "Kitchen Sink" lure as an excuse for rejecting the snares of novelism altogether. That is, by pursuing the inconsistent objective of Christian Roland, Clem in fact liberates herself not only from the marriage plot, but from all novelistic plots, and commits herself to a future grasped in the key of media other than the novel. In other words, I am suggesting that this novel is above all about its own status as a novel, since it is probing the very conditions of possibility of a novelistic voice in a social situation where radio, tape recording, telephony, television and the cinema are jamming the standard literary signals and generating entirely new scenes and images out of energies that baffle the narrative voice. The voice is pulled towards them in a manner that, I want to end by suggesting, adumbrates a new decade, a "1960s-to-come", which waxes apocalyptic for the institution of the novel itself.

---

3   See Brigid Rooney, "'White, fierce, shocked, tearless': *The Watch Tower* and Harrower's Electric Interiors", this volume.

10 Projecting the Sixties: Mediation and Characterology in *The Catherine Wheel*

Electronic Village

But first to establish that Christian Roland is less a literary character than a loosely assembled media construction projected into Clem's two rooms by the power of electrical circuitry. (He is not, we should now admit, a creature of celluloid after all, since he has to "affect an interest in the movie camera given him by Mrs Carruthers" (316); no doubt, insofar as *A Streetcar Named Desire* circulates in the media ecology of late-1950s London, it does so as a television broadcast first and foremost.) It is fitting that, in a novel whose opening sentence confounds the very orders of nature and the media – "The wind from Siberia as announced by the BBC came down Bayswater Road . . ." (3) – Christian should never be too far from the soundtrack provided him by the ubiquitous wireless sets of postwar London. Indeed, he actively seeks this soundtrack for his sexual exploits, as when during an early tryst he insists: "'It needs music too', he continued, starting to look about for the wireless. It was beside him, under the table. He found a record programme and, fumbling with the knob, turned it low" (158). Fumbling with his knob indeed. During his first serious assault on Clem's honour we read: "At this moment, by some freak of electricity, the wireless croaked as if clearing its throat and the volume rose" (161). Of course it did: the radio is a pivotal element of the electronic media system that Christian incarnates. That its electromagnetic surges and croaks should be cued to his playbook as a seducer is scarcely surprising; "freaks of electricity" both, the radio and Christian enjoy an ontological resonance that makes for mystifying coincidences in the novelistic plot. Even his faultless impersonations of others are routed through a cognate medium: "As if he were a tape-recorder, he mimicked the artless contributions of typist, manager and drivers . . ." (159). Such similes bear disproportionate semantic weight in a novelistic discourse characterised by a sense of defensive brittleness before the new media onslaught. Christian's paranoid suspicions, too, take an electronic bent. In a late scene, after a disburdening of Christian's accumulated guilt, Clem finds herself "finger[ing] the little white knob of the electricity switch" (286), as if trying to turn him off. His reaction clinches the extent to which his very imagination is distributed across an electronic domain:

> "I suppose you haven't got someone planted in the cupboard?" he looked up . . . very cagily. "Hearing all this? Or a tape recorder." (286)

It's above all on the telephone, of course, that Christian develops his unique fascination for Clemency: the crucial stage of his effective seduction of her is coterminous with the period they spend physically separated, during which they can only converse by phone. His purely electronic presence as a disembodied telephone voice is what triggers her deepest desire for him. "The telephone became my master. Between morning and midnight it was suddenly customary for Christian to ring me every few hours. The calls came like despatches from the front, and like an editor I lived for the telephone and the news. Every absence from the room was an emergency . . ." (142-3).[4] And what does the telephone yield in the way of an acousmatic voice? Something uniquely liberated

---

4 See Michel Chion, *The Voice in Cinema*, trans. Claudia Gorbman (New York: Columbia University Press, 1999).

from the ambiguities and equivocations of literary discourse: "His pronouncements came without a glimmer of doubt. He spoke with a warm impetus, in a way that was quite marvelous. None of the think-thinking, the 'ifs' and 'buts', the alternatives and consequences, that went on in my head and most of the heads I knew" (143-4) – which is to say, in the heads of novelistic people, round characters, liberal educated "selves". Christian, not being much of a self, thrives on a post-novelistic discourse of disposable sincerity. Exposure to it over any length of time engenders a useful new parrying technique, something Clem describes as a "looser, vaguer weapon" than adherence to the laws of gender (never argue, never judge): "the kind of mental passive resistance movement I had improvised during the long days and nights when we'd had telephone communication only" (191). Nevertheless, its apodictic flow, its steady "warm impetus", is increasingly addictive. Unplugging from it amounts to a kind of withdrawal. "*Was that the upstairs telephone?* I listened with electric attention to that distant perfect double-ringing of the telephone" (150-1). Clem thinks she hears it while sitting down to watch television with the rest of the house – that newest medium with which she has already learned to identify something intimate about Christian, who has related (fantastically) a job opportunity "with a television company. 'The electronics side,' said Christian . . . 'The money's good in electronics'" (146), about which Clem herself must confess complete ignorance, as must Christian too in his sobriety. But the link is forged – Christian, electronics, television. And his vision of the future is televisual, too: "In New York I'll break into television. They'll love my accent there" (247).

With enough of this sort of electric current mediating between Chris and Clem, we are not surprised to read that, eventually, their relations attain to the mystical status of perfect transparency: "Intense concentration made it seem that syntax and vocabulary flowed automatically from my head to his, suffering no loss or confusion. We became complementary machines. A switch had been touched and a current of knowledge passed between us" (200). John Durham Peters' history of the idea of communication plays insistently with this pervasive fantasy of transparency, which tends to come into increasing definition and focus around moments of media revolution.[5] What is particularly interesting here is that the intimate space of electric circuitry effectively transcends the ambiguous articulations and separations enforced by syntax and grammar. What is more, we are in a well-nigh computational space here, with these two perfect, digital "complementary machines" hooked up wirelessly to allow a communicational utopia of noise-free, post-literary intercourse.

It is from the post-human vantage point offered by this accord between our narrator and the new-media palimpsest of Christian Roland that the older, "novelistic" characters like Lewis begin to seem more or less redundant in a mediatic sense. Listening to Lewis being particularly informative one night, in a bookish sense, Clem reflects:

> Once I might have been enthralled; now, dully, without reverberation, the words and phrases dropped dead in my mind. I asked no questions, but Lewis, his eyes fixed thoughtfully in space, made point after point in his lucid unselfconscious style, reasoning, contending, convincing, unaware that his expressions were not mirrored in

---

5   See John Durham Peters, *Speaking into the Air: A History of the Idea of Communication* (Chicago: University of Chicago Press, 1999).

my face, unaware of any impression he might be making, conscious of himself for the moment as no more than a transmitter of ideas. (204)

Lewis has not learned the great and paradigmatic lesson of the 1960s to come, a lesson that Christian seems already to have intuited in his every gesture: *the medium is the message*.[6] What so fascinates Clem about Christian is his living, breathing incarnation of this principle. Lewis, on the other hand, is all message without a living medium; his is the dead medium of literature, of books and journals and reports now made obsolete by the light-speed flow of electrons and the BBC Light Programme. Lewis has a position on these new media, of course, as he tries to communicate to her:

"- mass entertainments on the working-class mind," he was saying.
    Mass entertainments on the working-class mind, my head echoed, unintelligibly, and closed down.
    "Yes," I said, trying not to seem as glazed as I felt, "It does sound - er -"
    The phone rang (241)

Of course, the phone call is from Olive, Christian's long-suffering paramour, with some news about Christian. Clem's distraction reads as a media interference pattern. Literary intelligence fails to transmit its judgements and opinions in an atmosphere electrified by radio and telephone. The sentiments and affects have been colonised by these new media forces, leaving the attention to drift across the stolid mass of literary data like dust over Miss Havisham's dining table. Meanwhile, Clem's other suitor is equally censorious and alarmist about the new electronic village. "Bertrand had completed a prodigious research project and was tonight to address a student organization on some such subject as 'Advertising, Television and Youth'" (292), just to underscore the opposition being suggested here.

As against these clean, boring novelistic channels of literary information, Christian has the glamour of a rude savage pieced together like a collage by electronic alchemy; he is a babble of the mediatic multitude. "The rapid bated changes of mood, expression and tone, the enormous confusion of voices and emotion gave the nightmarish effect of twelve stricken men arguing out some mysterious and tragic event in their common past" (295). Deleuzian schizophrenia? Perhaps. But again: the medium *is* the message. Clem has no idea *what* he is saying: but *that* he is saying it, as a polyphony of channels all switched on at once, *is* (in effect) *what* he is saying. And it is irresistible. His is a speech beyond speech, red-shifted by alcohol into the society of the spectacle: "Nothing intelligible, no single word. Yet up and down went the tone of the noises, small animal noises, a travesty of speech" (299). You can't turn away, can't turn it off. And so it begins, inevitably, shouting "Stella! Stella!" (299). "Christian had just hauled off his white T-shirt and was washing his face with the ineptitude of a four-year-old" (301). Back on the right channel again, the signals can clarify. Christian is less a person or literary character than he is a spontaneous effusion of the electronic village's "Niagara of [audio-]visual gabble", as Robert Hughes once put it.[7] If David Bowie's character in *The Man Who Fell to Earth*

---

6   Marshall McLuhan, *Understanding Media: The Extensions of Man* (New York: Mentor, 1964), 1.
7   Robert Hughes, *The Spectacle of Skill: New and Selected Writings of Robert Hughes* (New York: Knopf, 2015), 88.

entertained himself by watching an array of a dozen TV sets at once, then Christian Roland is the composite figure distilled out of such multi-channel entertainment, a "travesty of speech" that eventually coheres into an avatar of televisuality.

Demographies of the Post-imperium

Radio, telephone, tape-recorder, television: Christian is presented via this quadrilateral image of the electronic village. In a way, he is born for it, this son of a successful tenor recording star and a "small-time actress of no great talent but enormous ambition" (95) with a slew of little pink pills – but the novel doesn't particularly ask us to psychoanalyse or trace a complex genealogy for this sum of all contradictions. Rather, it leaves us to speculate on its function in the present, which I am now peremptorily going to characterise as a "masking" device for something else lurking ominously in the novelistic discourse's rear-view mirror. And that lurking thing is, concisely stated, *other people*. Not "other people" in the strictly limited existential sense elaborated by postwar French philosophical discourse, but in the world-historical sense made actual by the global wave of anti-imperial liberation movements that began in the late 1940s and consolidated itself heroically across the 1950s:

> The independence of Ghana (1957), the agony of the Congo (Lumumba was murdered in January 1961), the independence of France's sub-Saharan colonies following the Gaullist referendum on 1959, finally the Algerian Revolution [1957-1962] – all of these signal the convulsive birth of what will come in time to be known as the 60s:
>> Not so very long ago, the earth numbered two thousand million inhabitants: five hundred million *men* and one thousand five hundred million *natives*. The former had the Word; the others merely had the use of it.
>
> The 60s was the period when all these "natives" became human beings, and this internally as well as externally: those inner colonized of the First World - "minorities," marginals, and women – fully as much as its external subjects and official "natives."[8]

On this narrative, then, the emergence of so many novel "subjects of history" in the postwar era, stimulated by the waves of decolonisation and subsequent migrations, signals an irreversible rise in the tide of human "otherness" that the paradigmatic Western subject is henceforth obliged to recognise, name and hail. It is a question of the transformation of the very existential horizon of being-in-the-world, a momentous reconfiguration of the textures and sensory impressions – let alone of the names that will identify and classify these latter – of everyday life itself.

> We need to explore the possibility that there exists, in what quaintly used to be called the moral realm, something roughly equivalent to the dizziness of crowds for the individual body itself: the premonition that the more other people we recognize, even within the

---

8   Fredric Jameson, "Periodizing the 60s", in *The Ideologies of Theory: Vol. 2, The Syntax of History* (London: Routledge, 1988), 180–1. The indented quotation is from Sartre's preface to Fanon's *Wretched of the Earth*.

mind, the more peculiarly precarious becomes the status of our own hitherto unique and "incomparable" consciousness or "self."[9]

Which is as much to say, of course, that there exists a fundamental parallelism or historical analogy between the kind of psychic fragmentation and dispersal that we noted above for the logic of electronic mediation, and these new demographic crises of perception and interpellation in the postwar period. At risk, here in this unprecedented welter of migratory folkways and representations, is nothing less than the very integrity of the traditional bourgeois ego itself, whose stabilisation and reproduction it had been one of the primary ideological functions of the novel as a form to vouchsafe.

But at one critical level this demographic revolution was always and already a matter of media as well: the "emergence of new subjects . . . new people, 'others' who were somehow not even there before"[10] is very much a media development in its own right, since it depends upon the registration in our collective, Western consciousness of available images, stereotypes, names, representatives that have become current in the late-modern mass-mediated "public sphere". And with this complex dialectic of political self-representation and subsumption within the evolving mechanisms of corporate and state media institutions, all the old postmodern anxieties about "authenticity" and "co-optation" invariably rear their heads: to the degree that a "people", "minority" or "group" is established as a recognisable imago or figure within the semiotics of electronic mediation (in the daily news cycles, on sit-coms, in an evening's documentary, or what have you), so too is its material basis in the structure of daily life progressively abstracted and transmuted into a mere token of value specific to "spectacle" or image society as such. The referential reality of "Jamaican migrants" or "South African émigrés" recedes behind the circulating media avatars of those types; Baudrillard's simulacrum extends its empire.

At any rate, it is just this burgeoning of an ill-defined new public sphere that we detect in *The Catherine Wheel* in so many passing glimpses and lateral visions: Clem herself, of course, the archetypal colonial girl looking to accrue the cultural and educational capital of a London legal education; the "race riots at Notting Hill" (12) through which Chris has to escort Miss Evans early on; or the character of Lewis, who works for "an international welfare organization", "sent on occasional missions to the east" (25), and himself sends "working-parties to help underdeveloped countries" (122), meanwhile speaking on "the Real Challenge to the West" (335) or "talking on the crisis threatening in Africa" (27) (referred to on several occasions), or is found "wrangling" with his sister "over – of all things! – the United States' strategy during the latest crisis" (122) and to whom, to express the depth of her alienation from him, Clem blurts out "'It's like Suez!'" (207); or for that matter Bertrand himself, who whispers this telling mantra to shame Clem's apostasy from middle-class imperial liberalism: "The Middle East. The Middle East" (123); or the racist landlady Lucy Turner who mutters, "'[O]f course in a place like this I meet all kinds – foreigners, all sorts. Often enough we don't know ten words of a common language . . .'" (151). Foreigners like the African student Johnny Matowen whom Christian convinces his landlady to accept as a tenant (145), or the nice young Indian boy who briefly occupies the room next door to Clem's, and who laterally smuggles into the text its overt philosophical

---

9 Fredric Jameson, *Postmodernism, or, the Cultural Logic of Late Capitalism* (London: Verso, 1991), 358.
10 Jameson, *Postmodernism*, 357.

statement on Satyagraha, Gandhi's doctrine of non-violent resistance which broke the back of Empire in the 1940s and seems to be Clem's spontaneous ethical position (271; 308). And you don't really get more "sixties" than that: middle-class white girls embracing Eastern philosophemes to register their moral difference from the status quo.

Finally, to be sure, all of this comes to bear on the awkwardly hovering marriage plot itself, which is immanently undone, not by the intrinsic unworthiness of the suitors, but by this incandescent explosion of Otherness the world over, the demographic revolution that looms in the liberal collective unconscious as a kind of reproductive prophylactic: "'The world's over-populated. I hate crowds. There are plenty of people'" (277-8) she tells Chris when he suggests having children. "'I've got a social conscience. Children now are self-indulgence'" (278). Clem's epochal misgivings over the reproductive cycle, backed up by a nascent discourse of "overpopulation" and a dimly recycled Malthusianism, mark the intrusion of a crowded geopolitical unconscious into the immemorial plot mechanics of heterosexual coupling and comic resolution. This unique historical interference between two orders of textual productivity – between the obsolete generic matrix and the emergent ideologemes that mark the text's contemporaneity – stymies the flow of narrative energies and creates a certain ideological impedance.

My sense is that all of this signals a radically novel structure of feeling, one that the novel as a form has never had to internalise before, never before had to integrate into its aesthetic substance. This explosion of people, of sheer human numbers, in any number of new national, ethnic, religious, sexual and gendered forms, jostles the residual liberal humanism of the form's "national" ideological bedrock; just as the explosion of new electronic media contest the novel's moral hegemony as a social institution. Over the decade after the publication of *The Catherine Wheel*, something called "postmodernism" would gradually have to be invented to take cognisance of this alarming double-flanked assault on the waning legitimacy of the novel as a form; but on the cusp of this transition, we are looking not for clear and determinate positions or revolutionary new aesthetics. Rather, what we tend to find are awkwardly allegorical forms, raising the constitutive contradictions implicit in the historical situation into manageable representative shapes. So it is that, in Harrower's London novel, the mercurial Christian is set off against the redoubtable, dull, rounded characters, to demonstrate his spontaneous commensurability with a world fast changing beyond recognition. And as a native inhabitant of the electronic media – associated with them via an inexorable web of insistent figurations – he also takes a markedly different approach to the new world's rising tides of Otherness. While Lewis and Bertrand take the high road of elitist humanitarianism, Christian embraces the populist manner of his coming moment in a more intimate fashion.

This is not to say that he doesn't have a politics, but inasmuch as he does, it is decidedly a politics of the image, and not of the substantive educated views cultivated by his rivals. "No wholesome sense, no liberal attitude, was ever new to him" we read (145). We learn about "his disapproval of racial discrimination, anti-Semitism, and signs of neo-McCarthyism", all supported "with anecdotes that proved his good faith" (145), such as the story of his African friend Johnny Matowen: "very black, Christian said, as if that made it somehow much better" (145). Christian is the incarnation of a coming type: the post-imperial "beautiful soul", enamoured of his own capacity to "love his neighbor" whatever his colour, and willing at all times to advertise this capability. But therein lies the rub: the incessant PR campaign betrays the will to power implicit in all this leftier-than-thou posturing. At its back there lurks the suggestion of total indifference: "Behind his almost over-readiness to sympathize with the oppressed I sensed a sort of fundamental derision of the attitude he'd chosen to adopt" (145). These protestations of exquisite sensitivity are quintessentially a politics of the image, of being perceived to be "right on" rather than having to transform any aspect of one's own existence. And it is with the politics of the image that the immense demographic and political revolutions of the postwar era would inevitably come to be managed, not as a reason to reconstruct the edifice of social relations, but as a glib discourse of rights behind which lurked a darker sentiment.

In his remarkable 1973 audiovisual text called *Télévision*, and disseminated first of all on that medium, Jacques Lacan reflected on the inexorable "rise of racism" in postwar societies in this way:

> with our puissance going off the track, only the Other is able to mark its position, but only insofar as we are separated from this Other. Whence certain fantasies – unheard of before the melting pot. Leaving this Other to his own mode of jouissance, that would only be possible by not imposing our own on him, by not thinking of him as underdeveloped . . . [H]ow can one hope that the empty forms of humanhysterianism [humanitairerie] disguising our extortions can continue to last?[11]

That is to say: the historic humanitarianism of the immediate postwar period – achieving its ultimate expression in the Universal Declaration of Human Rights (10 December 1948) – cannot truly survive the seismic demographic and migratory events of decolonisation that are coeval with it. Our Western "mode of *jouissance*" must revert necessarily to extreme racism, albeit masked behind a mediatised screen of diplomatic political correctness. Christian Roland, packaged for us in the telltale vestments of the electronic media – a projection of the TV screen – is precisely that mode of *jouissance*, his inveterate narcissism a screen on which the rise of racism can be played off against "sincere" protestations of its contrary.

From this vantage point, we can see the investment of the "rounded" liberal characters like Helen, Lewis and Bertrand in liberal humanism as so much empty "humanhysterianism", staving off the inevitable backlash. Christian Roland, on the other hand, is a brilliant fetish, a fascinating masking device in which both the panoply of new electronic media and the new racism detonated by the demographic revolution can somehow be both concentrated and forgotten about. He serves a tremendously useful purpose, then, in two directions at once, and allows the novel to go about its real business, which is precisely allowing itself to be tempted by this fetish, to be divided against its native home base in the calm, comfortable monotony of the Oxford gang, by going in for the newer solicitations and alarms of the dawning era. Where this contest is properly tested is not so much in the nature of Clem's "decision" (in a way the decision is made for her by the trump card of Kitchen Sink charismatics), but in the quality of her voice as a narrator throughout. And here I cannot help submitting the view that Clemency James is one of the more impossible narrators in the tradition; signally devoid of any interest in sustained self-reflection; rushing to precipitous judgements and outrageously wounded feelings; immediately overturning those affects in the form of their opposites; brittle in mood as she is syrupy in sentiment, despite her superegoic rigour; cold, alienated, but then

---

11 Jacques Lacan, *Television: A Challenge to the Psychoanalytic Establishment*, ed. Joan Copjec, trans. Denis Hollier, Rosalind Kraus and Annette Michelson (New York: W.W. Norton, 1990), 32–3.

suddenly elated, oceanic, brimming. The one thing it seems correct to conclude about her voice is that it is properly schizophrenic, but in such a way as to highlight one quality above all: it is beyond good and evil. It thinks without a moral compass. Rather, its reactions are aesthetic, not moralistic, as when she presents her situation to herself as follows:

> Jealous woman throws open the door unexpectedly on love and other woman in heavy embrace! Really! It was too melodramatic, too unsophisticated, for my taste. (164)
>
> What had I to do with people who were hit on the head with pokers, who half-throttled other people to defend themselves, and rushed out of houses clutching rolls of money belonging to someone else? (172)

This quality of voice is tremendously generative and formally useful, and it is a qualitative leap out of the lumbering ethical narratological circuits of 1950s fiction, into a brave new world where, as she insists, "If someone chose to drop a bomb we could be something less than dust tomorrow" (250).

And what is the allegorical significance of Clem's conclusion? It is better to choose the ephemeral electronic matrix than to be "a snug Insider" (255) of the 1950s, with "[a] worthy career and a reasonably high standard of living", like her sober novelistic friends (265).

> I was alive, and the way was ahead, and unsupported I would have to stand and walk. I was too tired, too old, to have to grow up any further [she is still twenty-six]. Was there no end to it? Why pick on me? The world was full of infantile adults. I knew a thousand not enrolled for kindergarten yet. (323)

And here we are left, on the threshold of a new decade when that generation of infantile Baby Boomers will gradually assume dominance, shopping, channel surfing, bleating about their egos, filtering the rest of the world through a few serviceable stereotypes, fucking out of wedlock, and now and then suddenly being gripped by a cause. "Why pick on me?" It is the 1960s, the 1950s are over, and Clem, a narrator uniquely uninterested in her own interiority, is there to switch on the flashlight, walk us down the aisle and let us take our seats in the gathering dark. The movie is about to begin.

References

Chion, Michel. *The Voice in Cinema*. Translated by Claudia Gorbman. New York: Columbia University Press, 1999.
Harrower, Elizabeth. *The Catherine Wheel*. (1960) Melbourne: Text Publishing, 2014.
Hughes, Robert. *The Spectacle of Skill: New and Selected Writings of Robert Hughes*. New York: Knopf, 2015.
Jameson, Fredric. "Periodizing the 60s". In *The Ideologies of Theory: Volume 2, The Syntax of History*. London: Routledge, 1988.
———. *Postmodernism, or, the Cultural Logic of Late Capitalism*. London: Verso, 1991.
Kazan, Elia, dir. *A Streetcar Named Desire*. Warner Brothers, 1951.
Lacan, Jacques. *Television: A Challenge to the Psychoanalytic Establishment*. Edited by Joan Copjec. Translated by Denis Hollier, Rosalind Kraus and Annette Michelson. New York: W.W. Norton, 1990.

McLuhan, Marshall. *Understanding Media: The Extensions of Man*. New York: Mentor, 1964.
Peters, John Durham. *Speaking into the Air: A History of the Idea of Communication*. Chicago: University of Chicago Press, 1999.
Rooney, Brigid. "'White, fierce, shocked, tearless': *The Watch Tower* and Harrower's Electric Interiors". In *Elizabeth Harrower: Critical Essays*. Edited by Elizabeth McMahon and Brigitta Olubas, 81–95. Sydney: Sydney University Press, 2017.

11
Traversing "the same extreme country" in *The Watch Tower* and *Daniel Deronda*

Megan Nash

Over the course of 1961, the *New Yorker* published Hannah Arendt's reports on the trial of Nazi war criminal Adolf Eichmann. Her articles would give rise to a controversy in which Arendt would lose friends, as well as the support of many in the Jewish community. They also gave rise to one of the most significant philosophical concepts to emerge in the aftermath of the Holocaust: the idea of the banality of evil. Arendt painted a picture of Eichmann as a bureaucrat and a follower, who committed atrocities not out of ideology or hatred, but rather through a pronounced inability to think for himself. She writes,

> [I]t would have been very comforting indeed to believe that Eichmann was a monster, even though if he had been Israel's case against him would have collapsed or, at the very least, lost all interest. Surely, one can hardly call upon the whole world and gather correspondents from the four corners of the earth in order to display Bluebeard in the dock. The trouble with Eichmann was precisely that so many were like him, and that the many were neither perverted nor sadistic, that they were and still are, terribly and terrifyingly normal.[1]

When faced with Eichmann's actions, the more "comforting" alternative in Arendt's estimation is to picture him as a fabled villain like Bluebeard. And yet, she suggests, this prospect was belied by the unsettling reality that he was in fact quite normal.

Five years after the publication of these reports, Elizabeth Harrower would release her novel *The Watch Tower* (1966), where – knowingly or not – she would explore Arendt's provocative concept. Max Harris traces Harrower's interest in this theme back to her first two novels *Down in the City* (1957) and *The Long Prospect* (1958), where, he suggests, she delves into "the evil in the ordinary, the destructive seeds within the average mind" or "the Australian norm".[2] But there is a peculiar resonance between Arendt's description of Eichmann and Harrower's depiction of Felix Shaw from *The Watch Tower*, a tyrannical husband who dominates the lives of his wife Laura Vaizey and her younger sister Clare. Like Arendt, Harrower presents her reader with the "comforting" possibility that Felix

---

1 Hannah Arendt, *Eichmann in Jerusalem: A Report on the Banality of Evil* (New York: Viking Press, 1963), 129.
2 Max Harris, "The Novels of Elizabeth Harrower," *Australian Letters*, vol. 4 no. 2 (1962), 18.

might be a Bluebeard – at one point he is even given a china statuette of this wife-murdering villain. While a number of commentators have consequently understood his character as an "embodiment of total, inexplicable evil",[3] this may be to overlook what is most disturbing about him, for in many ways Felix – like Eichmann – is "terribly and terrifyingly normal". There is certainly a strong sense of banality about him; his acts of evil are not grandiose, but tend towards the small-minded, the petty and materialistic. As R.G. Geering notes, "the kind of business [sic] Felix goes into are, significantly, trivial – making boxes, chocolates, artificial flowers".[4] Even though Felix's evil is tied to his mundaneness, it is in no way mitigated by it; taking Arendt's lead in her representation of the banality of evil, Harrower refuses to diminish either term by the association.[5]

Deidre Coleman notes that this depiction of Felix finds a precedent in the poetry of Sylvia Plath. She suggests that his characterisation is reminiscent of the male figures in poems like "Daddy" and "Lady Lazarus", published in Plath's posthumous collection *Ariel* (1965). In these texts "the speaking voice is that of the woman-as-Jew, victim of the holocaust [sic] and of a Nazi father-husband figure".[6] In *The Watch Tower* the narrator actually refers to Felix's personal admiration for Adolph Hitler (59), and so it is no great leap for the reader to position him as the "Nazi husband figure" Coleman describes. It is a comparison that speaks to the troubling imbalance of power that can exist within heterosexual relationships. Indeed, Plath's famous assertion from "Daddy", that "every woman adores a fascist", seems to capture something of the way Harrower's female protagonists are often unaccountably drawn to insecure and domineering men.[7] By contemplating this kind of tyranny within intimate relationships, and in looking at the evil that pervades everyday life, Harrower follows Plath and Arendt into contentious but productive territory with her novel.

Due to the oppressive power wielded by characters like Felix, and to the fact that Harrower's novels tend to depict only a handful of characters in a confined setting, her works are known and admired for their claustrophobic intensity. This propensity of her fiction is generally aligned with her public perception as an author. While Harrower lived in England for several years, and produced a London novel in the form of *The Catherine Wheel* (1960), she has not been viewed as cosmopolitan in the manner of her near contemporaries Christina Stead or Shirley Hazzard. Commentary on her novels has, in consequence, been relatively unconcerned with their transnational trajectories. However, Harrower's most recent work, the much belated *In Certain Circles* (2014), offers something of a departure from the confinement of her earlier novels, broadening their tight focus to open gaps in the space and time of the narrative. *In Certain Circles* is a text that serves to elucidate some of the important preoccupations and patterns of Harrower's previous fiction, and this departure from form calls attention to the fact that certain expansive, global concerns were always already at work in her novels. They are apparent, as

---

3   Laurie Clancy, "Fathers and Lovers: Three Australian Novels," *Australian Literary Studies*, vol. 10, no. 4 (1982), 463.
4   R.G. Geering, *Recent Fiction* (Melbourne: Oxford University Press, 1974), 144.
5   Elizabeth McMahon to Megan Nash, 2 June 2017.
6   Deirdre Coleman, "*The Watch Tower*: Bluebeard's Castle," in *(Un)common Ground: Essays in Literature in English*, eds. Andrew Taylor and Russell McDougall (Adelaide: Centre for Research in the New Literatures in English, 1990), 104.
7   Nicholas Birns to Megan Nash, 4 December 2015. See Syvia Plath," Daddy" in *Collected Poems*, (New York: HarperPerennial 2008), 222.

suggested above, in the way she has imbued Felix's character with meaning derived from the international crisis of the Holocaust. The aim here is to further consider how *The Watch Tower* is oriented with respect to the world outside its stifling suburban living rooms, and how it negotiates the relationship between these disparate spheres.

In the preceding chapter of this volume Julian Murphet argues that throughout *The Catherine Wheel* Harrower runs a "generic interference", one that pits the characters and conventions of different genres against each other.[8] Taking Murphet's lead, I would suggest that in *The Watch Tower* Harrower's approach to the relationship between the personal and the global is characterised by a kind of "rhetorical interference", one in which she is frequently shifting the terms of her discourse. The various models and rhetorical devices Harrower employs to negotiate this relationship sometimes work at cross-purposes, and often refuse to enforce a certain meaning or interpretation. Key among these devices is the associational grammar of parataxis, something she deploys extensively at the level of both sentence and structure. At other points she navigates the relationship between the two spheres by posing questions of scale, by accessing a cultural reservoir of traumatic imagery, or by drawing on literary models and antecedents. Harrower's shifting discourse appears to underlie her positioning of the reader, who is prompted to make connections or infer meanings, but is repeatedly asked to rethink or reconfigure them at a later point.

In contemplating how Harrower encourages her reader to form these connections, it is instructive to look at Rebecca Walkowitz's analysis of the way twentieth-century novelists like Virginia Woolf, Kazuo Ishiguro and W.G. Sebald have negotiated the relationship between the personal and the global. Walkowitz offers an insightful summary of their strategy in the introduction to her book *Cosmopolitan Style: Modernism Beyond the Nation* (2006):

> The novels I examine approach large-scale international events, such as world war and immigration, by focusing on the trivial or transient episodes of everyday life. One way to view these novels is to say that in focusing on the trivial and the transient, they are little occupied with political or international conditions. But one might observe, instead, that these novels are testing and redefining what can count as international politics: they may emphasize incidents that seem to be trivial in order to reject wartime values of order and proportion, or they may emphasize what seem to be only personal experiences in order to expand what we know of global processes.[9]

Like Woolf, Ishiguro and Sebald, Harrower tends to depict world events through the prism of private life, not because she is "little occupied with political or international conditions", but rather because she is complicating accepted values of "order and proportion".[10]

---

8   Julian Murphet, "Projecting the Sixties: Mediation and Characterology in *The Catherine Wheel*," this volume, 108.
9   Rebecca L. Walkowitz, *Cosmopolitan Style: Modernism Beyond the Nation* (New York: Columbia University Press, 2006), 10. Not incidentally, this passage is also cited by Brigitta Olubas in *Shirley Hazzard: Literary Expatriate and Cosmopolitan Humanist* (2012). While the cosmopolitan contours of Hazzard's life and work are far more pronounced than those of Harrower, this speaks to the fact there are important similarities in the way these authors negotiate the relationship between the personal and political in their fiction.
10 Walkowitz presumably borrows the term "proportion" from her reading of *Mrs Dalloway* (1925). Specifically, from the character Woolf offers as a critique of the medical profession, the aristocratic

Walkowitz's analysis of Woolf's fiction is perhaps most pertinent with respect to Harrower's. She points to Woolf's assertion that "novelists need to discard the 'custom' and 'convention' that keep them from representing 'what is commonly thought small,' such as the 'dark places of psychology' and the daily experience of women."[11] She describes Woolf's approach to this problem of scale as a mode of "entanglement", a practice of "displaying self-consciously, perhaps aggressively, topics that will seem inconsequent alongside those that, traditionally, are thought more significant."[12]

It is this practice of "entanglement" that Harrower takes up in *The Watch Tower*. For while her novel is clearly focalised through the perspectives of the Vaizey sisters, there are various points at which significant global events are depicted through this lens. In one instance, the girls go to the local cinema, where they watch clips of the Second World War:

> On Saturdays at the pictures, newsreels showed the bombed cities of Europe and later still the deserts of the Middle East and the northern jungles, streaming jungles where trees walked and killed. Callow, shallow, safe, ashamed, the Vaizey girls were part of an audience that witnessed the destruction of the light of the world from cushiony red seats in the lilac-scented disinfected dark. They were pressed back on themselves and their few square inches of knowledge and experience.[13]

The "cushiony" and "lilac-scented" theatre connotes the apparently safe and materially privileged lives that the girls lead in remote Australia, far removed from the dangerous realities of war-torn Europe. While world events are here projected onto the big screen, Laura and Clare's experience takes up only a "few square inches". Harrower thus sets up a spatial contrast between the global and the domestic as the "big" and the "small", one that seems to be an example of the "metageography" that Robert Dixon identifies in her fiction. Elsewhere in this volume he discusses Harrower's use of cartographic or spatial forms of representation in order to contemplate or problematise ideas of national and personal identity.[14] Through Harrower's use of entanglement, she actually tends to emphasise the connections that persist across these different spheres, thus performing the kind of "scalar mediation" or "defamiliarisation" that Dixon suggests is inherent to the innovative practice of metageographical fiction.[15]

One of the connections that seems to persist across these different spheres in *The Watch Tower*, is that between experiences of oppression and suffering. Paralleling her depiction of Felix as a fascist figure, Harrower persistently represents the experiences of the Vaizey sisters by drawing on what Griselda Pollock and Max Silverman have referred to as the "concentrationary imaginary". This describes a "cultural reservoir of images" employed

---

physician Sir William Bradshaw. Maintaining "a sense of proportion" serves as a kind of maxim for Sir William, who insists on its centrality to health, to the practice of medicine and to life in general. His ethic of order and proportion seems to coincide with the values and expectations of the social establishment. It is, however, unable to save the shell-shocked veteran Septimus Smith from suicide.

11   Walkowitz, *Cosmopolitan Style*, 8.
12   Walkowitz, *Cosmopolitan Style*, 100.
13   Elizabeth Harrower, *The Watch Tower* (Melbourne: Text Publishing, 2012), 37–38. All subsequent references to this edition will appear in parentheses in the text.
14   Robert Dixon, "'The wind from Siberia': Metageography and Ironic Nationality in the Novels of Elizabeth Harrower," this volume, 50.
15   Dixon, "The wind from Siberia", 50.

in representations that are historically removed from the events of the Holocaust, but which "nonetheless reassert aspects of the apoliticizing logic and dehumanizing effects beyond the limits or the zone of the camp".[16] Thus when Laura prepares to leave business college to work at Felix's box factory, the description of her experience draws from this reservoir of images:

> She felt a sensation that was hard to identify. She half-thought to put it down to the loss of her hair, which had never been cut before … She was like someone who, having gone bravely through preparations for an operation that would almost certainly truncate her life, realised with a terrible twisting of her heart just as the anaesthetist's mask descended, that this shocking thing was truly happening, inevitable: shrieking resistance was of no avail. (19–20)

In having her hair cut and experiencing the sensation of being gassed, the passage all-too-vividly recalls the horrors of the concentration camp. This is similarly the case with the "two pairs of striped pyjama trousers" that Laura's mother watches flapping on the clothes line next door (24), as it is with the novel's title, which in this context, evokes images of the haunting guard towers that were characteristically spaced around the perimeters of the camps. While it is one thing to posit the ubiquity of tyranny, and to suggest that it might be found in suburban figures like Felix, it is seemingly quite another to associate the suffering of fictional characters with that of the victims of the Holocaust. The Holocaust is an event that has been surrounded by what Michael Rothberg describes as a "uniqueness discourse", and he notes that "In its extremity, it is sometimes even defined as only marginally connected to the course of human history."[17] According to this discourse, the way that Harrower entangles the event with the domestic abuse suffered by the Vaizey sisters could risk flattening two disparate and incommensurable forms of traumatic experience, exposing her novel to charges of insensitivity or irresponsibility. Harrower does, however, seem acutely aware of the risk, which might in part account for the fact that she often sets up the association between the personal and the global according to the logic of parataxis.

In grammar, parataxis denotes the placement of distinct phrases or clauses alongside one another, without words that determine their particular coordination or subordination. Rebecca Walkowitz draws on Adorno's lecture about this kind of syntax in the poetry of Friedrich Hölderlin. She suggests that it is one Woolf often employs in her entanglement of the personal and political, bringing together disparate ideas through "lists of phrases and images that appear within a single sentence".[18] Like Woolf, Harrower adopts this grammatical device in *The Watch Tower*. Most notably, it occurs in a passage that elaborates on the idea of the banality of evil, suggesting that this phenomenon is not limited to Felix, but pervades the suburban Australian society to which he belongs. In an expressionistic scene reminiscent of Samuel Beckett, Clare imagines herself waiting at

---

16   Griselda Pollock, "Introduction," in *Concentrationary Imaginaries: Tracing Totalitarian Violence in Popular Culture*, eds. Griselda Pollock and Max Silverman (London: I.B. Tauris, 2015), 33.
17   Michael Rothberg, *Multidirectional Memory: Remembering the Holocaust in the Age of Decolonisation* (Stanford: Stanford University Press, 2009), 17.
18   Walkowitz, *Cosmopolitan Style*, 93.

"life's bus stop". She catches fragments of people's conversations as they pass, which when assembled seem to offer a broad-strokes depiction of her cultural milieu:

> Then, because she happened to be standing in the queue, voices addressed her in unending soliloquies, burrowing like parasites for space inside her brain. "I've told him again and again not to shape my hair in like that at the back of my head. It's old fashioned – The skirt's going to have six yards in it, and underneath there'll be this petticoat with layers of frills – Ten cartons of Nutty Roughs – With all this funny weather our suitcases were covered with green mould – Hitler's got the right idea about the Jews, they can say what they like – Napoleon, there was a man! Where's your female Einstein, your Rembrandt? Women! Why were all the Greek and Roman statues of men? Because male beauty is superior in every way – When I win the lottery – The neckline's down to about *here* – After the war this block of land'll be worth three times what we gave for it. (105–6)

Harrower here uses what Adorno calls a "serial technique", where "what is lined up in sequence, unconnected, is as harsh as it is flowing."[19] She uses it to draw some disturbing associations; observations about a favourite hairstyle, the price of real estate and the shape of a neckline, are placed tellingly and frighteningly alongside statements that denigrate women, and that express support of Hitler. It associates the sinister with the mundane to perfectly dramatise the "interdependence of thoughtlessness and evil" that Arendt describes.[20] Moreover, by bringing together ideas of anti-Semitism and misogyny, the passage further reiterates *The Watch Tower*'s alignment between the oppression of Jewish people and the oppression of women. The scathing critique of postwar Australian suburbia offered in passages like this one suggest that it is complicit in Felix's treatment of Laura and Clare.

According to Adorno, parataxis can be extrapolated beyond the individual sentence to describe "forms that could as a whole be called paratactic in the broader sense".[21] Adorno suggests that Hölderlin's use of this device – both as syntax and structure – was something that tended to eschew conventional strategies for conveying meaning; it was a method by which "Hölderlin attempted to rescue language from confirmity".[22] Again, Walkowitz suggests that Woolf constructs certain episodes according to this logic, assembling "scenes that follow without immediate rationale" in order to produce an "arrangement of political imperatives and everyday pleasures".[23] Harrower, too, draws many associations in this way. It is how she first aligns Felix with Adolph Hitler, by placing the two figures side by side on the page; a scene in which Clare contemplates the actions of the German dictator is immediately followed by a passage describing Felix (35). At this point Harrower does not go so far as to draw an explicit metaphor or analogy between the two, but by placing them alongside one another she nonetheless renders them – in Walkowitz's words – "neither homogenous nor entirely distinct."[24]

---

19 Theodor Adorno, *Notes to Literature, Volume Two*, ed. Rolf Tiedemann, trans. Shierry Weber Nicholsen (New York: Columbia University Press, 1992), 133.
20 Hannah Arendt, *Eichmann in Jerusalem*, 129.
21 Adorno, *Notes to Literature, Volume Two*, 132.
22 Adorno, *Notes to Literature, Volume Two*, 137.
23 Walkowitz, *Cosmopolitan Style*, 93.
24 Walkowitz, *Cosmopolitan Style*, 100.

Harrower takes a similar approach in a passage where the narrator announces the outbreak of war. At this stage of the novel the sisters are still living with their mother, who treats them more like servants than her children. Here Laura mops the floor while her mother sits idly by, contemplating whether to withdraw Clare from school as a means of further reducing their expenses in the wake of her husband's death:

> Laura took a deep breath through her mouth, pressed her lips together and lunged away with the mop, starting to push it to and fro over the varnished boards surrounding the emerald carpet. "No. They only give them domestic science courses here. I've got this rise. We'll manage."
>
> "If your father had thought of this instead of those stupid investments of his—" Popping the other half of the biscuit into her mouth, she dusted her fingertips lightly together. "Look, I've sprinkled crumbs on your clean floor."
>
> * * *
>
> In September, a war started.
> "What are they doing it for?" Clare asked, and her mother said, "You can read. There's the paper. Find out." And the reasons were listed there in order of merit.
> People were dying. (33–4)

The scene registers Laura's mounting resentment towards her mother, whose careless crumbs seem to offer a clear and final provocation. Thus the announcement of war is at first likely to be read in reference to their relationship, as a declaration of domestic hostilities. But by continuing on, we find that the narrator is in fact referring to the Second World War. Harrower here sets up a relationship of contiguity between the personal lives of the Vaizey sisters and the international conflict breaking out in Europe, and her use of the indefinite article to announce '*a* war' allows the statement to apply to both. This unobtrusive and slight remark is rendered a kind of fulcrum that might tip toward either meaning, or allow the reader to remain poised between the two, thus illustrating the refusal of "confirmity" that Adorno ascribed to paratactic association.

Moreover, as this means of connection specifically eschews indicators of subordination between clauses or ideas, it enables Harrower to bring together world event and personal experience without necessarily subordinating one to the other. It also allows the implications of the association to work in both directions. On the one hand it makes us consider the significance of the conflicts that Laura and Clare face in their own home. On the other, it prompts us to reflect on the individual lives that are inevitably swept up in a monumental historical event like the Second World War or the Holocaust, each one with its own interiority and personal experiences of fear or suffering. These multidirectional implications also point to fact that while the difference between the personal and the global can be conceived as one of scale or magnitude, it should also be considered as a difference of kind. While personal lives are the basic unit by which all forms of human collectivity are comprised, in the sense that the personal involves subjectivity, it is always less abstract or conceptual than collective terms that are tied to a particular geography or imaginary, such as a community, a nation, or the world.

As if prompting her readers to think through some of the issues attendant on such associations, Harrower has the Vaizey sisters explicitly reflect on their own lives compared to those of the Holocaust victims. While we should not impute Laura and Clare's opinions to Harrower or to her narrator – who tends to maintain an ironic distance from the protagonists in the novels – the sisters' marked equivocation still serves to accentuate the novel's persistent refusal to enforce meaning. Not only do Laura and Clare adopt different perspectives, but the perspectives of both appear to shift in the course of the novel. For example, early on, Harrower has Clare refuse to "judge, pronounce and theorise" when reflecting on the events of the war:

> "What's the use? We don't know. We don't know. I mean—" She only meant it felt something like blasphemous, something like licentious, for their ignorance to speak, improvise opinions, consider its emotions in this situation. "I mean – we don't know anything". (38)

While Clare here rejects any suggestion of parity between her own experience and that of the victims of war, she begins to reassess this question once she has spent several years living with Felix. When Laura attempts to rebuff Clare's complaints she offers up the platitudinous justification that Clare should consider herself relatively fortunate: "'Think of the poor souls in concentration camps!" she would say with pious heat. 'How lucky we were in the war not to be thrown into the gas ovens!'" (222). While Laura defers to the accepted notion that her problems are inconsequential next to the suffering endured in the Holocaust, Clare is no longer entirely convinced:

> Some suffering must be clean compared with this, she thought. There was collusion here. There was nothing not depraved, perverted. There was no feeling of sufficient grace to earn the august name of suffering.
> And yet, she thought, I think we are probably very unhappy. (222)

Conscious of her and Laura's "collusion" in their abusive relationship with Felix, Clare denies that their experiences constitute anything like the "suffering" suggested by her sister's reference to the Holocaust. That said, she cannot help but persist in the belief that she is "very unhappy", and that her own experience is not to be discounted.

Laura's opinion is also shown to be in flux when she approaches the question of comparison hypothetically. When her colleagues ask her "But what do you make of these new bombs?", she suggests that, "I can only think – if someone's killed, what would the brand of the bomb matter?" (140). The reader is likely to draw a connection with Laura's own situation here: although not literally killed, she suffers a kind of figurative death at the hands of her husband, one that is said to leave her "Empty, salty, laid waste, not a person at all" (150). The implication of course being that if Laura is effectively "laid waste", it makes little difference whether the result is achieved by an atomic bomb or Zyklon-b, or alternatively through the destruction wreaked in the home by someone like Felix. Like Laura and Clare with their shifting points of view, the novel seems constantly to vacillate between drawing the Holocaust association, and drawing back from it. It is thus tempting to read Clare's initial doubts as a revealing moment of authorial intrusion, where Harrower might be questioning whether it could indeed be "blasphemous" or "licentious" to speak on this point.

Harrower's hesitancy could perhaps account for the way she constructs the character of Bernard. A Dutch war refugee and a presser at Felix's factory, Bernard comes to convalesce at the Neutral Bay house when he collapses during work. There is some intimation that he may be a Holocaust survivor, for he reflects at one point that it is "Better not to be reminded of what his life was before. There was nothing good to remember – my sister being killed, being imprisoned himself [sic]" (253). And a number of commentators have unquestioningly read Bernard's character in this way. Yet the details of his life remain purposely vague, and his wartime experiences are largely undefined. Moreover, his name does not identify him as Jewish in the way that, for example, Patrick White's own fictional Holocaust victim "Mordecai Himmlefarb" does.[25] The ambiguity surrounding Bernard might suggest that Harrower was reluctant to directly recruit the experience of a Holocaust survivor for the purposes of her novel.

The "collusion" that Clare refers to in the passage above, is an aspect of *The Watch Tower* that has always troubled readers. Particularly unsettling is the way that Laura partakes in her own destruction, and assists Felix in his domination of Clare.[26] In one instance, she even threatens to commit suicide if Clare leaves her alone with her husband (189). In being thus made guilty of "committing murder by proxy" (169), Laura's problematic actions seem to recall the way that many Jewish people were also reluctantly involved in the degradation and death of others during the Holocaust. Indeed, part of what ignited the controversy surrounding Arendt's reports on Eichmann was the fact that she criticised the actions of certain Jewish leaders. The Holocaust survivor Primo Levi has also addressed this problem of complicity. He describes the ways that Jewish people served at all levels as functionaries for their Nazi persecutors, some were even made to work as *Sonderkommandos* who transferred the dead from gas chambers to crematoria after extracting clothes, gold teeth and hair. Levi has argued that National Socialism "degrades its victims and makes them similar to itself, because it needs both great and small complicities".[27] He would come to describe the ambiguous moral space occupied by such collaborators as "the gray zone", which he suggests exists "not only in Nazi Lagers [camps]", but in all cases of persecution, between all victims and their tormentors. It is perhaps this space that Laura comes to occupy in *The Watch Tower*. While she is undoubtedly a victim herself, her willingness to do Felix's bidding seems to place her in this ethically ambiguous zone. By addressing this problem of complicity and the idea of the banality of evil, Harrower demonstrates that despite setting her novel in an Australian suburb, she is able to contemplate key moral questions shaped by the war.[28]

Her willingness to draw these associations with the problems of totalitarianism and the Holocaust might speak to the postwar milieu in which she lived and wrote. In his book *Multidirectional Memory: Remembering the Holocaust in the Age of Decolonization*, Michael Rothberg posits that during the 1950s and 1960s, writers were engaged in

---

25   Mordecai Himmlefarb appears in White's 1961 novel *Riders in the Chariot*.
26   Nicholas Mansfield, "'The Only Russian in Sydney': Modernism and Realism in *The Watch Tower*," *Australian Literary Studies*, vol. 15 no. 3 (1992), 133; Frances McInherny, "'Deep into the Destructive Core': Elizabeth Harrower's *The Watch Tower*," *Hecate*, vol. 9, no. 1 and 2 (1983), 125; Robyn Claremont, "The Novels of Elizabeth Harrower," *Quadrant*, vol. 23, no. 11 (1979), 20.
27   Primo Levi, *The Drowned and the Saved*, trans. Raymond Rosenthal (New York: Summit Books, 1988), 68.
28   In a review of *In Certain Circles* Delia Falconer points to the important role that the war plays in determining the novel's ethical considerations, noting that she "was especially struck by how World War II is shown to wrench the moral warp of its characters' world, and how important this sense is, on reflection, to [Harrower's] other novels." Delia Falconer, "Triumphant Final Fugue." Review of *In Certain Circles*, by Elizabeth Harrower, *The Weekend Australian*, 26–27 April, 2014, 20.

"markedly more comparative forms of memory than would come to predominate in later decades."[29] Against the "uniqueness discourse", he argues that the cultural memory of the Holocaust actually emerged in comparative dialogue with ongoing processes of decolonisation and civil rights struggles.[30] His book has a particular focus on texts that engage in a comparative exchange between the Holocaust and the fight for independence in Algeria. While Harrower takes on problems facing white, middle-class women rather than colonised subjects, she still participates in the kind of comparative practice that is said to be characteristic of her historical moment.

According to Rothberg, the more recent tendency to avoid such comparative thinking is due to the fact that cultural memory is now often conceived in terms of competition, as a "zero-sum struggle for preeminence".[31] But he proposes that comparison need not always be competitive, and that it might alternatively "provide the grounds for new forms of collectivity that would not ignore equally powerful histories of division and difference".[32] In *The Watch Tower* Harrower seems to envisage such a "new form of collectivity". While her hesitancy in drawing the Holocaust association acknowledges the irreconcilability of this experience with that of the Vaizey sisters, she nonetheless entertains the possibility that they might really share something with one another, even if this be only a shared vulnerability. Indeed, despite Bernard's wartime experiences, he seems to recognise Laura as a fellow-victim, who "suddenly seemed to Bernard, who had seen many victims, to represent them all" (315). And his experience is similarly compared to Clare's when the narrator observes that "she and Bernard had traversed the same extreme country" (261). Deploying the conceit of a "country", Bernard is here made to imagine a community of sufferers, one whose borders are defined not by geography, but by experience. Although Robert Dixon is specifically concerned with matters of geography in Harrower's novels, he comes to a similar conclusion regarding the ending of *The Watch Tower*. Just as Clare need not be located in war-torn Europe in order to know suffering, Dixon notes that her final liberation does not require a "physical expatriation". Despite the fact that Harrower often "appears to associate personal becoming with the contemporary discourses of global travel and expatriatism", he suggests that Clare's freedom turns out to be "as much epistemological as it is topographical".[33]

This conceit of experience as a "country" also recalls Virginia Woolf's famous assertion in *Three Guineas* (1938) that "[A]s a woman, I have no country. As a woman I want no country. As a woman my country is the whole world".[34] Woolf's statement is at once a declaration of exclusion and belonging. Not afforded equal rights and protections under patriarchal governance, she does not see herself as properly belonging to the country of Britain. She does, in consequence, find herself belonging to a "country" or "society of outsiders", not unlike Harrower's community of sufferers.[35] *Three Guineas* has further resonance with *The Watch Tower*, for in it Woolf points to the similarities between male power and fascism. She outlines her refusal to subscribe to an English anti-fascist

---

29 Rothberg, *Multidirectional Memory*, 26.
30 Rothberg, *Multidirectional Memory*, 17, 26.
31 Rothberg, *Multidirectional Memory*, 13.
32 Rothberg, *Multidirectional Memory*, 27.
33 Dixon, "'The wind from Siberia'", 60.
34 Virginia Woolf, *A Room of One's Own, Three Guineas*, ed. Morag Shiach (Oxford: Oxford University Press, 1992), 313.
35 Virginia Woolf, *A Room of One's Own, Three Guineas*, 314.

organisation on the grounds that the sexism perpetrated by her country's patriarchal institutions is reminiscent of fascism's assaults on freedom.[36] Woolf, Plath and Harrower thus converge on this point, but in the latter's alignment of the oppression of women with the oppression of Jewish people, she seems to have modeled her approach on the work of another great female author, specifically, on George Eliot and her late novel *Daniel Deronda* (1876).[37] It is a text that appears to have been of some significance to Harrower, and is discussed in a letter written to her in 1972 by her friend and contemporary Patrick White:

Dear Elizabeth,
I received the *Spoils of Poynton* for which I thank you very much, though I may not be able to read it until my next fiction orgy. I am almost at the end of *Daniel Deronda*; then I think there will be just time for *L'Education sentimentale* (re-reading of) before I start the final version of my own. There are wonderful things in *Deronda* (the development of Gwendolen Harleth) but I also find a lot of it sadly stodgy (most of the Jewish bits, and Deronda himself; but of course all this has been said many times before).[38]

White's comments seem to be framed as a reply. He moves straight from his acknowledgement of Harrower's most recent gift on to *Daniel Deronda*, perhaps intimating that she sent him the novel or suggested that he read it. In any case, his brief critique assumes her prior familiarity with the text, so even though only one side of the correspondence is available,[39] their implied discussion inevitably calls to mind a number of resonances between Eliot's novel and Harrower's own.

This is at first readily apparent in the depiction of the marriages at the centre of both texts, for Laura Vaizey's predicament distinctly recalls that of Eliot's heroine, Gwendolen Harleth. Like Laura, Gwendolen finds her family in sufficiently dire financial straits to induce her to wed the wealthy Lord Grandcourt, who is not dissimilar to Felix Shaw. In her marriage the once vivacious Gwendolen is "brought to kneel down like a horse under training for the arena".[40] Grandcourt's domination of Gwendolen is enforced by strategies of passive aggression and emotional manipulation, as "His words had the power of thumbscrews and the cold touch of the rack" (680). Although Felix is, by contrast, prone to outbursts of physical violence, he is reminiscent of Grandcourt in his ability to control Laura and Clare with "the blows from his eyes and his words" (82). In such respects Eliot's villain provides a useful archetype not only for Felix, but for the tyrannical husbands that

---

36 Virginia Woolf, *A Room of One's Own, Three Guineas*, 303.
37 In an essay on Christina Stead's *For Love Alone*, Brigid Rooney suggests that Stead's early novel is modeled on George Eliot's masterpiece *Middlemarch* (1874). Rooney notes that Stead avoids explicit quotation, but draws on Eliot's novel through "unmarked doublings or parallels". In *The Watch Tower*, Harrower appears to take up *Daniel Deronda* in a similarly inexplicit manner. Brigid Rooney, "Manifesto of the Senses: Blind Sightedness in Christina Stead's *For Love Alone*." *Australian Literary Studies*, vol. 24, no. 3–4 (2009): 53–65.
38 Patrick White to Elizabeth Harrower, 1972, in *Patrick White Letters*, ed. David Marr (Sydney: Random House Australia, 1994), 398.
39 Harrower has donated her personal papers to the National Library of Australia, but has not made them publicly accessible.
40 George Eliot, *Daniel Deronda* (London: Penguin Books, 1995), 320. All subsequent references to this edition will appear in parentheses in the text.

recur throughout Harrower's oeuvre, including Stan Peterson of *Down in the City* and Stephen Quayle of *In Certain Circles*.

More specifically, *Daniel Deronda* seems to offer a model for the entanglement of the global and the personal spheres that is established in *The Watch Tower*, for like Harrower, Eliot places the private suffering of women alongside the collective trauma of the Jewish community. It is an association that underlies the double narrative structure of Eliot's text, with private female suffering represented by the storyline of Gwendolen and Grandcourt, and Jewish trauma represented by that of the siblings Mirah and Mordecai Cohen. The character of Daniel Deronda moves between these two spheres, and these two narrative strains; he is the ward of Grandcourt's uncle, and befriends Mordecai and Mirah after rescuing the latter from suicide. Consolidating his connection to the brother and sister, it later emerges that Deronda is himself of Jewish descent. His character is made to contemplate the domestic suffering that takes place within Gwendolen's unhappy marriage, but he is also confronted with Mordecai's political world, with the oppression of the Jewish people and the cause of Zionism. This bipartite structure is visualised in a scene of personal reflection where Deronda imagines himself torn between the two spheres: "on the one side the grasp of Mordecai's dying hand on him, with all the ideals and prospects it aroused; on the other this fair creature [Gwendolen] in silk and gems, with her hidden wound and her self-dread" (564).

While Eliot's depiction of Gwendolen Harleth is attended by an appropriate amount of irony with respect to the character's egoism and inexperience, the novel still makes an important claim about the significance of such women's lives. Anne Cvetkovich contemplates this aspect of Eliot's novel in her book *Mixed Feelings: Feminism, Mass Culture, and Victorian Sensationalism* (1992), drawing attention to the following reflection of the narrator in *Daniel Deronda*:

> Could there be a slenderer, more insignificant thread in human history than this consciousness of a girl, busy with her small inferences of the way in which she could make her life pleasant? . . . What in the midst of that mighty drama are girls and their blind visions? They are the Yea or Nay of that good for which men are enduring and fighting. In these delicate vessels is borne onward through the ages the treasure of human affections. (124)

With respect to this passage, and to the double narratives of the novel, Cvetkovich notes that "By suggesting that the story of a girl's mind may be as important as the history of wars, the narrator offers a feminist critique of what counts as history".[41] The critique Cvetkovich identifies, in its comparison of private female experience and historical event, bears great resemblance to Harrower's own. In *The Watch Tower* she has effectively repeated and updated Eliot's fictional maneuver. At her historical moment the most pressing crisis facing Jewish people is the recent horror of the Holocaust, so this is the event she draws alongside the private struggles of the Vaizey sisters. Moreover, in the character of Bernard, Harrower seems to have followed Eliot in deploying a Deronda-like figure as a link between the global and personal spheres.[42] If one accepts the reading of his

---

41 Ann Cvetkovich, *Mixed Feelings: Feminism, Mass Culture, and Victorian Sensationalism* (New Brunswick, N.J.: Rutgers University Press, 1992), 132.

character as a Holocaust victim, Bernard serves to connect the personal lives of Clare and Laura with the political events of the war and the genocide.

Although Laura and Clare might initially have been described as "shallow" and "safe" when faced with newsreels of the war, in the course of the novel their lives are shown to be much more intricately entangled with the international conflict than they at first appeared. Harrower sets up connections between their experiences and those of the victims of the Holocaust, but by opening these associations to shifting interpretation and even refutation, she constantly asks the reader to rethink the relationship between the personal and the global. By way of these tentative connections, Harrower seems to suggest that despite the incommensurability of different scales and forms of suffering, there may actually exist between them some common ground – some of "the same extreme country" – irrespective of whether that country is located in war-ravaged Europe, or in the quiet suburban landscape of Sydney's North Shore.

References

Adorno, Theodor. *Notes to Literature, Volume Two*. Edited by Rolf Tiedemann. Translated by Shierry Weber Nicholsen. New York: Columbia University Press, 1992.
Arendt, Hannah. *Eichmann in Jerusalem: A Report on the Banality of Evil*. New York: Viking Press, 1963.
Cathcart, Michael. Interview with Elizabeth Harrower. *Books and Arts*, ABC Radio National, 9 November 2015. http://ab.co/1Qe2oxN.
Clancy, Laurie. "Fathers and Lovers: Three Australian Novels." *Australian Literary Studies* 10, no. 4 (1982): 459–67.
Claremont, Robyn. "The Novels of Elizabeth Harrower." *Quadrant* 23, no. 11 (1979): 16–21.
Coleman, Deirdre. "*The Watch Tower*: Bluebeard's Castle." In *(Un)common Ground: Essays in Literature in English*. Edited by Andrew Taylor and Russell McDougal, 97–107. Adelaide: Centre for Research in the New Literatures in English, 1990.
Cvetkovich, Ann. *Mixed Feelings: Feminism, Mass Culture, and Victorian Sensationalism*. New Brunswick, NJ: Rutgers University Press, 1992.
Dixon, Robert. "The wind from Siberia': Metageography and Ironic Nationality in the Novels of Elizabeth Harrower," In *Elizabeth Harrower: Critical Essays*. Edited by Elizabeth McMahon and Brigitta Olubas, 49–64. Sydney: Sydney University Press, 2017.
Eliot, George. *Daniel Deronda*. (1876) London: Penguin Books, 1995.
Falconer, Delia. "Triumphant Final Fugue." Review of *In Certain Circles* by Elizabeth Harrower. *Weekend Australian*, 26–27 April 2014.
Geering, R.G. *Recent Fiction*. Melbourne: Oxford University Press, 1974.
Harris, Max. "The Novels of Elizabeth Harrower." *Australian Letters* 4 no. 2 (1962): 16–18.

---

42 This is a structural device that Harrower uses again in *In Certain Circles*, where the character of Russell Howard stands in as the figure that connects the personal and political in the novel. Russell actually offers a closer approximation to Eliot's protagonist; spending his life helping others "like some angel of God consoling us sinners for not being perfect". He is reminiscent of Deronda, who, with respect to his charitable nature is described as a "rescuing angel to many"f (808). The traumatic historical event that Harrower draws on in *In Certain Circles* is that of the Second World War prison camp, and Russell's time in an unnamed camp introduces one of the novel's central themes of imprisonment. Harrower is particularly interested in the forms of imprisonment that arise within human relationships. Elizabeth Harrower, *In Certain Circles* (Melbourne: Text Publishing, 2014), 116.

Harrower, Elizabeth. *In Certain Circles*. Melbourne: Text Publishing, 2014.
——. *The Watch Tower*. (1966) Melbourne: Text Publishing, 2012.
Koval, Ramona. Interview with Elizabeth Harrower. *The Monthly Video*, October 2014. http://bit.ly/2pGhjKU.
Levi, Primo. *The Drowned and the Saved*. Translated by Raymond Rosenthal. New York: Summit Books, 1988.
Mansfield, Nicholas. "'The Only Russian in Sydney': Modernism and Realism in *The Watch Tower*." *Australian Literary Studies* 15, no. 3 (1992): 131–40.
McInherny, Frances. "'Deep into the Destructive Core': Elizabeth Harrower's *The Watch Tower*." *Hecate* 9, nos 1 and 2 (1983): 123–34.
Murphet, Julian. "Projecting the Sixties: Mediation and Characterology in *The Catherine Wheel*," In *Elizabeth Harrower: Critical Essays*. Edited by Elizabeth McMahon and Brigitta Olubas, 107–177. Sydney: Sydney University Press, 2017.
Pollock, Griselda. "Introduction," in *Concentrationary Imaginaries: Tracing Totalitarian Violence in Popular Culture*, eds. Griselda Pollock and Max Silverman. London: I.B. Tauris, 2015.
Rooney, Brigid. "Manifesto of the Senses: Blind Sightedness in Christina Stead's *For Love Alone*." *Australian Literary Studies* 24, nos 3 and 4 (2009): 53–65.
Rothberg, Michael. *Multidirectional Memory: Remembering the Holocaust in the Age of Decolonisation*. Stanford, Calif.: Stanford University Press, 2009.
Walkowitz, Rebecca L. *Cosmopolitan Style: Modernism Beyond the Nation*. New York: Columbia University Press, 2006.
White, Patrick. *Patrick White Letters*. Edited by David Marr. Sydney: Random House Australia, 1994.
Woolf, Virginia. *A Room of One's Own, and Three Guineas*. Edited by Morag Shiach. Oxford: Oxford University Press, 1992.

12
Moments of Being in the Fiction of Elizabeth Harrower

Elizabeth McMahon

In her poetic catalogues of being and experience, Emily Dickinson records the chasm between the visibility of the world, including the poetic image, and the invisibility of inner transformation. In one such poem she writes: "We can find no scar / But internal difference – / Where the Meanings, Are –".[1] Elizabeth Harrower's fiction investigates this "internal difference" in both its invisibile and its hypervisible effects, and understood in the related senses of transformation, individuation and self-division. In these representations, Harrower deploys a very particular version of the modernist epiphany or moment of being. In her novels and short stories this epiphany characteristically interweaves and disentangles the subjects and objects of the narratives. One recurring revelation exposes the ways some human subjects wire themselves and others through the objects of postwar consumer culture to expose how (mostly) women can become relegated to object status in and through these dynamics. In another mode, Harrrower's narratives record moments of instant, electrical connection between strangers, who are otherwise isolated. Across the spectrum of these interactions, as this essay will investigate, the revelations experienced by Harrower's characters are always intersubjective – even if the ultimate revelation is solitary and about the condition of being solitary in the world. This essay will identify at least some of the key properties of Harrower's epiphanies and consider how they relate to narrative mode and genre by moving between her short fiction and the novels. Ranging across these different genres, in view of their respective relationships to realism and their capacities to represent temporality and causality, underscores the operations of her particular postwar, postmodern epiphany and its centrality to her understanding of being in the world.

The moments of revelation experienced by Harrower's characters are figured according to the convention of awakening as illumination, even enlightenment, especially regarding knowledge of self. So, too, these epiphanies are premised on inherent contradiction and irresolution in their evocation of both life and death and their capacity to constitute and disperse the self – as occurs in the modernist moment of being in Joyce, Woolf and Proust. These characteristics defined the modernist epiphany against its romantic source for, as John McGowan argues, the modernist epiphany was a radical reduction from the romantic hope that such moments provide existential or metaphysical

---

1 Emily Dickinson, "There's a Certain Slant of Light", in *The Complete Poems* (London: Faber & Faber, 1976), 118.

coherence.[2] Rather, as McGowan identifies, for Woolf, Joyce and Proust, the revelatory moment resonates only for the perceiver and the coherence gained refers only to them.[3] This understanding also informs scenes of revelation in Harrower's fiction where, as for Woolf, Joyce and Proust, the focus is on the self-sensate quality wherein the subject experiences her own mind, becomes present to herself, which, indeed, is part of the meaning and the partiality of that meaning.

Critics from the 1970s onwards have identified ways the modernist epiphany evolved and mutated across the twentieth century to its self-conscious and ironic deployment in postmodern texts from the 1960s. Building on Morris Beja's landmark study from 1971, Arthur M. Saltzman distinguishes between high modernist and postmodernist epiphanies to show how the later works display a more conscious awareness of the role of poetic language interpolated into prosaic text and context in the construction of what might be termed, after Todorov, the "epiphany effect".[4] Writing of the epiphany in Thomas Pynchon and Seamus Heaney, Ashton Nichols also stresses the role of poetic language to observe that these moments of being become reflections of how "cognitive aspects of human experience are transformed, via literary language, into moments of resonance more significant for having occurred in a mind (brain) than for any precise meaning they might contain".[5] That is to say, the postmodern epiphany lays stress on its experiential, phenomenological qualities and downplays what John Barth famously termed the "felt ultimacies" understood as intrinsic to the revelation itself.[6] In this way, ironically, these later epiphanists return to Pater's belief in the moment for its own sake. As Pater writes in *The Renaissance* (1868): "Not the fruit of experience but experience itself, is the end".[7]

The epiphanic moments in Harrower raise similar questions of form, register, cognition and phenomenology in which dilemmas of identity, knowledge and experience are acted out and crystallised. The first period of Harrower's published work (1957 to 1966), the recent re-issues of these works and the publication of new work from 2013, span a crucial time in the mutation of the literary epiphany from its modernist source. Her fiction wears the marks of high modernism but also belongs to the postwar, pre-feminist decades of the 1950s and 1960s and, now, to the second decade of the twenty-first century – a long if interrupted span of philosophical and aesthetic thought. Specifically, Saltzman's argument regarding the self-conscious shift from prosaic to poetic registers in late-modernist epiphanies accurately describes such moments in Harrower's fiction, which characteristically shifts lexicon, rhythm and cadence at heightened moments. In Harrower, these shifts are not confined to the distinction between prosaic and poetic language but

---

2   See Ashton Nichols, *The Poetics of Epiphany: Nineteenth-Century Origins of the Modern Literary Movement* (Tuscaloosa: University of Alabama Press, 1987).
3   John McGowan, "From Pater to Wilde to Joyce: Modernist Epiphany and the Soulful Self", *Texas Studies in Literature and Language* 32, no. 3 (1990): 420.
4   Morris Beja, *Epiphany in the Modern Novel* (Seattle: Washington University Press, 1971); Arthur M. Saltzman, "Epiphany and Its Discontents: Coover, Gangemi, Sorrentino, and Postmodern Revelation", *Journal of Modern Literature* 15, no. 4 (Spring, 1989): 497–518.
5   Ashton Nichols, "Cognitive and Pragmatic Linguistic Moments: Literary Epiphany in Thomas Pynchon and Seamus Heaney", in *Moments of Moment: Aspects of the Literary Epiphany*, ed. Wim Tigges (Amsterdam and Atlanta, GA: Rodopi, 1999), 469.
6   John Barth, "The Literature of Exhaustion", in *The Friday Book: Essays and other Non-Fiction* (Baltimore, MD: Johns Hopkins University Press, 1984), 67.
7   Cited in McGowan, "From Pater to Wilde to Joyce", 421.

perform what Julian Murphet identifies as a "pattern of generic interference"[8] to include interpolations from theatre and film. In the scenes of revelation, this compound of genres obscures and multiplies meanings for the characters, who cannot focus on or decode one system to orientate themselves within experience. The insight may be quarantined within the genre of its representation with no capacity for effect beyond it, or it may be misdirected along the conventions of one or other of the genres in play. Furthermore, these lyricised, dramatic and cinematic moments are often re-circumscribed within the dominant narrative mode, which, in Harrower, involves an unflinching, naturalist dissection of the human psyche and human behaviour. In all these ways, Harrower's epiphanies also ironise and distort Pater's insistence on the value of the experiential moment rather than its "fruits" – what we might also name its implications or consequences. For when placed into the context of Harrower's naturalism, the encapsulation of these moments within the narrative often forestalls any effect – that is, there may be no discernible "fruits". Alternatively, these "fruits" may be misdirected or intensified by the interplay of genres to produce consequences so profound that they utterly determine future events, especially the plight of Harrower's female protagonists.

A further multiplication of effect in Harrower's moments of revelation is produced by a distinctive focus on human subjects. In both Pynchon and Heaney – as for Elizabeth Bowen, with whom Harrower is more closely aligned – the moment of psychic awakening centres on objects.[9] In Harrower's texts, however, this moment occurs between people. Every scene of revelation in her texts includes the shared gaze of recognition and misrecognition, charged with desire. This reciprocal gaze at times echoes John Donne, as the poet writes to his lover: "My face in thine eye, thine in mine appears", replete with the same confusion of subject and object, of self and other.[10] Or, in Hegel's terms, the viewer catches sight of the void that is the self, the "night of the world", when s/he looks "human beings in the eye".[11] The following reading of the texts will show how this vision of the interior self, which is achieved in this mutual gaze, marks the point where flesh meets psyche and dream meets reality, and where the conscious self encounters the unconscious. Character and reader steal a glimpse of the screen of the unconscious as at that moment when we feel a dream slipping away as we wake from sleep. Revelation is conventionally understood as waking us from sleep into awareness, from unconscious being to consciousness; in Harrower's fiction these revelations are experienced in the fantasmatic state between sleeping and waking and reveal the often dangerous interplay between these orders of experience and their compelling hold on the human subject.

---

8   See Julian Murphet, "Projecting the Sixties: Mediation and Characterology in *The Catherine Wheel*", this volume, 108.
9   Ashton Nichols notes *The Crying of Lot 49*. See Carmen Concilio, "Things That Do Speak in Elizabeth Bowen's *The Last September*". Susan Sheridan has compared Harrower and Bowen in "Pity's Cost", *Sydney Review of Books*, 12 August 2014, http://bit.ly/2pVSKKW.
10 John Donne, "The Good Morrow", in *Collected Poems of John Donne* (London: Wordsworth Editions, 2002), 1.
11 George Wilhelm Friedrich Hegel, *Hegel and the Human Spirit. A Translation of the Jena Lectures by Leo Rauch* (Detroit, MI: Wayne State University Press, 1983), 87.

In their compression, the short stories accentuate these operations.[12] The opening story in *A Few Days in the Country and Other Stories*, hitherto unpublished and the first story Harrower ever wrote, "The Fun of the Fair", contains familiar elements for readers coming to this belated collection of stories after the novels.[13] The story centres on a ten-year-old girl, Janet, an unloved, unwanted orphan, who is shunted between various triangulated relationships in which she is the third wheel: her aunt and cousin Hector, with whom she lives; this same cousin and his girlfriend, Leila. The lovelessness of these triangulations is elucidated for Janet in a scene at a fun fair, when she is called up on stage and placed between two figures, a husband and wife, one a "giant", the other a "dwarf", and is asked to shake each of their hands in a demonstration of scale. Through her participation in this performance, Janet understands not only the falsity of the stage couple's performance of affection, but also the loveless position she holds in relation to the other couples in her life. Like *Hamlet*'s play within the play, it is the performance that exposes the truth.

This story also deploys the interplay of diurnal and nocturnal contexts and experiences, and the psychic correlatives of awakeness, sleep and fantasy, which characterise the novels. It opens with a storm and a blackout at a beachside pool at evening before the trio – Janet, Hector and Leila – ascend the hill to the fair:

> And then, if the lightning that ripped the sky apart wasn't enough, the lights round the edge of the swimming pool, and even the three big ones sunk into it on cement piles, went out.[14]

This first line of the first story Harrower wrote locates us in a "night of the world" where the sky has been ripped apart. It reads as an echo of Stan Parker's revelatory moment of disillusionment in Patrick White's *The Tree of Man*: "Then the paper sky was tearing, he saw. He was tearing the last sacredness".[15] As Danny Anwar argues for White's novel, this moment of revelation signals the mutation of the landscape in a "process of reduction into the profanity and particularity of post-modernity".[16] As Kate Livett and Ivor Indyk separately note in this volume, Harrower's universe is a godless space. It is animated by powerful elemental and primal forces from the weather to the human psyche. The storm scene that opens "The Fun of the Fair" rehearses Janet's annihilation and rebirth in which the external, indeed universal, domains are wired through her. She is first "plunged" into darkness, which she compares to the "astronomical darkness into which she had been plunged last year when they took out her tonsils" (1). This comparison reveals Janet's emergence from the blackness of the storm as being a drugged state between sleep and

---

12 Bernadette Brennan's review of *A Few Days in the Country and Other Stories* also observes the recurring themes shared between the novels and the stories. Bernadette Brennan, review of *A Few Days in the Country and Other Stories* by Elizabeth Harrower, *Australian Book Review* 377 (December 2015).
13 Elizabeth Harrower confirmed that this was the first story she wrote in correspondence to the author on 6 June 2016.
14 Elizabeth Harrower, "The Fun of the Fair", in *A Few Days in the Country and Other Stories* (Melbourne: Text Publishing, 2016), 1. All subsequent page references are to this edition and appear in parentheses in the text.
15 Patrick White, *The Tree of Man* (1955; London: Vintage, 1994), 334.
16 Danny Anwar, "The Island Called Utopia in *The Tree of Man*", *Southerly* 74, no. 1: 227.

wakefulness. As Žižek reads Hegel, the glimpse into this night, this abyss, is the predicate of the self emerging into the world, into language. It is in this condition that Janet enters the surreal and cinematic space of the fair and where she does, indeed, learn to articulate her subjectivity.

The opening sentence of the story also blurs the lines between the real and the surreal. Both Janet and the reader are located in a realist narrative but the scene equips them with a fantasmatic readiness. According to narrative sequence, the story presents a demarcation between the worlds inside and outside the fair ground; it appears to follow a journey from the quotidian domain over a threshold into the fair ground as a space of heterotopic discontinuity. But the fair ground proves to be continuous with the world outside it, even if shared elements are realigned and distorted across these terrains. For in the fair, Janet finds a replication of the circumstances of her life, which are clarified through distortion and performance. In this state between sleep and wakefulness, there is no clear break between the domains of experience. As Žižek argues for fantasy, it "does not dissimulate reality: rather, fantasy serves as the screen which enables us to confront the Real – as such, fantasy is on the side of reality, it guarantees the distance between (symbolically structured) reality and the horrifying Real".[17]

Indeed, it is the stylised theatricalisation of her situation at the fair, with all the distortion of a dream, that enables Janet's self-recognition, where she delineates herself as both an object and a subject. The scene carries the chilling force of the uncanny and its signals of malign intent. Janet meets the eyes of the female performer: "On a level, their eyes met, and Janet went cold, then colder, transfixed by the look and by a sudden strange sensation in her chest" (9). She is asked to shake both performers' hands, one to the left of her, the other to the right, and say "how do you do", a gesture loaded with significance, as in a nightmare. Having confronted this vision, Janet flees from Hector and Leila:

> "I don't love any of you. I'll never go back." Aimlessly, frantically, and twisting round caravans and tents, up and down the paths of trodden earth, pushing through the thinning crowds, she ran, not crying now, but brilliant eyed. (14)

Janet's assertion of self in this statement provides a narrative conclusion that is aligned with attainment. From the opening scene in which she has been "plunged" into the abyss of anaesthetised sleep to her concluding statement of (negative) desire, Janet has achieved the capacity to enunciate the "I" of a desiring subject. The reader may wonder what will happen to a ten-year-old girl on her own at night in a strange place, and if and how she will continue to live with the knowledge she has gained, and how she will live with others now she understands her aloneness, but this short story does not explore these questions. The story is not so bound to a longer narrative's obligation to consequence but can more readily end with a figure, in this instance a figure of vision, as Janet's illuminated eyes define her being.

The second story in *A Few Days in the Country and Other Stories*, "Alice", was first published in the *New Yorker* on 26 January 2015, and presents the eponymous heroine according to familiar qualities of many girls and women in Harrower: she is sensitive, intelligent, manipulated and unloved. In structural terms, this tale stands in sharp contrast

---

17   Slavoj Žižek, "From Desire to Drive: Why Lacan Is Not Lacaniano", from *Atlántica de Las Artes* 14 (Autumn 1996), http://bit.ly/2pbnszY.

to the episodic slice presented in "The Fun of the Fair", in that it presents a flat catalogue of the "events" of Alice's loveless and constrained life from youth to old age. Akin to "The Fun of the Fair", however, a moment of awakening occurs towards the end of the story. In this instance, a young woman visits the elderly Alice on the morning of her wedding. In all Alice's long life, this is the first and only moment of kindness and connection she has experienced. These two women also stand face to face, as true and distorted mirrors of each other. The language shifts from the objective chronicle of Alice's life, which has been recounted as a parodic fairytale in a tone of affectless dessication, into poetic description, metaphor and then to embodied subjectivity:

> At last, the man fed and sleeping again, Alice sat down alone. And then, from the top of the garden path, someone was calling her name, and through the greenery and the late-summer flowers the girl came in her wedding dress and shimmering veil, like a bird or an angel, on her way to the church.
> Wonder almost lifted Alice off the ground. Stopping cars, leaving bridesmaids at the gate, the girl floated down. She had thought of Alice, wanted Alice's blessing at this astonishing moment. Everything shone with light – the sky, the garden, the girl in white, and Alice. This was like nothing that had ever happened before. The girl and Alice smiled.
> Even after the girl left, in clouds and drifts of white, nothing seemed substantial. A buoyancy, an airiness, something quite amazing surrounded Alice. She had no idea what it was called. (30-1)

In one sense, the arrival of a bride on a late summer's morning provides the conventional conclusion of romance and fairytale, genres this story has repudiated through parody to this point. But the bridal conclusion does not constitute a resilement from the story's dominant perspective and tone, for the romance conclusion is oblique to the main tale of "Alice"; the bridal tale is an interpolation, a proxy from another story, from another life, that occupies or hovers in the evacuated space of Alice's own loveless narrative.

However, Alice's experience of intersubjective identification enables her, for the first time in the story, to articulate the subjective "I". This possibility is first signalled, ironically, by her wordlessness: "She had no idea what it was called". But from the vision of herself as the negated double of the young bride, Alice is rendered capable of articulating an "I" and attaching that "I" to "thought", thereby achieving an initial act of self-consciousness, self-reflexivity, self-transitivity. The "thought" says: "But *I* know. *I* know". As in "The Fun of the Fair", the achievement of insight in "Alice" is realised through the eye-to-eye contact with another. So, too, the meaning is not found in that relation but in the self it enables. "Alice" concludes with the observation that, "[a]fter this she looked the same, and her circumstances didn't alter, but she was a different person altogether" (39). The difference wrought upon her is internal, "[w]here the meanings are". But this internal difference also describes Alice's new-found self-division, a duality that constructs a dialogue between "thought" and the "I", and gives evidence of subjectivity. These alterations of identity are mirrored by the story itself, which performs its own duality. For, in its echo of the fairytale ending – both the bridal scene and the mimicry of collapsing all future history into one final sentence – irony and echo effect a doubling so that the story appears to almost stand beside itself.

The confusions and illuminations produced by the interwoven domains of fantasy, fairytale and quotidian life are played out from the opening scene of the narrative proper in Harrower's first published novel, *Down in the City* (1957), which takes an entire novel-length narrative to explore consequences left suspended in "The Fun of the Fair" and resolved entirely in terms of "internal difference" in "Alice". Like Janet's apprehension of the female performer's malice and the shaking of hands in "The Fun of the Fair", in *Down in the City* it is the locking of eyes and the touching of hands that changes everything for the unworldly, unloved heroine Esther Prescott when she is visited by the con-artist salesman Stan Peterson. The scene of their first meeting focuses on their faces, especially their eyes: "Esther had been conscious of his eyes on her";[18] "They stood face to face" (21); "'I assure—' she began, distracted by the flaring intimacy in his eyes and voice, in her own" (22). Then they touch:

> Stan leaned forward and grasped her hand. She sat, rigid, more frightened than she had ever been. Someone else's soft human skin was touching hers. The hand that had never touched a living thing was clutched in a stranger's human hand. (22-3)

But it is the eyes that seal the connection; she tells him her name: "'Esther,' she said, her eyes held by his, and in that moment they were joined" (24). By this gaze and touch, Stan wakes Esther, as Delia Falconer notes: "Esther Prescott is a Sleeping Beauty. Her mother died when she was small, and her father, for inscrutable reasons of waspishness and wealth, has kept her hidden from the world . . . Only the vulgar Stan Peterson can wake her from this spell".[19]

Like Janet, Esther is a virtual orphan, who is poised between the conditions of sleep and wakefulness, between the mythic structures of the unconscious and conscious choice and action. Esther recognises Stan – another orphan – as her chance at life, even though that life results in pain and debasement. The illumination achieved through the interaction of sight and touch in this first meeting is full of self-knowledge, even if that is not conscious knowledge. Indeed, this partial recognition or understanding, which assumes clarity and dominance in this moment, overshadows other processes of cognition, other recognitions that might have enabled Esther to have, for instance, taken the opportunity presented to her without complete sacrifice. But atomisation is one of the key properties of Harrower's scenes of illumination in her dissection of the epiphany phenomenon itself; in Harrower's revelations, the conventional synthetic power of the modernist moment of being is only partially realised. In the scene with Esther and Stan, the synthesis is far from complete; it is not a union of like minds, soul or bodies, but one in which the respective deprivations, opacities and fantasies of class and gender synthesise to momentous effect.

The central revelation experienced by the heroine of Harrower's second novel, *The Long Prospect* (1958), repeats this misalignment of fantasy and reality in the connection between the novel's young heroine, Emily, and Max, a scientist who has come to board with Emily's grandmother. At the time twelve-year-old Emily meets Max she is described as having just "woke[n]" to a new world as if she had gained "x-ray vision". In this condition, she avoids "shuttered adult eyes"[20] in which she deciphers dishonesty, including

---

18 Elizabeth Harrower, *Down in the City* (1957; Melbourne: Text Publishing, 2013), 21. All subsequent references are to this edition and appear in parentheses in the text.
19 Delia Falconer, "Oblivion at the Edges", introduction to Elizabeth Harrower's *Down in the City* (Melbourne: Text Publishing, 2013), vii–viii.

self-delusion. One crucial element of Emily's awakening is, ironically, her discovery of the dreamscape of cinema:

> For the third night in succession Emily had been to the Rialto where, on Wednesday, she had seen the archetype of her aspirations – someone apparently famous, of whom she had never heard. In what kind of fog had she been living, she wondered, that she had never known the extraordinary range of subtlety people had it in their power to command. This was how people should be – witty, wise, compassionate and clever. (65)

The description deploys the lexicon of opacity and vision across the literal experience of the cinema and into the clearing mental "fog" in which she had been living. It is in this suspended state – newly woken but also suspended in dreams – that Max walks into Emily's life in reality, as if she has conjured him. After her third successive night at the cinema, Emily "flew home through the dark streets plunged in a fantasy in which life-size portraits on the walls of the room gave way to visions of a private cinema and trips to Hollywood" (66). Like Janet in "The Fun of the Fair", Emily, too, is "plunged" into the uneven, misaligned condition between dreamlike fantasy and harsh illumination.

In her trip home from the cinema, Emily is also like Roland Barthes, who, in his essay "Leaving the Movie Theatre", writes of the hypnotic lure of the cinema and the subsequent walk home.[21] Barthes states that he prefers leaving the cinema at night to all other cinema experiences. He describes this experience as one in which he is emerging from hypnosis, where the screens of the cinema and the psyche are merged and in dynamic relationship with the surrounding world. Similarly, when Emily first meets Max she is "hynotised" (67) by him. She gazes at his face, which is "[u]nder the light" and "half in shadow" (66), like a close-up and between day and night. Her grandmother Lilian berates her: "Wake up!" (67).

Emily meets Max in this transitional state between hypnosis and consciousness, the moment when we wake and sense the dream of our unconscious theatre slipping away from us. Between Max and Emily, too, recognition is through a mutual gaze:

> Under the light . . . Looking now and again at *her*.
> She looked again at the man, idly, with more ease, at his eyes and saw with a shock of profound surprise that his grey eyes were turned on her and more than looking at – seeing her. (67)

This relationship, where her face is in his eye, and his in hers appears, constructs the screen of an enabling if also dangerous fantasy in the psychic terrain between what Lacan terms the Real and Imaginary domains. In this condition, the psyche shapes and reshapes a self as both an object and a subject (the internal difference between "Alice" and "I" discussed above) and between the self and an external object-subject of another. In *The Long Prospect*, this negotiation, as it plays out between Max and Emily, crosses the line of what is deemed acceptable between a middle-aged man and a twelve-year-old girl.

---

20   Elizabeth Harrower, *The Long Prospect* (1958; Sydney: Angus & Robertson, 1988), 65. All subsequent references are to this edition and appear in parentheses in the text.
21   Roland Barthes, "Leaving the Movie Theatre", in *The Rustle of Language*, trans. Richard Howard (New York: Hill & Wang, 1986), 345–6. Thanks to my colleague in film studies, Dr Lisa Trahair, for directing me to Barthes' essay.

The novel does not shy away from the precarious terms of this relationship, which must necessarily play out in the social sphere which deems it inappropriate and brings about its closure.

As with *Down in the City*, *The Long Prospect* examines, in painful detail, the personal and social implications of these intense moments of intersubjective recognition and misrecognition. In one sense, the events of the novels perform this education for their protagonists, as if different faculties learn the force, the meaning and the adjustments of the moment of being unevenly over time. At the conclusion of Harrower's third novel, *The Catherine Wheel* (1960), the narrator Clem admits:

> That survival was in no way easy I had always understood. But that anything in life, that any action, that to have virtue, or to lack it, that *love* demanded this exertion of soul, I simply had not known.[22]

The title of the short story "The English Lesson", first published in 1965, and published in *A Few Days in the Country* in 2015, announces this pedagogical process. In this story the protagonist Laura learns the meaning of being insulted after receiving a twelve-word piece of correspondence from a financial adviser that is not reproduced for the reader. Midway through this experience, she becomes half-aware what an insult means:

> Her heart hammered. She was insufficiently acquainted with physiology to know what else was happening inside her because of a dozen casual words, but she was learning. For instance, an insult recorded by the eye could cause an entire organism to react as though it had been violently smitten with an axe.[23]

Ultimately, in the story's concluding paragraph, she completes her lesson: "I know something, Laura thought before falling dead asleep. It [the offending letter] did not speak against me; it spoke to me. And I know what insulted means" (164). In the novels, however, these hard-won lessons, this clarity, do not diminish the "fog". At the conclusion of *Down in the City*, Esther steels herself to continue her life with Stan on increasingly debased terms. The novel concludes: "By no moisture of eye, or trembling of hands, by no frown did she betray the blankness of her spirit, the exhaustion of her heart. That she was she, that this was her life, her past and future, she most tiredly knew" (289-90). In *The Long Prospect*, Emily is locked in a tedious, repetitive performance of the materialist nuclear family. In *The Catherine Wheel*, the two main protagonists, Clem and Christian, have not gained something "durable". Clem has learned the lesson that a possible alternative to the present destruction of her relationship with Christian may exist but they have missed the moment of its transformative potential:

> Perhaps if we had found the strength to go down before each other, to be cut back, razed, we might have risen yet from the holocaust with something hardly gained and durable, instead of this.

---

22 Elizabeth Harrower, *The Catherine Wheel* (1960; Melbourne: Text Publishing, 2014), 324. All subsequent references are to this edition and appear in parentheses in the text.
23 Elizabeth Harrower, *A Few Days in the Country and Other Stories* (Melbourne: Text Publishing, 2015), 159. All subsequent references are to this edition and appear in parentheses in the text.

> But it wasn't likely. I wasn't sure. And now, anyway, it was too late. (324–5)

All of these revelations have brought understanding and wrought havoc. In another way, the effects of these illuminations are indiscernible, for the condition of the present extends unchanging, even in the face of increased understanding. The heroines have gained truths of self and others but this understanding does not lead to change. In her heroines' compulsion to replay the scene of their intersubjective constitution of self/eves, Harrower shows how the operations of fantasy become inextricable from the "I" that was activated in the electrical moment of connection with another. Consequently, the novels do not perform resolution. The conception of internal difference, where self-knowledge only compounds the inevitability of endless repetition, is its own form of nightmare.

This pattern is partly broken down in *The Watch Tower* (1966) in that the dilemma of entangled dualities (between self and self and between self and other) is bifurcated in the narrative into two sisters, Laura and Clare, which enables at least one, Clare, to escape. The pattern is broken completely in Harrower's most recent novel, *In Certain Circles* (2014), whose narrative concludes decades after the time of its opening. Akin to *The Winter's Tale*, this long duration enables the transformation of individual tragedies rehearsed by the characters of the preceding texts and, indeed, by the characters of *In Certain Circles*. The relationships entered into in youth are dissolved in middle age, which in *In Certain Circles* affords various forms of detachment. The first form of detachment, as we see in the scene of Zoe and Stephen discussing the failure of their marriage, is that of objective and unmalicious perspective.[24] The second is enabled towards the end of the narrative, when Zoe and Russell mistakenly believe that Anna has suicided. This staged death, a performance of psychic and emotional crisis, allows the undoing of attachments. In what is the final scene of Harrower's fiction to date, the fantasmatic demons of intersubjective identification are expelled at the conclusion of this novel, which ends with the line from Zoe, the female protagonist, reflecting on her process of education: "What a slow learner, she thought, slowly rising. Still, the day was lovely. And now she could move on" (252).

This final, undramatic statement of self-knowledge is stripped of the intensity that accompanies the emergence of self through intersubjective fantasy, which occurs throughout Harrower's fiction. One of Harrower's great contributions to fiction is her profound understanding of the precarious processes by which subjectivity is activated, becomes sensate to itself, and how subjects, especially women, return to this scene in the attempt to shape and reshape identity, indeed to have an identity at all. Her fiction presents some of the endless range of possibilities created in this process, each one conveying a truth of a kind. However, these illuminations are characterised by forms of blindness, misapprehension, misrecognition and misalignment. The multiple aspects of the body and psyche do not come together in one moment, they are not all equally or sufficiently developed: being half asleep, adolescent, orphaned, arrested or unreal. This driving and dangerous energy is spent in *In Certain Circles*, where it is the reader who is required, like the audience of *The Winter's Tale*, to accept the possibility of a second chance delivered by time.

---

24 Elizabeth Harrower, *In Certain Circles* (Melbourne: Text Publishing, 2015), 324. All subsequent references are to this edition and appear in parentheses in the text.

References

Anwar, Danny. "The Island Called Utopia in *The Tree of Man*." *Southerly* 74, no. 1: 217-34.

Barth, John. (1967) "The Literature of Exhaustion". In *The Friday Book: Essays and other Non-Fiction*, 62–76. Baltimore, MD: Johns Hopkins University Press, 1984.

Barthes, Roland. "Leaving the Movie Theatre". In *The Rustle of Language*. Translated by Richard Howard, 345-6. New York: Hill & Wang, 1986.

Beja, Morris. *Epiphany in the Modern Novel*. Seattle: University of Washington Press, 1971.

Brennan, Bernadette. Review of *A Few Days in the Country and Other Stories* by Elizabeth Harrower. *Australian Book Review* 377 (December 2015). http://bit.ly/2p8abmE.

Concilio, Carmen. "Things That Do Speak in Elizabeth Bowen's *The Last September*". In *Moments of Moment: Aspects of the Literary Epiphany*. Edited by Wim Tigges, 279-92. Amsterdam and Atlanta, GA: Rodopi, 1999.

Dickinson, Emily. *The Complete Poems* (London: Faber & Faber, 1976).

Donne, John. *Collected Poems of John Donne*. London: Wordsworth Editions, 2002.

Falconer, Delia. "Oblivion at the Edges". Introduction to Elizabeth Harrower's *Down in the City*. Melbourne: Text Publishing, 2013.

Harrower, Elizabeth. *A Few Days in the Country and Other Stories*. Melbourne: Text Publishing, 2015.

———. *In Certain Circles*. Melbourne: Text Publishing. 2015.

———. *The Watch Tower*. London: Macmillan, 1966.

———. *The Catherine Wheel*. (1960) Melbourne: Text Publishing, 2014.

———. *The Long Prospect*. (1958) Sydney; Angus & Robertson, 1988.

———. *Down in the City*. (1957) Melbourne: Text Publishing, 2013.

Hegel, George Wilhelm Friedrich. *Hegel and the Human Spirit. A Translation of the Jena Lectures by Leo Rauch*. Detroit, Mich.: Wayne State University Press, 1983.

McGowan, John. "From Pater to Wilde to Joyce: Modernist Epiphany and the Soulful Self". *Texas Studies in Literature and Language* 32, no. 3 (1990): 417-45.

Murphet, Julian. "Projecting the Sixties: Mediation and Characterology in *The Catherine Wheel*". In *Elizabeth Harrower: Critical Essays*. Edited by Elizabeth McMahon and Brigitta Olubus, 107–117. Sydney: Sydney University Press, 2017.

Nichols, Ashton. "Cognitive and Pragmatic Linguistic Moments: Literary Epiphany in Thomas Pynchon and Seamus Heaney". In *Moments of Moment: Aspects of the Literary Epiphany*. Edited by Wim Tigges, 467-80. Amsterdam and Atlanta, GA: Rodopi, 1999.

———. *The Poetics of Epiphany: Nineteenth-Century Origins of the Modern Literary Movement*. Tuscaloosa: University of Alabama Press, 1987.

Saltzman, Arthur M. "Epiphany and Its Discontents: Coover, Gangemi, Sorrentino, and Postmodern Revelation". *Journal of Modern Literature* 15, no. 4 (Spring 1989): 497-518.

Sheridan, Susan. "Pity's Cost". *Sydney Review of Books*, 12 August 2014, http://bit.ly/2pVSKKW.

White, Patrick. *The Tree of Man*. (1955) London: Vintage, 1994.

Žižek, Slavoj. "From Desire to Drive: Why Lacan is not Lacaniano". *Atlántica de Las Artes* 14 (Autumn 1996), http://bit.ly/2pbnszY.

———. *The Metastasis of Enjoyment: Six Essays on Women and Causality*. (1994) London: Verso, 2005.

Contributors

Nicholas Birns is an adjunct instructor at New York University's School of Professional Studies. He is a leading scholar of Australian literature and editor of *Antipodes*, the publication of the American Association of Australasian Literary Studies. He is the author of *Contemporary Australian Literature: A World Not Yet Dead* (2015), *Barbarian Memory: The Legacy of Early Medieval History in Early Modern Literature* (2013), *Theory after Theory: An Intellectual History of Literary Theory from 1950 to the Early 21st Century* (2010), *Understanding Anthony Powell* (2004), and, as co-editor, *Reading Across the Pacific: Australia–United States Intellectual Histories* (2010) and *A Companion to Australian Literature since 1900* (2007).

Michelle de Kretser was born in Sri Lanka and lives in Australia. She went to university in Melbourne and Paris, and is an honorary associate of the English Department at the University of Sydney. Her new novel, *The Life to Come*, will be published in October 2017. Her fiction is published across the world and has won many prizes, including the Miles Franklin Literary Award.

Robert Dixon FAHA is Professor of Australian Literature at the University of Sydney. His recent books include *Photography, Early Cinema and Colonial Modernity: Frank Hurley's Synchronised Lecture Entertainments* (2011) and *Alex Miller: The Ruin of Time* (2014). He is currently completing the book *Australian Literature, Scale and the Problem of the World*, which was supported by an ARC DORA research fellowship (2013–16).

Ivor Indyk is the Whitlam Professor in the Writing and Society Research Centre at Western Sydney University. He is the founding editor and publisher of *HEAT* magazine and of the award-winning Giramondo book imprint. His current research projects include the history of Australian literary publishing and the expression of emotion in Australian literature, with a particular interest in Patrick White, and such concepts as awkwardness, shyness, embarrassment and wonder.

Kate Livett teaches in the School of Arts and Media at the University of New South Wales. She researches in literary and cultural studies and has published extensively as a literary reviewer, including five years as the fiction and non-fiction reviews editor of *Southerly*.

Fiona McFarlane is the author of *The Night Guest* (2013) and *The High Places* (2016), which won the 2017 International Dylan Thomas Prize. She teaches creative writing at the University of Sydney.

Elizabeth McMahon teaches in the School of Arts and Media at the University of New South Wales. She has published extensively on Australian literature, literary islands, and representations of gender and sexuality. Her monograph, *Islands, Identity and the Literary Imagination* (2016) was recently awarded the 2017 Walter McRae Russell Award, given for the best work of literary scholarship on an Australian subject published in the preceding two calendar years. She also co-edits *Southerly*, Australia's oldest literary journal.

Julian Murphet is Scientia Professor in English and Film Studies at the University of New South Wales, where he co-edits the journal *Affirmations: of the modern*. He is the author of *Literature and Race in Los Angeles* (2001), *Multimedia Modernism* (2009), and *Faulkner's Media Romance* (2017), as well as many articles and book chapters on modern and contemporary cultural phenomena. He has co-edited a range of literary critical volumes, including *Modernism and Masculinity* (2014), *William Faulkner and the Media Ecology* (2015), *Rancière and Literature* (2016), and *Sounding Modernism* (2017).

Megan Nash is a PhD candidate and course co-ordinator at the University of Sydney. Her project is an investigation of affect and eyes in the eighteenth- and nineteenth-century novel. She is interested in Elizabeth Harrower's work with its focus on affect and interiority, its diverse literary antecedents, and its complex engagement with generic forms such as the melodrama and the gothic. Megan is an occasional reviewer for *Southerly* and for the Sydney film website 4:3.

Brigitta Olubas convenes the English, film studies and creative writing programs at the University of New South Wales. She is joint managing editor of *JASAL* (*Journal of the Association for the Study of Australian Literature*). Her most recent publication is an edited volume of Shirley Hazzard's nonfiction writings, *We Need Silence to Find Out What We Think* (2016). She is currently writing the authorised biography of Shirley Hazzard for Farrar Straus & Giroux and a monograph on the diverse cultural circles of Hazzard and her husband Francis Steegmuller.

Brigid Rooney teaches in Australian literature at the University of Sydney. She is the author of *Literary Activists: Writer-Intellectuals and Australian Public Life* (2009) and has published widely on twentieth-century and contemporary Australian fiction. She has recently co-edited collections of scholarly essays about transnational approaches to Australian literature as well as a special issue of *Australian Literary Studies* on Christina Stead. Her current book project investigates the relationship between novels and suburbs in Australian literature.

Elizabeth Webby AM FAHA is Professor Emerita of Australian Literature at the University of Sydney. Her publications include *Early Australian Poetry* (1982), *Colonial Voices* (1989), *Modern Australian Plays* (1990), *The Cambridge Companion to Australian Literature* (2000) and, as joint editor, *Happy Endings* (1987), *Goodbye to Romance* (1989), *The Penguin Book* *of Australian Ballads* (1993) and *Australian Feminism: A Companion* (1998). She has also published numerous book chapters, articles and reviews and been a contributing editor of *The Penguin New Literary History of Australia* (1988) and *The Macquarie PEN Anthology of Australian Literature* (2009). From 1988–99 she edited the journal *Southerly*.

Index

abuse 9, 92, 99, 123
addiction 73, 97–101, 106
alcohol 54, 55, 59, 72, 85, 87, 89, 92, 97–99, 105–106
allegory 38, 108, 114, 116
Anderson, Benedict 49, 51, 54
   The Spectre of Comparisons 49
antipodes 52, 55–56, 62
Alexander, Neal 50, 57, 63
Arendt, Hannah 62, 119–120, 124, 127
   Eichmann in Jerusalem 119, 127
artifice 102

Barthes, Roland 81, 83, 94
Birns, Nicholas 29, 51, 59, 82, 120
bomb 62, 76, 87, 88, 90, 122, 126
Bowen, Elizabeth 20, 92, 135
   The Heat of the Day 20, 92
Brayshaw, Meg 40
bride 138; *see also* marriage
Burns, D.R. 73, 97

captivity 9, 51, 53, 59, 60, 75, 83, 91
cartograph 15, 49–50, 59, 62
Catholic characters 19
childhood 21, 52, 61, 85, 94
children 61, 114
Christological, the 100–101
cinema 52, 53–54, 59, 84, 85, 108, 122, 140
city, the 15, 23–30, 46, 52, 56, 59–60
Cold War 51, 56, 87, 90, 108
commodity 11, 89
concentration camp 123, 126
Connell, Raewyn 33
cosmos 66, 71

crowds 24, 29, 91, 94, 112, 114
cruelty 18, 22, 27, 29, 54, 62, 69, 89

Davidson, Carol 99
Davidson, Jim 23, 27, 84
Davis, Lennard 98
Dean, Jodi 45
devotion 71, 97–99, 101, 104–106
Dickinson, Emily 133
Dixon, Robert 72, 83, 85, 91, 93, 122, 128
domestic interiors 31, 57–58, 71, 83–94
dreams 53, 54, 85

Ehrenreich, Barbara 36
electricity 54, 57–58, 72, 75, 90, 92–94, 98, 102, 105, 108–110, 133, 142
elements, the 66, 67, 76, 104, 105, 136
Eliot, George 34, 35, 43, 93, 129–130
   Daniel Deronda 129–131
   Middlemarch 34, 40, 129
Eliot, T.S. 67
enlightenment 75, 82, 133
entrapment *see* captivity
entropy 66, 68, 71–73, 75, 77
epiphany 75, 133–135, 139
exile 61, 63
expatriates 35, 51, 60–61, 63, 86, 93, 128
expressivity 17
eyes 17, 19, 22, 25, 27, 28, 38, 58, 102–105, 129, 135, 137–141

face, the 17, 36, 70, 101–105, 111, 135, 138–141
fairgrounds 136–139
fairytale 52, 53, 88, 89, 138
Falconer, Delia 127, 139

Index

family, the 29, 43, 44, 66, 67, 75, 86, 87, 92, 129
fantasy 89, 90, 135–142
feminism 36–38, 44, 130
Franklin, Stella Miles 41
   My Brilliant Career 41
Fraser, Nancy 37, 44

Gelder, Ken 40
gender 33–46, 53, 58–60, 67, 69, 110, 139
genre 133, 135, 138
geography 50, 56, 60, 63, 125, 128; *see also* metageography
Gerster, Robin 41
Gilbert, James 41
Gilbert, Jeremy 45
globalisation 50, 55, 63, 82; *see also* internationalism
God 17–18, 65, 66
godlessness 17, 66, 70, 76, 78, 136
guilt 18, 109

hands 9, 68, 101, 137, 139
Harrower, Elizabeth
   A Few Days in the Country 28, 39, 136, 137, 141
      "Alice" 137, 140
      "Summertime" 28
      "The City at Night" 28
   Down in the City 13, 14, 23–28, 34, 35, 40, 46, 52, 54, 55, 57, 60, 67–75, 130, 139, 141
   In Certain Circles 14, 30–31, 51, 61, 66, 74, 76–78, 120, 130, 131, 142
   The Catherine Wheel 13, 23, 24, 34, 35, 40, 49, 56, 61, 71–73, 82, 97–98, 107–108, 113, 120, 141
   "The Fun of the Fair" 65–69, 136–140
   The Long Prospect 13, 17–18, 19, 21, 26–28, 37, 40–42, 51, 54, 55–62, 68–76, 84–88, 92, 139, 140
   The Watch Tower 9, 10, 11, 13, 15, 19–20, 27, 29, 30, 33, 36, 41–45, 58–63, 73–77, 81–93, 119–130
Hazzard, Shirley 52, 56, 64, 120
Hegglund, Jon 49–51, 56, 63, 72
Hellman, Matilda 99
heteronomy 33, 40
heterotopia 137
history 51, 56, 62, 83, 88–91, 107, 112–114, 123, 125, 128, 130
Hollywood 18, 42, 53, 55, 107, 140
hysteria 33, 41, 89

internationalism 50, 61, 63, 121; *see also* globalisation
irony 17, 19, 27, 50, 51, 52, 54, 58, 59, 85, 138

James, Henry 40, 57, 93
   Portrait of a Lady 40
Jewish characters 19, 42, 124–130, 127
Joyce, James 50, 77, 133
   A Portrait of the Artist as a Young Man 50
   Ulysses 77

Kazan, Elia 107; *see also* Williams, Tennessee
   A Streetcar Named Desire [film] 107
Kelaita, Jasmin 68

labyrinth 59, 87, 89
Lawler, Ray
   Summer of the Seventeenth Doll 37
Lawrence, D. H. 34
Leavis, F.R. 34, 54–55, 58
literary character 75, 109, 111
literary language 50, 73, 93, 104, 110, 111, 134
London 14, 23, 49–57, 61, 71–72, 82, 85, 97, 107, 109, 114
Lusty, Natalya 34

maps 15, 49, 56, 59, 61
marriage 10, 26, 27, 29–31, 41, 42, 43, 44, 61, 68, 74, 86, 88, 89, 108, 114, 129
masculinity 33–35, 38–46
masochism 18
mass entertainment 111
McGowan, John 133
McLuhan, Marshall 82
McMahon, Elizabeth 65, 75, 120
media 44, 54, 82, 84, 85, 93, 108–109, 110–115
melodrama 42, 52, 54, 57, 85, 97
metageography 55–63, 72, 85, 91, 122
meteorological 65–66, 70
metropolis 42, 59, 63, 82, 91
mid-century 36, 41, 45, 51, 52, 53, 56, 62, 64, 87, 90, 97
misogyny 53, 124
modernist novel 50, 57, 61–63, 66–67, 77, 91, 94, 133–134, 139
modernity 51–57, 59, 62, 63, 70, 83, 92–94
Moffett, Alex 66–67
Moran, James 50, 57, 63
Murphet, Julian 72, 82, 135

narcissism 15, 34, 86, 89, 104, 115

Index

narrative 10, 26, 40, 50–57, 63, 67, 69, 70, 73–77, 82–94, 97, 99, 100–103, 105, 112, 114, 130, 133, 135, 137–139, 142
Nash, Megan 62, 71, 86, 91, 93
neoliberal 37–38, 51, 55, 62
Nichols, Ashton 134, 135
Nietzsche, Friedrich 65, 66, 69, 70, 71
novel form, the 108–114, 120–131, 139, 142

objects 9–11, 14, 22, 89, 133, 135
Olubas, Brigitta 71, 73, 121
otherness 52, 71, 89, 99, 112–115, 135

Perec, Georges 11
photography 43, 61
Plath, Sylvia 120, 129
Pollock, Griselda 122
postwar society 11, 28, 30, 51, 56, 63, 85, 107, 112–115, 133, 134
primitive 22, 38
primal forces 85, 94, 136
provincial 33, 42, 51–56, 58–63
Punter, David 100, 102

race 113
racism 115
radio 54, 82, 85, 89, 109, 111, 112
Rantala, Varpu 99
Reid, Susan 34
Richardson, Henry Handel 97, 103
  Maurice Guest 97, 103
Riddle, Naomi 33, 74, 89
Rohan, Criena 37
  The Delinquents 37
Roiphe, Katie 36
romance 53, 103, 107, 133, 138
Rooney, Brigid 52, 57, 75, 98, 108, 129

Saltzman, Arthur M. 134
Salzman, Paul 40
Sedgwick, Eve 99
sex and sexuality 18, 22, 36, 41, 42, 53, 105, 114
shock 18, 57, 75, 83–86, 90–94
Silverman, Max 122
Stead, Christina 14, 64, 120, 129
  Seven Poor Men of Sydney 14
suburban 10, 15, 29, 41, 54, 55, 70, 74, 81–94, 121, 123

Summers, Anne 37
Sydney 13–15, 23–31, 36, 51–62
  Kings Cross 13, 24, 25, 27, 36, 53
  North Shore 13, 27, 53, 85, 89
  Sydney Harbour 10, 13, 27–31, 59, 81, 87–92

technological, the 62, 84, 93, 97, 108
telephone 72, 84, 97–99, 109–112
Text Publishing 2, 23, 63, 93
theatricality 54, 57, 85, 97, 104, 108, 122, 137, 140
thermodynamics 66–68, 71, 72, 75–78
transnational 50–51, 53, 56, 63, 88, 120
trauma 75, 84, 85, 87, 91, 121, 123, 130, 131
travel 29, 56, 60, 63, 76, 93, 128
truth 38, 43, 75, 77, 85, 98, 101, 104, 136, 142

urban 36, 82, 85, 87; *see also* suburban

Walkowitz, Rebecca 61, 121–124
weather 49, 56, 65–78, 68, 70, 72, 74, 78, 81–94, 136
Weil, Simone 38
White, Patrick 17, 18, 19, 25, 52, 55, 56, 61, 64, 127, 129, 136
  Flaws in the Glass 18, 52
  Riders in the Chariot 19
  "The Prodigal Son" 25, 52
  The Tree of Man 136
Whitlam, Gough 26, 31
will 52, 66–77, 99, 103
will-to-power 66–71, 73–78, 114
Williams, Tennessee 34, 107; *see also* Kazan, Elia
  A Streetcar Named Desire [play] 34
Williamson, Geordie 40, 74
Wilson, Scott 104–105
wireless 53, 54, 83, 109; *see also* radio
Wood, James 18, 40, 53, 61
Woolf, Virginia 67, 91, 121–124, 128, 133
world wars 41, 121
  World War Two 24, 28, 30, 58, 86, 122, 125, 127, 131
writing 14, 17, 20, 57, 62, 66, 83
Wyndham, Susan 1

Zionism 130
Žižek, Slavoj 90, 137

www.ingramcontent.com/pod-product-compliance
Lightning Source LLC
Chambersburg PA
CBHW081827230426
43668CB00017B/2398